William Faulkner's
Absalom, Absalom!:
A Critical Study

Studies in Modern Literature, No. 85

A. Walton Litz, General Series Editor

Professor of English
Princeton University

Joseph Blotner, Consulting Editor

Professor of English
University of Michigan

Other Titles in This Series

William Faulkner's
Absalom, Absalom!:
A Critical Study

by
David Paul Ragan

U·M·I Research Press

Ann Arbor / London

Produced and distributed by
UMI Research Press
an imprint of
University Microfilms, Inc.
Ann Arbor, Michigan 48106

Library of Congress Cataloging in Publication Data

Ragan, David Paul, 1952-
 William Faulkner's Absalom, Absalom!: a critical study / By
David Paul Ragan.
  p. cm.—(Studies in modern literature ; no. 85)
 Bibliography: p.
 Includes index.
 ISBN 0-8357-1840-9 (alk. paper)
 1. Faulkner, William, 1897-1962. Absalom, Absalom! I. Title.
II. Series.
PS3511.A86A6768   1987
813'.52—dc19   87-23300
                                                                      CIP

British library CIP data is available.

In Memory of
Fannie Lookabill Ragan

Contents

Acknowledgments

My gratitude is due to many people who have helped shape my work on this project. Professor James B. Meriwether read an early version of this study, which profited heavily from his valuable suggestions. Other thoughtful advice was offered by Professors Keen Butterworth, Patrick Scott, and Joseph Blotner. For work on the tedious and important job of proofreading, I am grateful to Melissa Kaufman and Emily Wolfe.

Part of this study has appeared in revised form in the *Mississippi Quarterly*.

Abbreviations

All quotations from the novel refer to *Absalom, Absalom!: The Corrected Text*. New York: Vintage Books, 1987.

FIU   *Faulkner in the University*. Eds. Frederick L. Gwynn and Joseph L. Blotner. New York: Random House, 1959.

SLWF   *Selected Letters of William Faulkner*. Ed. Joseph Blotner. New York: Random House, 1977.

TS   *William Faulkner Manuscripts 13: Absalom, Absalom! Typescript Setting Copy and Miscellaneous Material*. Introduced and Arranged by Noel Polk. New York: Garland Publishing, Inc., 1987.

TSTF   *The Sound and the Fury*. New York: Cape and Smith, 1929.

USWF   *Uncollected Stories of William Faulkner*. Ed. Joseph Blotner. New York: Random House, 1979.

Introduction

When *Absalom, Absalom!*, William Faulkner's ninth novel, was published on October 26, 1936, it signalled the completion of what had been for the author his most time-consuming and difficult creative effort to date. Though it is impossible to determine with certainty the point at which the idea for the novel had occurred to Faulkner, a likely date is the late fall or early winter of 1933. Harrison (Hal) Smith, Faulkner's editor at Smith and Haas, had proposed a new collection of short stories. Faulkner was then engaged in working upon the first volume of the Snopes Trilogy, which became *The Hamlet*, published in 1940. He had written Ben Wasson that the contract called for publication of the novel by the fall of 1934 (*SLWF*, 74). Writing to Smith on "something October," 1933, Faulkner had postponed the expected date of completion of the Snopes book and responded to the query about the collection:

> I dont think the novel will be ready for spring. I have been at the Snopes book, but I have another bee now, and a good title, I think: REQUIEM FOR A NUN. It will be about a nigger woman. It will be a little on the esoteric side, like AS I LAY DYING.
>
> About a collection of short stories. It has been almost 16 months since I have written anything original or even thought in such terms. I dont know what I have in short stories. I will take a day off soon and go through them and see if we can get a book we wont be ashamed of. I'll let you know. (*SLWF*, 75)

The completion of *Requiem* would eventually be postponed even longer than the Snopes book, perhaps because the survey of stories for what would become *Doctor Martino* (1934) suggested to Faulkner another project. Elisabeth Muhlenfeld has suggested that Faulkner seized upon the unpublished story "Evangeline" as the foundation for a new novel.[1] Faulkner had submitted it to the *Saturday Evening Post* in July 1931.[2] Containing many of the elements which would later find their way into *Absalom, Absalom!*, the story was one of a group employing two speakers, an unnamed first-person narrator and his friend Don. As well as "Evangeline," the group includes "Snow," "Mistral," and "The Big Shot."[3]

"Evangeline" opens as the narrator is summoned to a small Mississippi town by his friend Don, who is an architect and amateur artist. The telegram he receives proclaims that Don has found a ghost for the narrator to investigate immediately. When the narrator arrives, Don outlines the story of a Colonel Sutpen's family in a bantering, sarcastic way which has little in common with the tone of narration in the novel. Sutpen had been "a florid, portly man, a little swaggering, who liked to ride fast to church of a Sunday" (*USWF*, 584); he had established a plantation on land acquired from the Indians and built a house designed by a foreign architect. His daughter Judith had married a friend of her brother Henry's named Charles Bon. Immediately after the marriage, Henry and Bon had left for the war. Bon had apparently been killed by Henry at the war's end when he had discovered him to be a bigamist, married to a woman in New Orleans.

Sutpen, whose role in the story is minor, dies in 1870, and some fifteen years later, after inviting Bon's other wife for a visit, Judith dies as well. Raby, Sutpen's half-black daughter, who tells the narrator a great deal about events, hints about some objection Henry had had to the marriage, but she does not explain. One of Raby's children sees a face in the house on the day of Judith's funeral, and since Raby had prepared Judith for burial without letting anyone else see her, Don and the narrator assume that the ghost is actually Judith herself, who had not died and had remained hidden in the house. The basic points of the plot are established in the story's first two numbered sections through a conversation between the two young men which at points anticipates the exchanges between Quentin and Shreve in the novel. When Don says, for instance, that Bon and Henry had been in the tenth graduating class at the University of Mississippi, the narrator replies " 'I didn't know there were ten in Mississippi that went to school then' " (*USWF*, 586), a barb which Shreve delivers to Quentin in slightly altered form in the novel: " 'I didn't know there were ten in Mississippi that went to school at one time' " (449).

With the story's third section, Don disappears as the narrator seeks to discover the identity of the ghost. He accepts Raby's challenge to get by the police dog which guards the house and learns from her about the conflict between the two men. Henry had objected to something which he had discovered on a trip with Bon to New Orleans. But Raby tantalizingly withholds a piece of information which is vital to making sense of the story. The narrator's puzzling about this key information is similar to comments made by Mr. Compson in chapter 4 of the novel (124):

> But still I couldn't understand it. If Henry didn't know they were married, it seemed to make him out pretty much of a prude. But maybe nowadays we can no longer understand people of that time. Perhaps that's why to us their written and told doings have a quality fustian though courageous, gallant, yet a little absurd. But that wasn't it either. There was something more than just the relationship between Charles and the woman; something she hadn't told me and had told me she was not going to tell and which I knew she would not tell out of some sense of honor or of pride; and I thought quietly, "And now I'll never know that. And without it, the whole tale will be pointless, and so I am wasting my time." (*USWF*, 600)

The narrator is introduced to Henry Sutpen, whom Raby reveals to be the ghost who has been living in the house for the past forty years. He is moved by what he sees and decides not to write the story. As a result of his intense interest in the Sutpens, though, he declines to leave the house and returns to go over in his mind parts of his interviews with Henry and with Raby. The memories, like those in *Absalom, Absalom!* of Quentin's visit to Sutpen's Hundred with Miss Rosa, are inconclusive yet compelling. But they do not explain the objection which apparently had forced Henry to kill his friend. The puzzle is solved only after Raby sets fire to the house and the narrator discovers a metal case supposed to contain Judith's picture. After Bon's death she had hammered the lock closed, but the narrator pries it open to reveal the secret: a picture not of Judith, who had been blond, but of the other wife, a woman of mixed blood.

Much of the plot of the novel is rehearsed in the story, though there are some important differences, including the nature of the relationship between Judith and Henry, the relative prominence and character of Sutpen, the possibility that Bon was Sutpen's son, the subplot involving Wash, and the presence of Miss Rosa and her attitudes toward her brother-in-law. As Muhlenfeld demonstrates, Raby's role is split in the novel between Miss Rosa and Clytie, whom she resembles in many respects.[4] Still, "Evangeline" anticipates several of the novel's concerns and techniques. Most important of these is the structural device of withholding information until its appearance is most dramatic (used in many Faulkner works), usually at the end of sections.[5] The story's second part, for instance, ends with the revelation that a ghost has inhabited the Sutpen house for forty years; the ghost's identity is revealed at the end of section 3; as the following unit ends, Raby reveals that Henry Sutpen is her brother. The climactic information, that the New Orleans wife had been a woman of mixed blood, is withheld until the very end of the story, where it is literally sifted from the ashes of the past.

The overall structure of the story is also similar to that of the novel. In "Evangeline," the first part reveals what is generally known about the characters, both by Don and by Raby, leaving the narrator to draw his conclusions in the second half. In *Absalom, Absalom!*, much the same progression from "fact" to interpretation is used: Quentin learns about the Sutpen family from his father (who liberally sprinkles his recital of the facts with his own interpretation of them) and Miss Rosa. In the second half, reversing the order of narration in "Evangeline," he and Shreve piece together a coherent story from what they know about the events. The factor at which the story only hints and which gives *Absalom, Absalom!* so much of its emotional impact is the effect of the tragedy upon Quentin. Although the narrator of "Evangeline" is sympathetic and obviously moved by what he learns, he views the events with much more distance, much less personal involvement. Still, Faulkner must have recognized that "Evangeline" had great possibilities for a more extended and complicated treatment.

Another piece Faulkner may have encountered as he went through stories for the proposed collection dates from a period even earlier than "Evangeline." "The Big Shot" had been submitted to *The American Mercury* before January 23, 1930, and was subsequently sent to four other magazines (*USWF*, 707). On the basis of its style, Joseph Blotner assigns it to the period between Faulkner's New Orleans fiction and the more mature writing of the late 1920s, such as *Flags in the Dust* (*USWF* 707). "The Big Shot" is the story of how Dal Martin rises from poverty and obscurity to riches through bootlegging and other nefarious activities. He attempts to buy respectability and is concerned with acquiring the advantages of social position for his daughter. His efforts lead to the suicide of Dr. Blount, one of the prominent citizens he seeks to corrupt, and eventually to the escape of Popeye, a thug who works for Martin and is responsible for killing his daughter in an automobile accident.

Though not as successful a story as "Evangeline" when evaluated on its own merits, "The Big Shot" contains elements which reverberate in several of Faulkner's novels: Popeye, the warped villain of *Sanctuary* (1931) makes his first appearance; elements of Dr. Blount prefigure the characterization of Hightower in *Light in August* (1932); and aspects of Dal Martin suggest both Wash Jones of *Absalom, Absalom!* and Flem Snopes of the Snopes Trilogy. An incident in Martin's childhood anticipates a similar episode in Sutpen's boyhood. Martin is sent with a message to the owner of the plantation his family lives on, but the planter sends him to the back of the house with instructions that he should deliver his message to one of the "niggers." As he leaves, Martin is aware of the derision of the Negro servant standing behind the white man. The parallel with Sutpen's experience is obvious, even though a slave delivers the admonition to the young Sutpen. The reactions of the two youths are also very different, though neither comes to hate the white plantation owner: Martin watches him with fascination after the episode, much as Sutpen had before the insult. The narration implies that the experience had initiated in Martin a desire for both wealth and social position, but the effect of the experience is not so carefully delineated as in *Absalom, Absalom!*. Years later, when Martin owns his own store, he plays poker with the aging plantation owner and pours the drinks for him, just as Wash Jones pours Sutpen's drinks when the two play cards in the store Sutpen operates after the war.

The story may have triggered in Faulkner's imagination other means of expanding the materials provided by "Evangeline." In his desire for respectability and position, Martin suggests aspects of Sutpen's character. He attempts to manipulate people for his own purposes, giving little consideration to possible consequences. Ultimately his is a very destructive personality, and the results of his manipulations of social convention and the law return to destroy the very qualities of his life he seeks to preserve—his dubious respectability and position, both symbolized by his daughter. Her death, caused by Popeye, obviously pre-vents her entrance into society, an event which would have solidified Martin's position in the community; the circumstances of her death are sure to provoke a scandal, destroying what little respectability Martin has managed to acquire. His relative lack of interest in the fate of the injured woman insures Popeye's escape. Like Sutpen later, Martin has little understanding of human nature, relying upon his dedication to abstractions which the story demonstrates to be largely devoid of meaning. His relationship with the people around him looks forward to Sutpen's sublimation of others to his design. Martin would not have hesitated, we are told, to use the political figures of the town to gain his daughter an invitation to the Chickasaw Guards ball, "since . . . he would not have hesitated to make his illusions serve his practical ends, or vice versa if you will" (*USWF*, 516). He uses the underworld figures he commands " 'just as [he] would use a mule or a plow' " (*USWF*, 508).

At one point the language of the story also anticipates a comment in *Absalom, Absalom!*. Don Reeves remarks, "Have you noticed how people whose lives are equivocal, not to say chaotic, are always moved by the homely virtues. Go to the brothel or the convict camp if you would hear the songs about sonny boy and about mother" (*USWF*, 505). The idea is similar to Mr. Compson's question, " 'Have you noticed how so often when we try to reconstruct the causes which lead up to the actions of men and women, how with a sort of astonishment we find ourselves now and then reduced to the belief, the only possible belief, that they stemmed from some of the old virtues? the thief who steals not for greed but for love, the murderer who kills not out of lust but pity?' " (150).

The final story which contributes directly to the composition of *Absalom, Absalom!*, "Wash," was written in the fall of 1933; it was accepted by *Harper's* on November 2.[6] The specific motivation for the composition of "Wash" is unclear, though it grew out of Faulkner's work on the Snopes novel he had been struggling with at the time. In a letter to Malcolm Cowley on August 16, 1945, Faulkner explained how his work toward *The Hamlet* had led to various offshoots:

> Meanwhile my book [*The Hamlet*] had created Snopes and his clan, who produced stories in their saga which are to fall in a later volume: MULE IN THE YARD, BRASS, etc. This over about ten years, until one day I decided I had better start on the first volume or I'd never get any of it down. So I wrote an induction toward the spotted horse story, which included BARN BURNING and WASH, which I discovered had no place in that book at all.[7]

"Wash" appeared among a group of stories written or revised in the late fall of 1933, including "A Bear Hunt," "A Portrait of Elmer," and "Pennsylvania Station."[8] Muhlenfeld suggests that "Wash" may have arisen from Faulkner's work on the Snopes novel coupled with the possibilities suggested by Dal Martin's background in "The Big Shot" and the presence of Sutpen in "Evangeline."[9] Certainly Sutpen has undergone a transformation from "Evangeline," where his role is largely insignificant, to "Wash," in which he is one of the two major characters.

"Wash" may have been the turning point which suggested the means of combining the disparate elements of the three stories into a unified whole. Though after its composition Faulkner continued work on other projects, he would soon turn his attention exclusively to the book he would initially call "Dark House."[10] The character of Sutpen as he appears in that novel obviously owes a great deal more to his appearance in "Wash" than in "Evangeline." Indeed, his personality appears full-blown in "Wash," essentially the ruthless, overbearing character he would exhibit in the novel; the alterations Faulkner made in incorporating the story into chapter 7 of *Absalom, Absalom!* primarily result from the different narrative perspective.

The story focuses on Wash himself, his reactions to the seduction and eventual abandonment of his granddaughter by the man he had admired, almost apotheosized, for years. The basic elements of class conflict which the material explores in Mr. Compson's interpretation of Wash's behavior in *Absalom, Absalom!* are also present in the story. Wash associates the men who come to arrest him for the murder of Sutpen with Sutpen himself, men who had also fought in the war, who had themselves been recipients of citations of valor from the commanding generals. Some additions to this material in *Absalom, Absalom!* serve to underline Mr. Compson's own view of events, such as the imaginative picture voiced by Shreve in chapter 6 of Sutpen and Wash in the afterlife, drinking as they had in the scuppernong arbor, trying to remember the conflict which had divided them in life, and being unable to. But the essential traits of the story survive their being reworked in the larger and more complicated context of the novel.

Louis Daniel Brodsky's examination of different manuscripts of "Wash" and a typescript draft indicates that Faulkner conceived the full outlines of the plot almost from the beginning.[11] However, he experimented with the opening of the story in a manner similar to his later experimentation with the first chapter of *Absalom, Absalom!*. The manuscript drafts open with Wash in hiding, watching Sutpen emerge from his house.[12] The narration continues to allude to their afternoons drinking together, during which Sutpen would begin to threaten to kill Lincoln and Sherman. Following this version, Faulkner tried opening the story with the image of Wash himself justifying his absence from the war. Finally, Faulkner grafted on an introductory section, presenting Sutpen's discovery that Milly's child is a girl. The original opening follows the typebreak as it appears in published versions of the story. The revised opening forces the reader to view Wash through what the reader knows about Sutpen, and knowledge provided by the opening scene adds greater tension to the descriptions of Sutpen's seduction of the girl. The revisions provide a break in chronology and a more dramatic context for the story as a whole, giving the published text of "Wash" more in common with the techniques of *Absalom, Absalom!* itself. Perhaps the changes Faulkner made were consciously designed as a rehearsal of some of the problems he would encounter in the longer project, though they are certainly in line with the same sort of narrative experimentation which had concerned him throughout his career.

Internal evidence and the publication histories of the individual stories make possible some suppositions about Faulkner's plans for these materials in the late fall of 1933. Obviously, incorporating as it does some of the same characters as "Evangeline," "Wash" was most probably composed after Faulkner's reacquaintance with the earlier story. Though some of the family history is different—Sutpen's son being killed in the war, for instance—both Sutpen and Judith make appearances, and the ending of the story, in which Wash sets fire to his house, is reminiscent of Raby's burning the Sutpen mansion in "Evangeline." The character of Sutpen is transferred virtually intact from "Wash" into *Absalom, Absalom!*. Wash also appears with relatively few changes in personality or behavior.

It is also perhaps signficant that in assembling the stories for *Doctor Martino* Faulkner chose to include "Wash" but not "Evangeline." Though the changes required to incorporate "Wash" into *Absalom* would be extensive, they would not alter the basic plot, with the exception of the fire at the end; the fire at Sutpen's Hundred is borrowed more directly from "Evangeline." Faulkner may have been reluctant to include "Evangeline" in *Doctor Martino* because of the extent to which it would share traits in common with *Absalom, Absalom!*, upon which he was by then seriously engaged.[13] Neither would "The Big Shot" be included, though there were certainly sound aesthetic reasons for its rejection. "Evangeline" is a story which can stand on its own merits, one which would not have embarrassed its author had it been included in either *Doctor Martino* or *Collected Stories*, in which "Wash" also appeared. We must assume, then, that Faulkner had other reasons for ignoring it when assembling those collections. It might be argued that Faulkner did include other stories which would later be woven into his novels, but significant differences exist. Stories incorporated into the Snopes Trilogy, for instance, occupy the place of a single episode in the books where they appear in much the same manner that "Wash" is incorporated into *Absalom, Absalom!*. "Evangeline" bears a different relationship to the novel it anticipates; the story represents an assemblage of incidents which will be expanded throughout the novel as a whole, not limited to a particular chapter or episode.

Yet another publication project was on Faulkner's mind during the summer and fall of 1933 which quite possibly had an important impact upon the development of *Absalom, Absalom!*. Bennett Cerf of Random House had proposed a new edition of *The Sound and the Fury* with an introduction by Faulkner. The author had written two versions of the introduction[14] and had marked the Benjy section of the book in different colors of ink to indicate the shifting levels of time in Benjy's mind; he had forwarded the book to Random House, cautioning that he had used his only copy.[15] He made a trip to New York in November 1933, in part to discuss the proposed edition with Cerf.[16] Throughout his life Faulkner was reluctant to reread his work after it had been published, though later evidence suggests that he was quite thoroughly familiar with the published text of *The Sound and the Fury*. Maurice Coindreau, Faulkner's French translator who worked with the author on the translation of *The Sound and the Fury* in 1937, reported that Faulkner "seemed to know *The Sound and the Fury* by heart, referring me to such-and-such a paragraph, to such-and-such a page, to find the key to some highly enigmatic obscurity."[17] It would seem likely that this acquaintance dates from his work on the proposed Random House edition of the novel, since he reported that he had marked his only copy and that marked copy was never returned to him.

Thus, at the point when he realized possibilities of the "Evangeline"/"Wash" material, Faulkner may have had clearly in mind the anguish and despair of Quentin Compson and thereby arrived at the narrative strategy which would add so much to the Sutpen legends.[18] One of the stories composed during the fall of 1933, "A Bear Hunt," has an unnamed narrator who resembles Quentin, as does the narrator of "Fool About a Horse," which was probably written in the spring of 1934. Quentin is named as the narrator of "Lion," written around the same time, when Faulkner was well into the composition of *Absalom, Absalom!*. As Joseph Blotner points out, "This use of Quentin Compson may have reflected the fact that though short stories kept Faulkner from *Absalom, Absalom!* [in the spring of 1934] he was still considering technical problems in this novel in which Quentin would also narrate."[19]

Regardless of how the possibilities of this material may have begun to gestate in Faulkner's mind during the opening weeks of 1934, he still planned work on the novel he had written Smith about in October, *Requiem for a Nun*. A letter received by Smith on January 31, 1934, explained his future plans for two writing projects:

> About the novel. I still think that SNOPES will take about two years of steady work. I could finish the other one [*Requiem*] in good time, if only the Snopes stuff would lie quiet, which it wont do. However, I will have my taxes and insurance paid and off my mind by March first. Then I intend to settle down to the novel and finish it . . . . Perhaps the best thing as regards the novel would be for me to draw from you to the full amount of our agreement and get all this off my mind and concentrate on the novel. If I did this, I believe I might promise it for late fall printing—provided I could stop worrying about what I would use for money next year, with royalties already spent. Anyway, I will settle upon the one which I can finish soonest, and I will try to give you a definite promise by March first. (*SLWF*, 78)

Within two weeks Faulkner embarked on a totally different project which would take precedence over both the Snopes book and *Requiem*. Probably in February 1934, he wrote Smith that he had put both aside for a novel to be called *Dark House*, which he thought he could promise for the fall. He gave Smith a hint about the plot: "It is the more or less violent breakup of a household or family from 1860 to about 1910. It is not as heavy as it sounds. The story is an anecdote which occurred during and right after the civil war; the climax is another anecdote which happened about 1910 and which explains the story. Roughly, the theme is a man who outraged the land, and the land then turned and destroyed the man's family" (*SLWF*, 78–79). He also identified the narrator of the book as Quentin Compson, whose "bitterness which he has projected on the South" would be a means of keeping the novel on a level above that of the conventional historical fiction dealing with the antebellum South.

By this point, then, Faulkner seems to have devised a method of combining the stories he would use with Quentin as his main narrative persona. The two anecdotes to which Faulkner refers in his letter to Smith could be "Wash" and "Evangeline." That is, the events which occurred during and after the war (in "Wash" and the Judith/Henry/Bon triangle in "Evangeline") would provide the story; the method of making sense of that story would be a climactic explanation of elements which are otherwise a mystery, similar to the narrator's opening the metal picture case at the end of "Evangeline." As the composition of the novel progressed, however, the process of narration became considerably more complex. The projection of the completion date would be off by nearly two years.

The idea for the novel which would become *Absalom, Absalom!* apparently began to crystalize in the second week of February, 1934. Beginning with an opening similar to that of "Evangeline," Faulkner substituted two characters named Chisholm and Burke for the Don and I of the story. A trial opening is told entirely in dialogue, much lifted verbatim from the story. In the second section, a third-person narrator begins to characterize Sutpen until interrupted by Burke, who starts to sketch out the plot of "Wash." The manuscript fragment breaks off after three pages.[20] The draft indicates, as Muhlenfeld remarks, that even at this point Faulkner had hit upon the use of multiple sources of information about the Sutpen family. Burke identifies the source of some of what he knows as an "old bird that sets all day on a chair in front of the store" and tells him about an "old lady" Chisholm will have to talk to:

> "You bet," Burke said. "She's got the lowdown. She was engaged to Sutpen. He had come back from the war with his sword and plume and a citation from Joe Johnstone [sic] and not much else, including a widowed daughter and a half-ruined house and one family of negroes that had stayed on for some reason. And they were engaged to be married: the old guy in his fifties and this old lady who was a girl of 16 then. Nobody knew why. And then it was broken off, and nobody knew why again until Wash told them. Showed them."[21]

Though obviously Faulkner had in mind much of the plot of the novel, he would experiment with other openings before arriving at one he seemed satisfied with. One fragment describes the hot stale hotel room in which Chisholm and Burke discuss Sutpen before moving on to the dialogue between them.[22] Yet another attempt pursues a similar strategy but is broken off after less than a page.

Faulkner had already recognized the usefulness of contrasting his narrators, however: Burke is a northerner, while Chisholm is from the South.[23] Having made this distinction between the two young men, Faulkner was close to his solution: he transferred the locale from Mississippi to Massachusetts and gave the narrators the names Quentin and Shreve. Three manuscript fragments (two dated February 11, 1934) use a letter from Mr. Compson to Quentin to introduce the Sutpen story.[24] Shreve does not appear in all three versions, though. In one, the stifling hotel room of the Chisholm-and-Burke fragment becomes a room in Miss Rosa's house, and the two characters Quentin and Shreve have become divided aspects of Quentin's own personality, a convention which survives in the first chapter of the published novel.

As the process of composition continued, Faulkner began to refine his characters. Sutpen becomes more the dominating figure of Wash Jones's imagination and less the swaggering, portly man of "Evangeline." Rosa progresses from a witness and reporter of events to the obsessed harpy of the novel. The most dramatic changes, however, would continue throughout the process of composition and would involve the nature and extent of Quentin's involvement in the story.

Faulkner's progress on his new novel was to be interrupted often during the spring and summer of 1934. He attended the dedication of Shushan Airport in New Orleans, leaving on February 14. Blotner assumes that Faulkner continued work on the Snopes book, but that "whatever he had been able to do with the history of Colonel Sutpen seems not to have pleased him particularly" as of April 1934.[25] He wrote a story entitled "This Kind of Courage," which he would expand later into *Pylon* (1935), along with "Lo!" and the first three stories about Bayard Sartoris for the *Post,* which would later become the first three chapters of *The Unvanquished* (1938). During the summer he was further interrupted by a three-week assignment in Hollywood; he left on July 1.[26] He wrote his wife, Estelle, that he had worked on the novel "from time to time" (*SLWF,* 83).

His progress throughout the summer of 1934 must have been disappointing, however. In August, he informed Smith of where he stood:

> I wrote you in the spring that in August I would let you know definitely about the novel. The only definite news I can tell you is, that I still do not know when it will be ready. I believe that the book is not quite ripe yet; that I have not gone my nine months, you might say. I do have to put it aside and make a nickel every so often, but I think there must be more than that. I have a mass of stuff, but only one chapter that suits me; I am considering putting it aside and going back to REQUIEM FOR A NUN, which will be a short one, like AS I LAY DYING, while the present one will probably be longer than LIGHT IN AUGUST. I have a title for it which I like, by the way: ABSALOM, ABSALOM; the story is of a man who wanted a son through pride, and got too many of them and they destroyed him. . . . (*SLWF,* 83–84)

In addition to indicating the amount of work Faulkner had accomplished on the novel since February, this letter to Smith demonstrates that he had further refined his plot. Earlier he had described Sutpen as a man who had "outraged the land," though *Absalom, Absalom!* presents him as a faithful steward of his plantation. Faulkner now defines his crime in more classically tragic terms: his desire is for a son "through pride." Significantly, Faulkner explains this theme after announcing the title of the book, suggesting that the allusion to David's lament for his dead son represents a statement of Sutpen's fatal desire. In light of the completed novel, the title would have to be interpreted ironically, in a way similar to that in which the title *Sanctuary* functions.[27]

Perhaps in an effort to allow time for *Absalom, Absalom!* to coalesce in his mind, Faulkner turned his attention to other projects in the fall of 1934. In September and October he completed "The Unvanquished," "Vendee," and "Drusilla,"[28] and in mid-October he requested that his agent, Morton Goldman, return to him the story "This Kind of Courage" because he was making a novel out of it (*SLWF*, 85). The novel, *Pylon*, occupied Faulkner until the middle of December, when the final two chapters arrived in New York.[29] When Hal Smith came to Oxford in January 1935, he brought the galleys of the novel so Faulkner could go over them.[30] At the University of Virginia, Faulkner explained that he had written the novel "because I'd got in trouble with *Absalom, Absalom!* and I had to get away from it for a while so I thought a good way to get away from it was to write another book, so I wrote *Pylon*" (*FIU*, 36).

Financial pressures, however, meant that even with the completion of *Pylon*, Faulkner could not devote his full attention to *Absalom, Absalom!* in the spring of 1935. He worked on another group of short stories in March and April, including "Fool About a Horse," "That Will Be Fine," "Uncle Willy," and a revision of "The Brooch."[31] "Lion" and "Moonlight" also probably date from the same period.[32] The end of the month, March 25, was the publication date of *Pylon*; the first page of the manuscript of *Absalom, Absalom!* bears the date March 30.[33]

When questioned at the University of Virginia about the point at which he had put *Absalom, Absalom!* aside, Faulkner recalled his reasons for interrupting his work:

> I can't say just where it was that I had to put it down, that I decided that I didn't know enough at that time maybe or my feeling toward it wasn't passionate enough or pure enough, but I don't remember at what point I put it down. Though when I took it up again I almost rewrote the whole thing. I think that what I put down were inchoate fragments that wouldn't coalesce and then when I took it up again, as I remember, I rewrote it. (*FIU*, 75–76)

Faulkner's testimony is reinforced by the condition of the manuscript, now at the University of Texas; Michael Millgate describes it as follows:

The first page of this manuscript is close to the published text, but the manuscript as a whole is a composite, made up of material written at different times over what may have been a fairly long period. Many sections, some brief, some of one or more paragraphs in length, have been affixed to the base sheets, and these sections, like the base sheets themselves, are in a variety of different inks and even show minor differences in handwriting.[34]

Once the novel had become more clearly fixed in Faulkner's mind, he wrote it rapidly. Blotner reports that Smith received chapter 2 on June 29, with chapter 3 following in July and 4 in the middle of August, despite the fact that he had interrupted his writing in late July to work on some other short stories and had spent considerable time during the spring and summer flying.[35] In late August his work was again interrupted, and he did not return to it for nearly two months, during which time he did some flying and made a trip to New York in an attempt to improve his financial situation.[36] It was October 15 when he began the manuscript of chapter 5.[37] He would soon be interrupted again, however, by the death of his brother Dean on November 2, 1935.[38]

In his grief, Faulkner perhaps turned to work on the new novel as a release; he took the manuscript when he went to stay for a while with his mother and Dean's widow, Louise.[39] His progress must have been steady, since he wrote to Morton Goldman on December 4, 1935, that the novel would be completed in a month and that he thought it was "pretty good" (*SLWF,* 93). He would focus his attention as exclusively as possible until completing the manuscript, despite another assignment in Hollywood, for which he departed on December 10. There he worked with Howard Hawks on *The Road to Glory* but continued his progress on *Absalom* as well.[40] That he could come close to meeting his projected schedule is remarkable, for not only did he suffer a period of illness in California, he also met and fell in love with Hawks's secretary, Meta Carpenter.[41]

The last page of the manuscript bears the date January 31, 1936, and the locations where he had worked upon it: "Mississippi, 1935 / California, 1936 / Mississippi, 1936."[42] As was his usual practice, however, the process of typing the setting copy involved considerable revision, and with *Absalom,* especially, Faulkner would continue to make decisions which radically affect the reader's understanding of and response to the novel.

The preparation of the typescript occupied Faulkner through the late winter and spring of 1936. As in the writing of the manuscript, Faulkner worked on the typescript both in Mississippi and in California, to which he returned in late February.[43] On April 6, a new version of chapter 1 arrived in New York.[44] He continued a Hollywood routine of work on the novel in the morning, work at the studio during the day; in the evenings he usually saw Meta. As a tribute, he inscribed to Meta three typed sheets with manuscript corrections and a two-page typed chronology, also with manuscript additions, on May 15, 1935. On a copy of the final page of the typescript, he listed the date and the place, "Los Angeles, Cal."[45]

The chronology lists all the years from 1807 to 1910, with notations about what had happened during those years. It is probably a revision of a two-page manuscript listing of the same years which Faulkner had drafted earlier; several important differences distinguish the two versions.[46] The typescript chronology probably represents materials Faulkner had used during the preparation of the typescript setting copy to keep dates and ages straight. Often, he listed the age of a character after his name appears on the sheet; in some cases the age seems to be a later addition. On the left side of one of the sheets Faulkner added a manuscript notation concerning the weather: "60 days without rain, / 42 no dew." The working draft may have been the basis of the Chronology appended to the novel, along with a Genealogy and a handsome map of Yoknapatawpha County drawn by Faulkner himself.[47] As many critics have recognized, there are inconsistencies between the Genealogy and the Chronology, as well as between both and the text of the novel; some of these may represent Faulkner's changing conceptions of the characters as his work on *Absalom* progressed.

Such aids during composition were not unusual with Faulkner. He used them with *The Sound and the Fury* and *Go Down, Moses* (1942); he even recorded the chronology of major events for *A Fable* (1954) on the walls of his office at Rowanoak. Earlier in the preparation of the manuscript of *Absalom, Absalom!* he had developed a chart which indicated the channels through which Quentin acquired information about the Sutpen legends.[48] The chart shows Sutpen, his name then Charles, conveying information to General Compson, who in turn reveals it to his son, Quentin's father, who "tells Quentin." Another line descends from Sutpen to Rosa Coldfield, who also tells things to Quentin Compson, "21, about to go to Harvard." Thus, Faulkner had made working notes which he had drawn upon and revised from the earliest drafts of the novel to the completion of the typescript, when he made some final alterations in the chronology.[49]

Elisabeth Muhlenfeld has examined at some length the kinds of revisions Faulkner made in preparing the typescript of *Absalom, Absalom!*. Her summary indicates that "While most of the revisions are of greatest interest because of the stylistic nuances they achieved, several important kinds of revisions pertained to the plot itself."[50] For instance, Faulkner frequently postponed the revelation of information until a later point, where its effect would be more dramatic, thereby achieving greater suspense. He also apparently decided rather late in the composition process that "the fact of Bon's taint of black blood would remain speculation."[51] Other alterations Faulkner either made at the request of his editors or allowed to stand once the editors had made them. Most of these involve the removal of material the editors found repetitive or confusing, the shortening of sentences, and the substitution of proper names for pronouns that the editors took to be ambiguous. Michael Millgate remarks that Faulkner may have accepted editorial changes more readily since *Absalom, Absalom!* was the first of his novels to be published by Random House and "perhaps in the interests of getting the book into print with the minimum of delay and distraction"; for whatever reason, "he seems to have been prepared to make co-operative gestures which were unusual for him, at least at this stage of his career."[52]

Most of the editorial tampering occurs in the first half of the novel; in the last three chapters, editorial markings are infrequent, as if the copy editor had either finally understood Faulkner's method more clearly or—what is more likely—he had simply given up out of confusion or frustration. Most of the editorial comments and objections were apparently made by Hal Smith, who had joined Random House when the firm had acquired Smith and Haas,[53] though Noel Polk has suggested the presence of at least three editorial hands.[54] Muhlenfeld identifies these as Hal Smith, Evelyn Harter, and Saxe Commins.[55] None of the readers seems to have understood the nature of Faulkner's narrative method, though marginal notes in the typescript indicate they occasionally appreciated the raw power of the prose.

On June 1, Faulkner left Hollywood, but six weeks later he returned with his family.[56] By early September he had finished the galley proofs of the novel, apparently making further changes at this stage,[57] and by late in the month the page proofs were ready.[58] Random House correspondence files indicate that Faulkner twice requested Hal Smith to send him corrected galleys and that he made further corrections on the page proofs.[59] Obviously, he took great care with the proofreading of the novel.

One of the reasons for this care was the demonstrated lack of understanding evidenced by the copyeditors. Another was the extent to which Faulkner's conception of the novel had continued to change up to the very last stages of preparation of the typescript setting copy. Faulkner himself altered aspects of the chronology, for instance. At several points in the first edition, the period that Bon spent at Sutpen's Hundred, and thus the time during which he could have established a relationship with Judith, is listed as twelve days; on other occasions, the time is seventeen days. The typescript reveals that the alteration from seventeen to twelve was made by Faulkner himself, but it was not made consistently throughout. A similar instance concerns the period of Rosa's outrage: forty-three years in most references, forty-five in two others. Once again, the change appears to have been inconsistently made by Faulkner. Copyeditors apparently did not notice the discrepancies, which add to the reader's confusion when confronted with the uncorrected edition.

During the preparation of the typescript printer's copy in California, Faulkner had spent some time with Ben Wasson, who reports that Faulkner commented to him one day that *Absalom, Absalom!* was "a tortured story, and a torture to write it."[60] Not only had the process of composition been long and complicated, it had occurred during one of the most frustrating and difficult periods in the author's life. Faulkner must have greeted the publication of the novel with a tremendous sense of accomplishment and pride. He had referred to it to David Hempstead as "the best novel yet written by an American,"[61] and many critics since its publication have supported this view. A further measure of Faulkner's regard for it was his extraordinary gesture of donating the manuscript as a contribution to a relief fund for the Spanish Loyalists on October 24, 1939.[62] It was the first of his manuscripts he had parted with (indeed, one of the few during his lifetime), and his donation of it must have been for the author an assertion of the values he would later call the "old verities and truths of the heart."[63] His magnanimous gift could be seen as a gesture of affirmation during one of history's darkest periods, an offering of one of his most valued possessions to a cause which he saw his entire creative endeavor as supporting.

Absalom, Absalom! is Faulkner's most fully realized tragic novel.[64] His references to the book at the University of Virginia make clear that he thought of it as a tragedy, that he saw Sutpen as a tragic hero, one cast in "the old Greek concept of tragedy" (*FIU*, 35). Certainly readers of the novel cannot escape being caught up in Sutpen's story, realizing both the man's grandeur and his terrible crimes against human dignity and values. And yet the novel records far more than the downfall of the House of Sutpen. Indeed, it incorporates two tragedies among its complex bodies of narration—that of Thomas Sutpen and various members of his family, and that of Quentin Compson. For many readers, it is not Sutpen's downfall, but Quentin's reaction to it which is the foundation for much of the novel's undeniable power.

Several critics over the years have recognized the close relationship between *Absalom, Absalom!* and *The Sound and the Fury*, though few have been willing to state categorically that Faulkner expects the readers of the later novel to bring to it an understanding of Quentin's problems in the earlier. Richard Poirier, for instance, recognized the ties between the two novels over thirty years ago but declined to pursue them: "It is well to remember that Quentin's interest in Sutpen's story transcends any reference he finds in it for [his] personal problems, which, after all, we are acquainted with only from observing his activity outside the context of *Absalom, Absalom!*"[65] Later critics have likewise recognized the ties between the two novels, but have not examined them in detail.[66] Joseph W. Reed summarizes the position of critics who, acknowledging the connections, nevertheless insist that *Absalom, Absalom!* be evaluated solely on its own terms:

> *Absalom* pulls in *The Sound and the Fury* in much the same way "That Evening Sun" does. Each of the three Quentins is independent of the others, and each is legitimately read only in the light of his surrounding narrative. But Faulkner supports our temptation to see all three as one by subtle turns of the narrative. Quentin, in moving freely though his and Shreve's flexible—almost loose—narrative, raises the ante on incest and returns to it again and again. . . .[67]

Considerable external evidence, both before and after the completion of the novel, indicates that Faulkner used the same Quentin who had appeared in *The*

Sound and the Fury. Indeed, his 1934 letter to Hal Smith had stated that he had chosen Quentin *because* of his problems with his sister in *The Sound and the Fury* (*SLWF*, 78–79). Faulkner expressed essentially the same notion at Virginia:

> Q. Sir, speaking of those two books, as you read *Absalom, Absalom!*, how much can a reader feel that this is the Quentin, the same Quentin, who appeared in *The Sound and the Fury*—that is, a man thinking about his own Compson family, his own sister?
> A. To me he's consistent. That he approached the Sutpen family with the same ophthalmia that he approached his own troubles, that he probably never saw anything very clearly, that his was just one of the thirteen ways to look at Sutpen, and his may have been the—one of the most erroneous. (*FIU*, 274)

Faulkner proclaimed that the novel was indeed "Sutpen's story," but he acknowledged that "every time any character gets into a book, no matter how minor, he's actually telling his biography. . . . Quentin was still trying to get God to tell him why, in *Absalom, Absalom!* as he was in *The Sound and the Fury*" (*FIU*, 275). That Faulkner considered *Absalom* Sutpen's story may reflect the author's primary motivation in composing it; that is, *Absalom* is Sutpen's story in the same sense that *The Sound and the Fury* is Caddy's story. What we know of the process of composition indicates that at each stage Faulkner made revisions that gave greater prominence to Quentin and his reactions to the events he attempts to understand.

In the 1970s, critics began paying more attention to the obsessions established in *The Sound and the Fury* which Quentin brings with him to *Absalom, Absalom!* In 1975 John T. Irwin's *Doubling and Incest, Repetition and Revenge* took issue with the critical separation Poirier had called for in the early 1950s.[68] His reading of the two novels, largely psychoanalytic in orientation, brought to bear what we know about Quentin from *The Sound and the Fury* in understanding his peculiar obsessions with parts of the Sutpen history in *Absalom, Absalom!*. Two years later, Estella Schoenberg's *Old Tales and Talking: Quentin Compson in William Faulkner's Absalom, Absalom! and Related Works* went even further in exploring the relationship between Quentin's roles in the two novels. Schoenberg conflates the chronology of the books to maintain that Quentin's discussions with his father in *Absalom* occur in September 1909, immediately after those depicted in *The Sound and the Fury*, which had occurred in August of the same year.[69]

Neither Irwin's nor Schoenberg's book is completely satisfactory in exploring the relationship between the two novels, though each suggests approaches which might prove valuable. Schoenberg's critical analysis of Quentin is quite limited, and Irwin considers him within the context of larger speculations about the psychology motivating several characters in the two novels. There can be little doubt, however, that Faulkner chose Quentin Compson as a narrator for a reason, and that Quentin's concerns in *Absalom, Absalom!* bear a remarkable resemblance to those in *The Sound and the Fury*. Further, his father seems essentially the same character the reader is familiar with from the earlier novel.[70] Finally, conversation between father and son in an attempt to understand human motivation and behavior has been established as a sort of trademark of their relationship, which is certainly carried over into *Absalom*.[71]

Quentin dwells frequently in *The Sound and the Fury* on things he remembers his father as having said. Mr. Compson's cynicism and world-weariness are very much a part of Quentin's view of him. The comment of Mr. Compson's which Faulkner uses to introduce the Quentin section of *The Sound and the Fury* would work just as well in beginning to understand the young man's interest in the Sutpen story. Significantly, the occasion is when Mr. Compson presents his son with a watch inherited from General Compson, as the Sutpen story will later be a part of Quentin's heritage from his grandfather. Mr. Compson's remark concerns the value of time, one of the central subjects of both *The Sound and the Fury* and *Absalom, Absalom!*:

> Quentin, I give you the mausoleum of all hope and desire; it's rather excrutiating-ly apt that you will use it to gain the reducto absurdum of all human experience which can fit your individual needs no better than it fitted his or his father's. I give it to you not that you may remember time, but that you might forget it now and then for a moment and not spend all your breath trying to conquer it. Because no battle is ever won he said. They are not even fought. The field only reveals to man his own folly and despair, and victory is an illusion of philosophers and fools. (*TSTF*, 93)

Absalom, Absalom! presents in dramatic terms Quentin Compson's wrestling with his father's cynicism as reflected in the Sutpen story. Indeed, we might say that Quentin spends a great deal of breath in the later novel trying to conquer time. His effort takes the form of an attempt to reconstruct the past in such as way as to make it significant for his own understanding of human experience. His knowledge of the Sutpen story would tell him that battles are indeed fought, that men live and die in pursuit of ideals which have everlasting significance, despite his father's disclaimers. Thus, Sutpen's story is fascinating to Quentin precisely because *it is a tragedy*—a story of people whose mistakes led to the disruption or destruction of lives, but who saw themselves as affirming something that mattered.

In the conversation at the end of Quentin's section of *The Sound and the Fury*, Mr. Compson makes a point which Quentin might well have had in mind as he returns from his night visit to Sutpen's Hundred with Miss Rosa. Referring to the pain occasioned by Caddy's loss of innocence, Mr. Compson says:

> You cannot bear to think that someday it will no longer hurt you like this now were getting at it you seem to regard it merely as an experience that will whiten your hair overnight so to speak without altering your appearance at all you wont do it under these conditions it will be a gamble and the strange thing is that man who is conceived by accident and whose every breath is a fresh

cast with dice already loaded against him will not face that final main which he knows before hand he has assuredly to face without essaying expedients ranging all the way from violence to petty chicanery that would not deceive a child until someday in very disgust he risks everything on a single blind turn of a card no man ever does that under the first fury of despair or remorse or bereavement he does it only when he has realized that even the despair or remorse or bereavement is not particularly important to the dark diceman. . . . (*TSTF*, 220–21)

The passage illustrates how little Mr. Compson knows his son, who will indeed take the action his father seems sure he will avoid—suicide. But the ironies of the passage are multiplied by the fact that Quentin will commit suicide precisely for the reasons Mr. Compson outlines here: his discovery that neither the despair nor remorse nor bereavement is particularly important. Remembering Faulkner's comment that he used Quentin because he is "about to commit suicide because of his sister" (*SLWF*, 79), we must conclude that ultimately this fact is what he learns at Sutpen's Hundred and what he finds so disturbing. His confrontation with Henry reveals to Quentin the final outcome of his own obsessions. Far from being a confirmation of significance, a reward for the defense of honor, Quentin discovers a wasted man whose life has finally stood for nothing. His father's nihilism lies embodied before him, and he cannot bring himself to face its relevance to his own situation.

The following examination of *Absalom, Absalom!* does not attempt to establish that Quentin Compson must be seen as projecting his difficulties from *The Sound and the Fury* upon the Sutpen tragedy. Certainly the novel is explicable without such a premise, even if certain passages would prove to be rather puzzling if not interpreted in light of the earlier book. Faulkner, however, does nothing to prohibit bringing a wider knowledge of Quentin and his relationship with his father to a reading of *Absalom, Absalom!* On the contrary, he encourages such an approach on several levels. And no one can deny that such a possibility immeasurably enriches the complexities of *Absalom, Absalom!*, independently Faulkner's most complex work.

In *The Sound and the Fury*, Quentin accuses his father of reducing things of substance to hollow words, and Mr. Compson tacitly agrees. At issue in their conversation is the concept of virginity. Mr. Compson maintains that he had come to his position at the instant when he had realized "that tragedy is second-hand" (*TSTF*, 143). In *Absalom, Absalom!*, Quentin comes to the same conclusion, one which Shreve does not understand. Thus, his friend assumes that Quentin's feverish reaction to the story results from his hatred of the region which had given rise to such a man as Sutpen. Quentin's anguished reply that he does not hate the South is indeed accurate, for the despairing truth he has learned from Henry Sutpen transcends both time and location. For Quentin Compson, tragedy is secondhand, at least in *Absalom, Absalom!*, and he will escape from the despair occasioned by that discovery only by plunging into the cold depths of the Charles River.

1

"Because she wants it told":
Quentin's Encounter with Rosa

The first chapter of *Absalom, Absalom!* provides the careful reader with keys to the book's major structural techniques as well as introductions to the central characters, themes, and patterns of imagery. Moreover, from the very first page, Faulkner hints, however subtly, at the relationship between *Absalom* and *The Sound and the Fury*. The reader familiar with the earlier novel not only recognizes the character of Quentin, but cannot miss the references to things which obsess him there: the progression of time and the way Quentin marks its passing by observation of the changing angles of the sun's light, as in the opening of his monologue; the presence of the wisteria which torments him because he associates its over-sweet fragrance with both his sister's sexual experience and his own sexual frustrations. There is, of course, a danger in transferring knowledge of a character from one Faulkner work to another. Yet there is both internal and external evidence to substantiate a direct relationship between the character of Quentin in *The Sound and the Fury* and *Absalom, Absalom!*.

In the 1934 letter to Harrison Smith outlining his plans for the novel, Faulkner made clear the significance of Quentin's contribution to the book:

> The one I am writing now will be called DARK HOUSE or something of that nature. It is the more or less violent breakup of a household or family from 1860 to about 1910. . . . Quentin Compson, of the Sound & Fury, tells it, or ties it together; he is the protagonist so that it is not complete apocrypha. I use him because it is just before he is to commit suicide because of his sister, and I use his bitterness which he has projected on the South in the form of hatred of it and its people to get more out of the story itself than a historical novel would be. To keep the hoop skirts and plug hats out, you might say. (*SLWF*, 78–79)

To an unmistakable degree, Faulkner's use of Quentin in *Absalom, Absalom!* would change as he wrote the novel. Quentin is hardly an effective agent at keeping the story from degenerating into "complete apocrypha," given his and Shreve's conjectures in the second half, and the completed work would be considerably heavier than Faulkner's projection of it sounds. But Faulkner makes clear that in his original conception, Quentin's role in *Absalom* would be a direct outgrowth of the part he plays in *The Sound and the Fury*, and, indeed, at more than one point his peculiar involvement in the Sutpen story is practically incomprehensible to the reader unfamiliar with his reactions to events and concerns in the earlier novel.

Absalom opens with a description of Miss Rosa, a woman whose bizarre, contradictory appearance becomes for Quentin a personification of the past itself. She suffers in the dark stifling heat because "when she was a girl someone had believed that light and moving air carried heat and that dark was always cooler" (3), suggesting from the very beginning the impact of the past upon Miss Rosa's thinking. Her demeanor and her clothing suggest the peculiar nature of her strangely repressed life. Her feet fail to touch the floor, giving her the appearance of a little girl, and Quentin is aware of "the rank smell of female old flesh long embattled in virginity while the wan haggard face watched him . . . from the too tall chair in which she resembled a crucified child" (4). The description holds important clues concerning how what Miss Rosa says should be interpreted. She is in many ways still a child, having missed in her life most of the experiences which combine to create an adult sensibility. Chief among these is sexuality, and the references to marriage in her speech indicate that a large portion of her resentment of Sutpen derives from her own sexual frustration. Both Rosa's appearance and her interest in sex anticipate her longer speech in chapter 5, in which she explores in some detail the reasons for her extended childhood and Sutpen's alleged responsibility for her life of sexual frustration.

Quentin has been summoned to hear Miss Rosa's own account of how Sutpen had destroyed her and her family, but from the very beginning we find him listening selectively. He brings with him to the interview his earlier knowledge of the legends, those shared by the rest of the town and county, but he brings his own preoccupations as well. John T. Matthews offers a suggestion for Quentin's fascination with Rosa's story in terms of his own obsessions: "Quentin's behavior under the spell of Rosa's voice reveals that the story holds him—whatever the original bond—by the power of its similarity to his own."[1] Perhaps for this reason, before anything that Miss Rosa says to him is related in the text we find him retreating into his personal concerns, which at every point affect his perceptions of the story of Sutpen and his family. As Rosa talks, Quentin conjures his own vision of the man: "Her voice would not cease, it would just vanish" (4), and in Quentin's mind, "Out of quiet thunderclap he would abrupt (man-horse-demon) upon a scene peaceful and decorous as a schoolprize water color" (4). Thus, though Quentin's image of Sutpen blooms in his own mind, it represents sympathetically the picture which Rosa constructs for him—the heroic demon, larger than life and more terrible, who wrenches his plantation from the wilderness with a dramatic, indeed almost mythic power resembling God's own act of creation: "the *Be Sutpen's Hundred* like the oldtime *Be Light*" (5).

The very way Quentin hears the story foreshadows later events. He finds his personality as listener divided into two separate but by no means equal entities: the youth preparing for his freshman year at Harvard, leaving the South peopled by ghosts, and the tragic young man, himself a ghost, who must continually confront the image of Sutpen, a figure who could hardly be more different from Quentin himself, yet a figure to which the young man finds himself strangely compelled. The first telling of the outlines of Sutpen's story transfixes the latter of these two personalities, though Miss Rosa addresses the former, and it is the second Quentin who in Hugh Ruppersburg's term translates it for the reader:[2]

> *It seems that this demon—his name was Sutpen—(Colonel Sutpen)—Colonel Sutpen. Who came out of nowhere and without warning upon the land with a band of strange niggers and built a plantation—(Tore violently a plantation, Miss Rosa Coldfield says)—tore violently. And married her sister Ellen and begot a son and a daughter which—(Without gentleness begot, Miss Rosa Coldfield says)— without gentleness. Which should have been the jewels of his pride and the shield and comfort of his old age, only—(Only they destroyed him or something or he destroyed them or something. And died)—and died. Without regret, Miss Rosa Coldfield says—(Save by her) Yes, save by her. (And by Quentin Compson) Yes. And by Quentin Compson.* (5–6)

This first recitation of the Sutpen legend is invested with a tremendous significance for what follows. Superficially it outlines practically all the facts which can be known with certainty about the man, doubtlessly all the important ones.[3] Furthermore, it signals the central questions in his history: the ambivalence of Sutpen's relationships with the members of his family, the inability of the present characters to discern exactly what or who destroyed what or whom. More importantly, however, this passage underlines the means through which information about the Sutpen family is to be conveyed throughout the novel. Quentin's own musings are constantly amended by Miss Rosa's comments, expressing her own viewpoints. In effect, she "corrects" his interpretations. So will later pieces of information be interpreted and corrected, on the obvious level by the various narrators, but more significantly by the reader himself.

Beyond this level of correction as new information is discovered, we find Quentin beginning the process of assigning motives to the individual characters. Though in a sense Miss Rosa regrets Sutpen's death because through dying he has removed himself from her scorn and hatred, she certainly does not regret his death in the way that Quentin seems to indicate, certainly not the way Quentin himself regrets the loss. Indeed, her comment that he died "*without regret*" seems to reflect her own opinion of her feelings. Yet Quentin immediately contradicts her, perhaps identifying her obsessive need to talk about Sutpen with the (to him, at least) tragic events Quentin himself cannot forget. As the novel progresses, Quentin comes more and more to identify his own past and the members of his family with Sutpen's story and particularly with the conflict among the Sutpen children. Sutpen's death and the inability of the present narrators to figure out his history underline Quentin's own shortcomings in unravelling the tormenting threads of his relationship with his own father and his sister. It is in quite a different and intensely personal way that the death is regretted by Quentin Compson.

The image of the wisteria vine, blooming for the second time that summer, has significance not only for Quentin, but for Rosa as well, for it reminds her of her own "summer of wistaria." The blossoms link her with Quentin, both sharing an obsessive need to make sense out of Sutpen's destructive downfall and a desire to come to grips with how it affects their individual experience.[4] Rosa, of course, has no way of knowing about Quentin's independent interest, and she begins by suggesting to him a reason for hearing the story: "'So maybe you will enter the literary profession as so many Southern gentlemen and gentlewomen too are doing now and maybe some day you will remember this and write about it. You will be married then I expect and perhaps your wife will want a new gown or a new chair for the house and you can write this and submit it to the magazines'" (6).[5] But Quentin views her reasons differently, prefiguring his and Shreve's attempts later to assign motives to the characters of the drama or to revise motives assigned by the other narrators, particularly Mr. Compson. Quentin thinks, *"Only she dont mean that . . . . It's because she wants it told"* (7). His mind wanders to the moment he received the summons from Rosa, and the narrative voice reveals that perhaps because of his youth he did not recognize the "cold, implacable, and even ruthless" aspects of her character. But his understanding of her reason includes an intuitive grasp of the significance of the story to Rosa: to her, God had let the South lose the Civil War because only by such an apocalyptic cataclysm, *"only through the blood of our men and the tears of our women could He stay this demon* [Sutpen] *and efface his name and lineage from the earth"* (8). Immediately, however, he revises this idea. If Rosa had only wanted the story told, she is perfectly capable of telling it herself as the "county's poetess laureate" (8).

Quentin's ascribing motives to Rosa's summons and immediately revising these motives in light of new or reconsidered information signal one of the novel's major structural principles. He is probably wrong in thinking that to Rosa the war had been fought in order to resolve a family crisis, though this is an idea which will later arise again in his and Shreve's examination of the conflict between Bon and Henry. In both instances, Quentin's thinking follows similar lines. His own inability to assimilate experience suggests the need to ascribe great import to that experience. Thus, for Quentin, Sutpen's tragedy acquires dimensions which parallel those of the whole South. Understanding Sutpen and his family would mean understanding not only Quentin's personal problems and the circumstances which gave rise to them, but the problems of the entire region, the history of an entire people.

Miss Rosa's choice of Quentin proves a shrewd one. He is already knowledgeable of a great deal of the Sutpen story, part of it related by his father, part of it his heritage of community legends. As the narrative voice summarizes these legends, they are expanded, offering the reader more hints about Sutpen and his tragedy, hints which may be added to those in Quentin's earlier recital of what he knows. We learn how on a Sunday morning in June 1833 Sutpen "rode into town out of no discernible past and acquired his land no one knew how and built his house, his mansion, apparently out of nothing and married Ellen Coldfield and begot his two children—the son who widowed the daughter who had not yet been a bride—and so accomplished his allotted course to its violent . . . end" (9). Added to the earlier account is the conflict between brother and sister, a matter of vital interest to Quentin. Appropriately, the narration breaks off at this point to focus again on Quentin himself. He is presented in terms of a haunted building—recalling Sutpen's ghost which haunts Miss Rosa's voice "where a more fortunate one would have had a house" earlier in the chapter (4). Once again, though, the history of the region is linked with Quentin's own perception and experience: "He was a barracks filled with stubborn back-looking ghosts still recovering, even forty-three years afterward, from the fever which had cured the disease, waking from the fever without even knowing that it had been the fever itself which they had fought against and not the sickness . . ." (9). The fever represents the war, but the sickness suggests a much wider set of circumstances than mere slavery. To Quentin (no less than to Rosa), the sickness suggests the entire social structure which could produce a Sutpen and allow his tragedy to be played out. (The repetition here of the period of forty-three years—the length of Rosa's outrage—reminds the reader once more of the connections between speaker and listener; their personal fixations have a great deal in common.) Free of the disease, Quentin, like his fellow Southerners, is "not even aware that the freedom is that of impotence" (10).

The concept of physical and psychological impotence once again suggests *The Sound and the Fury*, and at this point in his narrative Faulkner introduces Mr. Compson in a parenthetical interruption of Quentin's musings. The passage jumps forward in time to Quentin's return home after his afternoon interview with Rosa. He questions his father about her motives, hinting both at the problems of the Compson family and those of the South: "'What is it to me that the land or the earth or whatever it was got tired of [Sutpen] at last and turned and destroyed him? . . . It's going to turn and destroy us all some day, whether our name happens to be Sutpen or Coldfield or not'" (10).

Mr. Compson's answer functions on a number of levels, both structurally and thematically. The entire passage anticipates chapters 2 through 4, in which Quentin listens to his father's interpretation of events, but Mr. Compson's cynicism in responding to his son recalls the tortured conversations they had had at the end of section 2 of *The Sound and the Fury*, conversations which had occurred the previous spring if the chronologies of the two novels are joined together.[6] The imagery Mr. Compson uses extends the chapter's emphasis upon spirits which are dead but still very much present: "'Years ago we in the South made our women into ladies. Then the War came and made the ladies into ghosts. So what else can we do, being gentlemen, but listen to them being ghosts?'" (10). Mr. Compson has accurately defined Miss Rosa's personality and her relation to the Sutpen story, but even further, he has accurately stated a truth about his ineffectual functioning as head of the family in his own home. The Quentin section in *The Sound and the Fury* dramatizes Mr. Compson's weakness, and it becomes a minor refrain throughout Jason's monologue as well. In *Absalom, Absalom!*, as Mr. Compson continues to attribute motives to Ellen and to Judith in his recounting of events, the reader legitimately questions the extent to which his view of these characters may be influenced by his relationship to his own wife and children.

Like Quentin, Mr. Compson offers a different motive for Rosa's choosing to relate her story to his son, discounting the reasons she herself provides. Since General Compson had been as close to being Sutpen's friend as anyone, perhaps Rosa assumes extensive knowledge on Quentin's part. Or perhaps she is telling the story for purely personal reasons and really wants it to stay in the family, so to speak. But Mr. Compson also relates a new piece of information: that Rosa herself had at one time considered marriage to Sutpen. As we later learn, that "engagement which did not engage, that troth which failed to plight" (10) was the crucial event confirming Rosa in the sterile pattern of death-in-life she had known since childhood. It was this broken engagement, not the war, which had turned her into a ghost, a fact which Mr. Compson seems to recognize. He postulates that she perhaps holds Quentin's family partially responsible for the waste of her own life.

Ultimately, however, Mr. Compson hits on Rosa's real motive without seeming to remark it: "'It's because she will need someone to go with her—a man, a gentleman, yet one still young enough to do what she wants, do it the way she wants it done'" (10). This comment foreshadows Quentin's crucial trip to Sutpen's Hundred, not described until the final chapter of the novel but present throughout as though an ominous, portentous threat. Brief references to it in the early sections culminate at the end of chapter 5 in Rosa's assertion that something has been hidden in the house for four years, something she and Quentin must investigate under cover of darkness.

Thus, her true reason is not made clear to the reader until the end of Rosa's monologue, three hours after Quentin enters her house. During this time she presents her view of Sutpen and of the other members of his family. To Quentin, they seem to emerge "in inverse ratio to the vanishing voice" (11), though the reader has likewise to wait until the end of chapter 5 to understand the full import of his fixation on a single part of the story. To him, Sutpen seems to arise out of hell, and around him are grouped the two children and wife. They become assimilated into "the conventional family group of the period" (12). Still, the image remains illusive, possessing "a quality strange, contradictory and bizarre; not quite comprehensible, nor . . . quite right" (12). This image sets the tone for Quentin's view of the participants: for him they will remain unapproachable, slightly beyond his ken.[7]

As Miss Rosa talks, Quentin pictures the major characters; however, his musing is directed not toward understanding them but toward the speaker's attitude, what it reveals about Miss Rosa. Her voice acquires almost a life of its own.[8] He wonders if at an earlier time the voice had been a "cry aloud . . . of young and indomitable unregret, of indictment of blind circumstance and savage event" (13–14). Once again the reader familiar with *The Sound and the Fury* is reminded of Quentin's concern there with fixing emotional pain in a realm where its meaning and significance remain always keen, always present. But this passage also introduces a long line of characters in *Absalom* who question the divine ordering of events and rebel against the circumstances in which they find themselves.

Rosa's recounting of events comprises roughly the second half of the first chapter. Quentin contributes only one-word responses, which punctuate her monologue. Rosa draws Sutpen as a villain, a demon. Her reason for this view lies largely in her ignorance of Sutpen's background—of the nature of his true motives as they were understood by General Compson, to whom he confessed them. She knows only of his behavior after his arrival in Jefferson, and his cold manipulation of her family can appear only demonic to her. She pictures him fleeing to remote Yoknapatawpha County in order to establish a front of respectability behind which he can hide. The tools he uses to achieve respectability are provided by Rosa's family, the Coldfields.

Rosa establishes yet another metaphor for the structure of the novel in explaining how her sister Ellen had fallen under Sutpen's spell: "'Oh, I hold no brief for Ellen: blind romantic fool who had only youth and inexperience to excuse her even if that; blind romantic fool, then later blind woman mother fool when she no longer had either youth or inexperience to excuse her . . . '" (13). The repetition of Rosa's epithet signals various other rehearsals of episodes as the novel progresses, usually with each subsequent one adding to the reader's understanding of events and of the characters who set them in motion. Likewise, Rosa proceeds to add further information to what the reader knows from the brief telescoping of the events at two points earlier in the chapter. For instance, the daughter (as yet unnamed) is now the "same as a widow without ever having been a bride and was, three years later, to be a widow sure enough without having been anything at all" (13–14).

She then returns to Sutpen himself, again emphasizing the fact that he was not even a gentleman, that he was a sort of outlaw.[9] Gradually, Rosa begins to support her interpretation of Sutpen's motivations and character, though the evidence she musters is weak indeed, reflecting almost exclusively her own hatred. She highlights his lack of background, of family relations, and assumes that his reticence about his origins masks something dark and terrible: "'Anyone could have looked at him just once and known that he would be lying about who and where and why he came from by the very fact that apparently he had to refuse to say at all'" (15–16). Her evidence for this point is Sutpen's youth: that there were easier ways for a young man to make money and acquire the respect of the community than clearing virgin land. Her view is again a barometer of her lack of understanding of Sutpen. In her wildly romantic interpretation, she refuses to give the devil his due. She ignores the perseverance and dedication to long hours of hard work which the reader later finds to have been integral to Sutpen's character.

As Rosa's narration proceeds, her focus shifts from Ellen's view of Sutpen to her own. Unlike her sister, she has no extenuating explanation for falling within the range of Sutpen's demonic power. Unlike Ellen when she had married Sutpen, Rosa had been a mature woman when she had agreed to wed him. She had indeed watched him all her life, since, as Mr. Compson hints, her life had ended with the broken engagement. Once again she summarizes the events of the Sutpen tragedy; once again further details are added, including the children's names. But with the added details comes a more passionate attitude revealed in the vivid language itself:

> "I saw Judith's marriage forbidden without rhyme or reason or shadow of excuse; I saw Ellen die with only me, a child, to turn to and ask to protect her remaining child; I saw Henry repudiate his home and birthright and then return and practically fling the bloody corpse of his sister's sweetheart at the hem of her wedding gown; I saw that man return . . . who had created two children not only to destroy one another and his own line, but my line as well, yet I agreed to marry him." (17–18)

In rationalizing her rashness, Rosa maintains that she is doing just the opposite. She refuses to plead youth, propinquity, or her own peculiar experience of living. But Rosa protests too much, and eventually the ambivalence which lies at the heart of her view of Sutpen begins to surface. To her he partakes, if only vicariously, of the glory she associates with those who had fought in the Southern Cause. She somewhat grudgingly grants him bravery; but if Sutpen had "valor and strength," he lacked "pity and honor" in her eyes. Her jaundiced vision cannot completely obliterate Sutpen's heroic qualities, but she continues to picture him as a demon. Recalling earlier suppositions about her reasons for telling her story, she demands of Quentin whether, supported by such men, " 'Is it any wonder that Heaven saw fit to let us lose?' " (19).

Rosa views the playing out of her family tragedy as the expiation of a curse, in part because of what she perceives to have been the absurdity of Sutpen's involvement with her family. She contrasts him with her father, a conventional merchant who, despite his unorthodox attitude toward slavery, had managed to exist within the social structure Rosa insists Sutpen had attempted to flout. She emphasizes Sutpen's alienation from the small community of Jefferson, and she offers his exploitation of the church as the ultimate affront to the values of that community. He enters the church only to serve his own need, three times, according to Miss Rosa: once when he had met Ellen, once to rehearse the wedding and once actually to marry her. Rosa, with her tendency to magnify the significance of events relating to her family (a tendency she shares with Quentin), can accept this outrage only as evidence of " 'a fatality and curse on our family' " (20). Like Quentin, she views the anathema pronounced upon the Coldfields as a paradigm of the larger curse placed upon the South.

As Miss Rosa begins to explain her perception of the curse, Quentin conjures a vision of her as a little girl. His conception is quite convincing, drawing upon the image Rosa herself provides, and it indicates how he will continue to approach all the characters in the novel—through his imagination. Rosa's language summons the sort of dream-vision associated with a fairy tale. In such a vision she sees her sister, nephew, and niece as she had viewed them in her childhood, when they had been largely forbidden to her. The only reason she could fathom for such an alienation from the members of her own family had been the influence of the demon Sutpen. Thus, when Ellen on her deathbed had requested that Rosa protect Judith, Rosa had responded, " "Protect her? From whom and from what? He [Sutpen] has already given them life: he does not need to harm them further. It is from themselves that they need protection" '" (22).

Rosa's evocation of a dream state in relating memories borne since childhood is reinforced when the narrative voice interrupts her story to focus on its impact upon Quentin. Time for him seems to have advanced faster that it actually had, as judged by the progress of the sunlight in the room. (His following the progression of time in terms of the sun is once again reminiscent of *The Sound and the Fury*.) To Quentin, Miss Rosa's story seems to be a dream itself, frozen in time, yet paradoxically drawing its imaginative involvement from an awareness of elapsed time. Throughout the novel the past will be seen as a kind of dream, and the imagery of dreams and shadows will intensify as various narrators attempt to exorcize the demons the past evokes.

As justification of her answer to Ellen and of the view of Judith and Henry which it implies, Rosa relates two incidents which had occurred while they were both children. She could have witnessed neither of them directly. Rosa's earliest memory is of seeing Ellen and the children arrive at the church Sutpen himself would not attend. Once more, she summons the language of dreams, or, in this case, of nightmares: " 'a glimpse like the forefront of a tornado, of the carriage and Ellen's high white face within it and the two replicas of his face in miniature flanking her . . .' " (24). She insists that Ellen, terrified, was holding " 'those two children who were not crying and who did not need to be held' " (24). Her interpretation ignores the natural fascination which children have with speed, with movement and color (perhaps out of sheer ignorance: Rosa continues to maintain that a childhood had been denied her). Instead, she sees evidence of the curse, derived genetically from Sutpen; resembling him physically, the children share his propensity for violence and for violating the codes of community conduct.

John Hagan sees a connection between Rosa and Sutpen implicit in the scene in which he and his family race to church. The picture conjured by Rosa is reminiscent of the Tidewater carriage of Sutpen's youth which had almost ridden down the boy and his sister. His racing along is a replay of that earlier event. Just as Sutpen's entire life is predicated upon events which had happened when he was a boy, as he explains to General Compson in chapter 7, so is Rosa conditioned for life by her early experiences, as she makes clear to Quentin in chapter 5.[10]

Though present himself at the first race, Sutpen accedes to the community pressure to conform, manifested by the minister, though the races to the church continue. In Rosa's view, they are instigated by Sutpen through his surrogate, the slave who drives the carriage; like his master he remains outside the rules governing conduct in the community and is further separated by the barrier of language. Rosa bases her interpretation on the fact that when one of the men had attempted to stop the slave from beating the horses for ostensibly running away, the slave had replied, " ' "Marster say; I do. You tell Marster" ' " (25).

Still maintaining that Judith and Henry had needed protection only from themselves, having inherited the Sutpen nature, Rosa relates how Ellen had then interceded with Sutpen. In Rosa's picture of the following Sunday, however, when the children are brought out of the house and see their mother's phaeton drawn by a gentle mare, Judith reacts violently and even has to be put to bed. Sutpen has indeed triumphed, forcing acknowledgment that his face had been present all the time in the carriage: Judith herself had been the instigator of the runaways. For Rosa, this is proof positive of her answer to her dying sister; not only is Henry inheritor of his father's nature, but so too is the daughter.

In telling what transpired when she had been taken to Sutpen's Hundred as a child of four on that Sunday, Miss Rosa emphasizes her heightened sense of perception. She maintains a foreknowledge of how the house itself and its inhabitants would look. (The scene anticipates the heightened perception Quentin demonstrates in chapter 9 when he visualizes Rosa's final trip to the rotting mansion.) Much of her supposed foreknowledge was certainly acquired later, in recalling the day through the filter of subsequent events, particularly her later view of Sutpen. She insists that even at the age of four she had wondered what Judith had seen in the phaeton to precipitate so vituperative a reaction, or worse, what she had missed. She is further immediately aware upon entering the house itself that Sutpen is not present in it, and she recalls being mesmerized at the sight of Judith asleep in her bed, suggesting that rather than sleeping she had been prey to a trance-like stupor. Again Rosa underlines the sentience of the house itself, its inimical presence in the quiet Sunday afternoon " 'louder than thunder, louder than laughing even with triumph' " (28).

Rosa does not tell Quentin very much about the conversation she had overheard between Ellen and her father. Mr. Coldfield cautions his daughter to think of her children, and Ellen's response indicates that she is virtually obsessed with their welfare. When questioned about her love for Sutpen, Ellen responds only " 'Papa,' " suggesting to Rosa that the question is irrelevant (29). Rosa again insists to Quentin that she could see her sister's face through the closed door, that she had understood her attitudes, her repressed hatred and fear of her husband. Once again, however, the reader must question the validity of Rosa's view of Ellen, tainted—as Quentin is aware—by forty-three years of her own hatred of her brother-in-law. Perhaps she merely projects her own fear and resentment onto the shade of her dead sister.

The second proof Miss Rosa provides duplicates the point of the first, though it intensifies the nature and extent of the struggle between Ellen and her husband. Rosa even goes so far as to suggest that Sutpen stages the slave fight for the sole purpose of demonstrating his victory over his wife: "'he now showed us why that triumph [of the carriage] had been beneath his notice. He showed Ellen, that is: not I'" (29). Throughout this part of her story, Rosa continues to stress the fact that though she understands the implications of the scene, she had not been present herself. It is now six years after the episode with the carriage. Sutpen continues his custom of staging fights among his slaves for the enjoyment of his guests, men Rosa describes as being as coarse as their host. The men would still gather at Sutpen's Hundred, but in deference to Ellen they would approach the stable from the back to witness the fights. At the end, Sutpen would himself enter the ring, forcing his son, Henry, to watch the spectacle. Henry rebels, screaming loudly enough to bring his mother running. Ellen condescends to grant Sutpen the right to force their son to witness the ritual, but she remains convinced that he had also invited Judith to the stable. Rosa, though, had not been there to see Judith's replica of the Sutpen face staring at the scene from the loft above, beside a Negro girl sharing the Sutpen features. Rosa accepts Sutpen's protestation of innocence; his supreme triumph—she implies—is that Judith has come to see the primitive masculine rite of her own accord. She *wants* to view it, unlike her more delicate brother.

In this first section of her long monologue, continued in chapter 5, Rosa has both signaled her attitude toward Sutpen and outlined the major events of his downfall. At the end of chapter 1 the stage is set, the characters roughly in place. But Rosa's account also identifies one of the central problems confronting the reader throughout *Absalom, Absalom!*—that of sorting fact from fiction, the difficulty of interpreting action and motivation, especially when confronted with narration prejudiced, as Rosa's is, by a peculiar bias. Miss Rosa is the only narrator who had actually witnessed part of the events she recounts, who had actually known some of the participants firsthand. Yet she constantly infuses her narration with factors forcing the reader to question her reliability: her tendency to view Sutpen as a demon, resulting primarily from her own broken engagement to him and her ignorance of his design; her need to identify with her sister, who has experienced living in a way Miss Rosa herself has not, while at the same time holding herself superior to Ellen in judgment and perception; finally, and perhaps most pervasively, her desire to have her own peculiar interpretation of events accepted by her young listener. She must have Quentin view her participation in the Sutpen tragedy sympathetically in order to persuade him to accompany her to Sutpen's Hundred later in the evening. But from a broader perspective, Quentin's approval would provide at least a partial vindication of her decision forty-three years before to renounce Sutpen and flee into the outraged exile which characterizes the remainder of her life.

"A day of listening": Sutpen's Early History in Jefferson

The opening line of chapter 2 resonates throughout *Absalom, Absalom!*: "It was a summer of wistaria" (34). It anticipates Miss Rosa's summer of wisteria in the fifth chapter as well as recalling the imagery of the opening paragraphs of the novel. Here, as there, it also echos important image patterns in *The Sound and the Fury*, image patterns reinforced by the added description of Mr. Compson talking to Quentin on the front porch of their house.[1] The time, significantly, is twilight, the original title of the earlier novel[2] and the setting of several crucial events in its first two sections. Quentin is talking with his father about Sutpen, his curiosity piqued by what Miss Rosa has told him earlier in the afternoon and by the anticipation of accompanying her out to Sutpen's Hundred later in the evening. The odors of the wisteria and of Mr. Compson's cigar anticipate the scene in the last four chapters of the book as well, for five months later these odors would be carried by Mr. Compson's letter "up from Mississippi and over the long iron New England snow and into Quentin's sitting-room at Harvard" (34). The reader encountering *Absalom* for the first time hardly notices this throwaway reference to Mr. Compson's letter announcing Miss Rosa's death, which precipitates the discussion between Shreve and Quentin in the final sections. Having absorbed so much of Miss Rosa's view of Sutpen from chapter 1, the reader is now anxious to learn more, as is Quentin himself.

The first sixteen pages of chapter 2, related by the semi-omniscient third-person narrator,[3] indeed disclose a great deal about Sutpen. Like Quentin, the reader is forced to revise his opinion, for much of what he discovers here conflicts with Miss Rosa's testimony.[4] As in the narrative method of the first chapter, Faulkner provides a metaphor for the book's structure and clues to the reader's responsibility in approaching the story of Sutpen and in sorting out what and (perhaps more importantly) how Quentin knows what he does about it. The narrator outlines Sutpen's history from his arrival in Jefferson to the point of his choosing Ellen Coldfield as his bride. Picking up an idea first alluded to in the preceding chapter, the narrator begins with what Quentin knows about the story as his heritage from the town, drawing a pastoral view of Jefferson in 1833, then little more than a village on the edge of the wilderness. The Sunday church bells ring on a peaceful morning in June—the image recalls the setting of section 4 of *The Sound and the Fury*—as the stranger rides into town.

But the narration serves a broader purpose than merely summarizing what Quentin knows about Sutpen's early career in Jefferson. Faulkner also provides a complex study of how the information is accumulated over the years, how gossip about the stranger spreads, how assumptions are made and later proved incorrect, and how the portrait of the man Sutpen gradually emerges. The image does not develop clearly, however, either to Quentin or to the reader: Sutpen remains something of an enigma to the community in general and to Quentin and his father in particular, as subsequent chapters illustrate.

Faulkner's concern in presenting Sutpen's early history, then, focuses not directly on the events themselves, but on the community's perception of those events and how that perception is passed along through a variety of individual participants: General Compson, the coon-hunter Akers, and various unnamed citizens who witness Sutpen's early history. Firsthand observers pass along information to later generations in the town, symbolized by Mr. Compson and Miss Rosa (privy in some cases to more direct sources than the others), who in turn pass along what they know to Quentin. The narrator continually evokes Quentin as the final repository of knowledge, and thus the information this passage provides about Sutpen is always filtered through his perception. At times, Miss Rosa's picture of the demon intrudes on the generally more sympathetic view provided by Mr. Compson, a view he has inherited in turn from his father, Sutpen's only friend in Jefferson. Yet the narrative persona defines specific limits to the nature of that friendship, as well as specific reservations concerning General Compson's understanding of Sutpen.

Even the anonymous community observers are drawn with considerable care, and their perception of Sutpen's actions is limited by a number of factors: social station, extent of contact with the man, fear of his ability with a pistol, even gender. Certain common attitudes accrue, however. Sutpen is presented as a man shrouded in mystery, one driven with great energy to achieve goals only dimly perceived. His background is assumed by almost all to have been dubious, and his reluctance to talk about himself, added to his manipulation of his slaves and the architect he brings with him, creates the generally held view of his ruthlessness.

Sutpen enters Jefferson on that Sunday in June 1833, and "for almost a month" the only thing the town knows about him is his name. The early gossip predictably focuses on his appearance. His age could not be accurately guessed because Sutpen appears to have been ill with "some solitary furnace experience which was more than just fever" and which he had survived at a cost "not so much physical as mental" (36). His beard resembles a disguise, and "his pale eyes had a quality at once visionary and alert, ruthless and reposed in a face whose flesh had the appearance of pottery" (36). Even the physical description bears traces of interpretation Quentin has heard. The disguise of the beard reinforces Miss Rosa's view of Sutpen as a criminal seeking refuge in the Mississippi hinterland, while the visionary quality of the eyes reflects General Compson's theory of Sutpen's design, related in chapter 7.

There is agreement, though, about the stranger's skill with his pistols. General Compson witnesses him "ride at a canter around a sapling at twenty feet and put both bullets into a playing card fastened to the tree" (36). Calvin Brown points out that Sutpen uses single-shot pistols,[5] so he is equally accurate with either hand; understandably, his demonstration gains him instant respect, requiring that further investigations into Sutpen's personality and background be carried out obliquely. He tells the men at the Holston house that he does not drink, but later evidence disproves this assertion. General Compson concludes that "at this time Sutpen lacked not only the money to spend for drink and conviviality, but the time and inclination as well" (37). We are not told at what point the General had come to this realization, but his interpretation hints that his insight had occurred after Sutpen revealed something of his early life to him in 1864: "that he was at this time completely the slave of his secret and furious impatience" (37) that drove him until the conception of his son, an idea clearly prefiguring the "design" which Sutpen explains to Quentin's grandfather.

Town legend enshrines Sutpen's purchase of one hundred square miles of land, the deed recorded with an exotic gold Spanish coin. The gold coin occasions considerable speculation concerning his origins and his intentions among the townspeople:

> But he owned land among them now and some of them began to suspect what General Compson *apparently knew*: that the Spanish coin with which he had paid to have his patent recorded was the last one of any kind which he possessed. So they were certain now that he had departed to get more; there were several who even anticipated in believing . . . what Sutpen's future and then unborn sister-in-law was to tell Quentin almost eighty years later: that he had found some unique and practical way of hiding loot and that he had returned to the cache to replenish his pockets. . . . (38–39, emphasis added)

Presumably, unless the records had been destroyed or lost, Sutpen's patent could have been verified. Once again, as throughout the narrative passage at the beginning of the chapter, the point is not the event itself, but how it is perceived and transmitted. General Compson *seems* to know things which he may or may not actually know. The narrative persona specifically points out that Rosa had not even been born, yet she has theories about Sutpen's behavior at this point, even before his involvement with her sister Ellen. The persona hints that even if reliable information had been available, the passing of eighty years before Quentin receives it would make much of it suspect. Later in the same paragraph we discover that it was "years later" before the town discovered that the architect had come from Martinique "on Sutpen's bare promise" (39), an opinion which corrects Rosa's interpretation in the first chapter that he had been forced against his will. No information is offered about how the town discovered these facts, though supposedly they would have to have come from Sutpen himself. The narrator even goes to the length of pointing out that it *was not* General Compson who stopped to look into Sutpen's covered wagon "and into a black tunnel filled with still eyeballs and smelling like a wolfden" (40).

Gradually the reader comes to understand that practically none of what he learns about Sutpen can be trusted without reservation. The information evolves from a variety of conversations between witnesses and interested parties, conversations which the novel does not present, such as that (or those) in which General Compson relates what he knows to Quentin's father.[6] Moreover, the narrator ascribes several pieces of information to Miss Rosa's conversation with Quentin, which had occurred earlier in the afternoon. She ostensibly had told Quentin about Sutpen's pistols (36), about his stashing his loot (39), about the parties of men who would meet at the Holston House before going out to Sutpen's plantation (41), about the mud the workmen had spread over their naked bodies as protection against the mosquitoes (39), about the occasions on which Sutpen would fight with his slaves, once forcing Henry to watch (45), and finally about how the women of the community had viewed Sutpen during the period before his marriage (47). None of this information could have been gathered by Miss Rosa as a direct witness; moreover, the novel actually presents her relating only *one* portion of it to Quentin—the episode of Sutpen's fighting with his slaves, which she covers at the close of the first chapter. The reader must accept that the other "facts" have been conveyed in portions of her conversation which the novel records neither in chapter 1 nor in her lengthy monologue, chapter 5.

The point may appear insignificant on the surface, but later episodes will indicate that it is of primary importance. At the end of Rosa's monologue, Quentin recalls yet another portion of her story which is not presented directly in the text, and interpretation of the entire Sutpen tragedy hinges on what Quentin may have learned later in the evening when he visits Sutpen's Hundred and supposedly learns things not directly recorded. In these passages in chapter 2, ideas conveyed by Rosa in unrecorded conversations form a fabric with what Quentin learns from other sources, with what the community at large knows about Sutpen. They seem no more prejudiced nor no more outlandish than the suppositions of others, unlike some of Miss Rosa's statements recorded elsewhere in the novel. And the narrative voice even seems to support them over Rosa's version, specifically pointing out on at least one occasion that Miss Rosa did not understand the nature of her father's dealings with Sutpen (48–49) and generally undercutting her authority elsewhere by providing plausible explanations for events which she attributes to his demonic nature.

Similarly, the narrator refuses to grant extensive knowledge to General Compson. He *apparently* understands things about Sutpen on some occasions; on others, such as his comprehending Sutpen's desire for a splendid plantation house, we are told that "even General Compson did not know yet" what Sutpen's reason had been (43–44). The implication is that he would understand more later, but the passage underlines the fact that his knowledge has definite limits. Referring to Sutpen's overall plan, a mystery to most of the residents of Jefferson, we are told only that "General Compson claimed to have known" what the town clearly does not understand (44). Later, it is General Compson who *seems* to know Sutpen well enough to lend him some seed cotton and to offer to lend him money (46), an offer which Sutpen declines. The general is thus led to expect Sutpen to attempt an advantageous marriage, suspecting that he "intended to marry" the money to complete his house and furnish it (44). Like others who shared this opinion, Compson is proven wrong. Clearly, there is no outright endorsement of General Compson's opinions or interpretations of the story; on the contrary, he is shown drawing the wrong conclusions, equally capable of underestimating Sutpen or of misunderstanding him as any of the men who merely observe him from a distance. A narrative endorsement is offered to none of the characters in *Absalom, Absalom!*

Using such an amalgamation of sources, the narrative persona advances the recital of Sutpen's early history in Jefferson. Sutpen builds his house, allowing the architect to curb his desire for grandeur, finishing it as far as the resources of his plantation will allow. One tangible piece of evidence remains—Quentin knows the house, which even after seventy-five years retains the qualities which had prompted his grandfather to refer to the architect as an artist, not only because of his skill, but because "only an artist could have borne Sutpen's ruthlessness and hurry and still manage to curb the dream of grim and castlelike magnificence at which Sutpen obviously aimed" (43).

Following the completion of the mansion, Sutpen seems to have paused for a period of three years, and his future plans now become the object of speculation not only by the men who occasionally ran into him or rode out to his house as it was being built, but by the women of the community. To the men, Sutpen has a perfect dream, his house a "halfacre gunroom of a baronial splendor" (45), a notion which perhaps betrays some hint of Mr. Compson's misogynism. Sutpen now hosts the parties at which he pits his slaves against one another, himself sometimes challenging the victor. Led by General Compson, the community assumes Sutpen is searching for the proper marriage to complement the edifice which he had begun but had not the means to complete. They wrongly assume he would turn to the marriageable daughter of a landed planter; instead he chooses the daughter of a man without means—Mr. Coldfield. The reaction of the community is shock.

The reason for the reaction is simple: "Because the town now believed that it knew him" (48). The point is, of course, that it did not. As the long narrative passage gives way to Mr. Compson's recounting of Sutpen and Ellen's courtship and marriage, the persona summarizes the town's view of Sutpen which Quentin has inherited. Largely, this view is developed through contrasts between Sutpen and his prospective father-in-law. Mr. Coldfield is "a man with a name for absolute and undeviating and even puritan uprightness in a country and time of lawless opportunity, who neither drank nor gambled nor even hunted" (49). Superficially, Sutpen would appear to be Mr. Coldfield's antithesis: he drinks, hunts, (presumably) gambles, and his very lack of a definable past suggests the opposite of puritan uprightness—a man with few if any strengths of character. But the narrator has continually undercut the perception of the community, and the reader is encouraged to look beyond what the people of the time saw.

Because he is an outsider unwilling to justify himself, Sutpen is denied the very virtues he exhibits. His reluctance to drink until he is able to provide his measure of the liquor indicates a literal-minded respect, if not for moral principles, at least for fairness among men he takes to be his equals. (He is also wary of becoming indebted to his new neighbors.) His bringing an architect indicates a healthy respect for training and skill in areas where his own instincts and abilities are deficient. His refusal of General Compson's offer of a loan indicates independence and a desire for self-reliance, as well as a wariness of owing favors if he can avoid doing so. (Presumably his need of seed cotton had been much greater, his level of indebtedness to Compson less than a loan of cash would have been, since he accepts the seed.) Even his entering the ring with his slaves reveals a man who exults in his physical ability, his masculine strength; his domination over his blacks arises from more than mere chattel slavery.[7] Finally, all the accounts would point to Sutpen as a man of tremendous energy and initiative; he sets himself goals and dedicates himself to achieving them with a singlemindedness which can only be perceived as ruthlessness.

Instead, the community prefers its own conception of the man, no matter how far true of the mark. When Sutpen establishes his relationship with Mr. Coldfield, the onlookers forget that the storekeeper has a daughter of marriageable age: "They did not consider the daughter at all. They did not think of love in connection with Sutpen. They thought of ruthlessness rather than justice and of fear rather than respect, but not of pity or love" (49). Various signals suggest that the reader should be less harsh in judging Sutpen's character, at least in this portion of his career.

A mystery is created as Mr. Compson prepares to resume the story in his own voice. No one, we are told, including Miss Rosa understands the relationship between Sutpen and Mr. Coldfield; no one can explain how Sutpen could use Coldfield "to further whatever secret ends he still had" (49). This much appears sure: Sutpen himself is now aware of his path; his pattern of living changes. After three years of inhabiting the unfinished mansion, he quits inviting the men out to hunt and drink and fight. What the town now learns must come from an even more distant observation. Interpretation will be magnified as evidence diminishes. Significantly, Mr. Compson takes over at this point.

Initially, Compson tells the story with little change in emphasis. His concern remains the town's view of Sutpen, how the citizens react when he persuades Mr. Coldfield to hire and dispatch four wagons which return to Jefferson with the furnishings for the house. Following the pattern of community misunderstanding, the general assumption is that Sutpen has robbed a riverboat, even murdered a traveler in order to rob him. The coon-hunter who had earlier brought word of Sutpen's wild slaves seems to confirm the impression: " ' "Boys, this time he stole the whole durn steamboat!" ' " (51).

Adding specific details he recalls from his father, Mr. Compson relates how a vigilance committee of outraged citizens convinced of Sutpen's guilt rode out to the plantation to question him. General Compson had described to his son how Sutpen appeared as he accosted the men he met on his way into town: " 'Your grandfather said that his eyes looked like pieces of a broken plate and that his beard was strong as a curry-comb. That was how he put it: strong as a curry-comb' " (51–52). As Mr. Compson continues his story, he interjects specific observations made by his father, as well as the general's interpretations of Sutpen's behavior, including that he was "underbred" (46).[8] Telescoping the town's view of Sutpen's character, the general remarked, " 'anyone could look at him and say, *Given the occasion and the need, this man can and will do anything*' " (53).

One of the major differences between the voice of the narrative persona and Mr. Compson's style lies in the subtle humor Compson manages to invest in the story. He recognizes the absurdity of the town's "acute state of indigestion" (53): the conviction that a crime had been committed, though there is no proof, and the general unwillingness to confront Sutpen with the community's suspicions and demand an explanation. Partially because of this humorous detachment Mr. Compson begins to emerge as a distinctive personality through the story he tells. His attitude is one neither Rosa nor Quentin can muster, though Quentin communicates something of it when relating the architect's escape to Shreve in chapter 7. Mr. Compson seems to relish the discomfort the members of the growing posse must have felt when remembering Sutpen's pistol demonstration. And he seems rather cynically to appreciate the fact that Sutpen is faced with such a trial on his way to becoming engaged to Ellen.

Doubtless, in relating the events to Quentin, Compson embellishes them to a degree. That the number of men who had gathered to arrest Sutpen when he emerged from Mr. Coldfield's house was exaggerated seems certain given the size of Jefferson in the 1830s. The level of interest the entire town manifests in the episode as it transpires reflects the conventions of the old southwestern humor tradition: " 'They took him back to town, with the ladies and children and house niggers watching from behind curtains and behind the shrubbery in the yards and

the corners of the houses, the kitchens where doubtless food was already beginning to scorch, and so back to the square where the rest of the able-bodied men left
their offices and stores to follow . . . ' " (55).

Despite General Compson's earlier (apparently imagined) description of
Sutpen's expression as he studied the original eight members of the vigilance
committee, Quentin's grandfather now appears with Mr. Coldfield to make
Sutpen's bail. Once again, General Compson supplies specific details about
Sutpen's appearance; Mr. Compson mentions his father's observations three
separate times to show how Sutpen had matured physically in the five years he had
been in Yoknapatawpha County: " 'He actually filled his clothes now, with that
quality still swaggering but without braggadocio or belligerence, though according to your grandfather the quality had never been belligerence, only
watchfulness' " (56).

Mr. Compson's personality again rises to prominence in his analysis of
events preceding Sutpen's wedding; he relies less directly on his father's reporting
and allows his own imagination freer play. His thinking follows a tortuous path in
which he weighs the motivations of each of the participants against his own values
and prejudices. In speeches such as this one we become more aware of the
presence of Quentin as audience, and we recognize that Compson intends to
instruct his son in human behavior as well as to recount a story which has
fascinated him over the years. As Joseph W. Reed, Jr. explains: "The tone of his
telling is almost precisely consistent with the conversations he has . . . with
Quentin in *The Sound and the Fury*. He is an ironic moralist for whom assumption
and subtlety have replaced curiosity and a sense of (or even need for) a general
design."[9]

The wedding took place " 'in the same Methodist church where he saw Ellen
for the first time, according to Miss Rosa' " (56). The fact that Mr. Compson cites
not only his father but Miss Rosa as authority indicates that Quentin has at least
partially informed his father of what he had learned earlier in the afternoon (unless
Mr. Compson has had independent conversations with her, a possibility which
seems unlikely). Mr. Compson views the wedding as portentous—an indication of
the tragedy which the children of this union will initiate. Not only does the bride
cry—Miss Rosa, by contrast, stresses Ellen's later lack of tears, drawing a
distinction between her view of her sister's character and reaction to events and
Mr. Compson's—but the wedding takes place in ominous rain, though Mr.
Compson insists that the wedding itself, not dread of the groom, had been the
source of the tears.

Further reflections of Mr. Compson's character and cynical outlook are
provided when he interrupts his story to meditate on the nature of marriage,
particularly women's view of the ceremony. His opinion that a big wedding tends
to cement a relationship more permanently underlines the sterility he finds at the
heart of practically all human relationships, a sterility his letter to Quentin five

months later confirms. (The notion also looks forward to his theory of the contention between Henry and Bon in chapter 4, which Compson attributes to a wedding ceremony.) To him women view themselves as perpetual brides, despite the evidence of children and the process of aging: "'they still have in their minds the image of themselves walking to music and turning heads, in all the symbolical trappings and circumstances of ceremonial surrender of that which they no longer possess'" (57). Readers familiar with *The Sound and the Fury* will recognize echoes of his views in that novel and, remembering scenes such as Mrs. Compson's approach to Herbert Head, will understand something of the foundations for Mr. Compson's attitudes. Regardless of the origins of his opinions, however, what Mr. Compson says to Quentin in this passage is important in evaluating his interpretation of Ellen Sutpen, whom he sees differently than Miss Rosa in several important respects.

Despite what he says about women, Mr. Compson insists that it is Sutpen who had wanted the big wedding. His source is something General Compson "let drop" one day, something not specified in the text, which Mr. Compson is convinced Sutpen had also revealed in a similar way. The idea supports Miss Rosa's view that Sutpen had desired respectability above all. If Quentin has repeated this part of her conversation to his father, her notion may also have influenced his theory. Compson offers no definite proof; on the contrary, we are told that at the last minute Sutpen "'refused to support [Ellen] in her desire'" for a large wedding (57).

Mr. Coldfield's desire for a small wedding reflects—in Compson's view—his puritan parsimony. He was not interested in a large affair that would redeem his future son-in-law in the eyes of the community. Indeed, in the perception of the town, the fact that Mr. Coldfield had signed his bond was sufficient vindication. Though the nature of the business arrangement between Coldfield and Sutpen remains a mystery, Mr. Compson suggests that Mr. Coldfield had lost money on the proposition when he withdrew from the partnership at the "'point where his conscience refused to sanction it'" (59). Still, though maintaining a position as an upright man in the community, he had entered into the original dubious agreement and had permitted his daughter to marry a man of "'whose actions his conscience did not approve'" (59). This moral lapse in Coldfield's actions parallels Compson's behavior in regard to his own daughter when she becomes pregnant in *The Sound and the Fury*. His refusal to further indict Mr. Coldfield possibly results from Mr. Compson's recognition of similarities in their makeups, however different their outward characteristics.

Mr. Compson agrees with Miss Rosa that the big wedding would have cemented Sutpen's place in the community. Though the aunt had been the one to persuade Mr. Coldfield to accept the big wedding, Sutpen "'did want, not the anonymous wife and the anonymous children, but the two names, the stainless wife and the unimpeachable father-in-law, on the license, the patent'" (59). Still,

Sutpen remembers his precarious position only two months earlier, and despite both pride and bravery, he refuses to support Ellen's desire for the big wedding. According to Mr. Compson, this refusal contributes to Ellen's tears.[10]

Compson admits that Sutpen had not actually expressed himself on the issue. Quentin's father merely theorizes, but his interpretation provides an important balance to Rosa's vision. Mr. Compson is more willing to grant Sutpen the attributes of pride and bravery than Rosa; his view is more sympathetic, though Compson's interpretation of Sutpen's motives is no more sound than hers. His ideas are too bound up in his own theories of the opposed nature of men and women, and his narration amply illustrates his tendency to ignore evidence that contradicts those views. Though we are told that Sutpen had made no statement to Ellen about the wedding, Mr. Compson shows him really wanting the impressive ritual, reluctant only because of his reputation in the community. This would seem a curious supposition, considering Mr. Compson's description of Sutpen's uncon-cern with the members of the vigilance committee on the day of his arrest.

To a degree prefiguring Shreve's later creation of the lawyer to explain occurrences which otherwise make little sense to him, Mr. Compson ascribes much of the motivation for the disastrous wedding to Ellen's aunt. Again, there are apparent contradictions in his view of her character. On the one hand, she represents the women of the community who " 'had agreed never to forgive him for not having any past, and who had remained consistent' " (61). On the other, she feels the need to justify her brother's involvement with Sutpen and her own reputation as a member of the family that had agreed to the match. Perhaps sensing that the contradiction is too great to provide a reasonable answer, Mr. Compson falls back on his cynicism to offer an explanation of her actions: " 'Or maybe women are even less complex than that and to them any wedding is better than no wedding and a big wedding with a villain preferable to a small one with a saint' " (61).

Mr. Compson then switches the focus from the aunt to Sutpen himself. Anticipating the town's reaction to the church wedding, Sutpen became grave and watchful, an attitude Compson suggests Sutpen had cultivated since he first had departed from the world of his childhood. Mr. Compson thereby places the wedding within the much broader context of Sutpen's entire life and design. Like Rosa, he surveys the entire history of the Sutpen family and allows what he knows to influence his theories of behavior. To Compson, the wedding is the first step in the working out of Sutpen's tragic destiny, what he calls his "doom."

Understandably, Mr. Compson sees Sutpen as the lonely figure, put upon by the women who " 'never plead nor claim loneliness until impenetrable and insur-mountable circumstance forces them to give up all hope of attaining the particular bauble which at the moment they happen to want' " (63). Mr. Compson even suggests that when no one attended the rehearsal, Sutpen had offered to postpone the wedding and had been vetoed by the aunt. Once again, Compson adds a bizarre touch of humor in describing the machinations of the spinster aunt to force the acceptance of the wedding. She moves from house to house, followed by one of the women servants "'perhaps for protection, perhaps just sucked along like a leaf in the wake of that grim virago fury of female affront'" (64). Quentin's grandmother provides another witness, for the aunt comes to the Compson house too, "'not to invite her to a wedding but to dare her not to come'" (64).

In relating the story, Mr. Compson is forced to provide several details from his own imagination: that Ellen had not been aware of the aunt's actions, that the aunt had expected them to have the effect she had intended, that Sutpen would have warned her that they would not have the desired effect, but that he knew she would not believe him. Anticipating trouble, Sutpen sends for more of his slaves, so that the scene before the church recalls a Mexican standoff: the Sutpen slaves with torches guarding the door and the invited guests remaining in their carriages across the street, there not to attend the wedding but to witness the fray. Incomprehensibly, Mr. Compson assumes that neither Ellen nor the aunt had been aware of any difficulty until the wedding party had emerged from the church. Once again, his interpretation of Ellen's actions is influenced by his general view of women as capriciously unconcerned. He depicts her going through the ceremony as though nothing were wrong, though she must have been aware that the church was nearly deserted. Once out of the church, however, she seeks the privacy of her carriage so that she may cry. Protected by Sutpen, who must shield her and the aunt from the refuse being thrown and command his servants not to attack, she finally secures that privacy and soon forgets the affront, as Mr. Compson romantically suggests.

But Sutpen does not forget. His separateness from the community is confirmed by the wedding, which is the culmination of his arrest two months earlier. Mr. Compson thinks that though he would occasionally invite parties out to the plantation for cock fights or bouts between his slaves, the events of that somber wedding night had a lasting impact on Thomas Sutpen. Though he would remain in Jefferson, he would never become a part of its social fabric, never really share the civic or political views of his neighbors, as his spurning the night raiders after the close of the war demonstrates.

The reference to the fights in the stable links the close of chapter 2 with that of chapter 1. The view of Ellen at the end of the two chapters, however, is radically different. Miss Rosa had pictured a desperate and terrified mother trying to shield her children from an overbearing, barbaric tyrant. Mr. Compson, on the other hand, sees her as vain, silly, even unconcerned. To him, the rain the night of the wedding is emblematic of the troubles which would befall the Sutpen house; the mistress of the house would simply wash the night "'out of her remembering with tears'" (69).

3

"An instrument of retribution": Mr. Compson's Rosa

Mr. Compson's conversation now turns to Miss Rosa. Responding to Quentin's question about why she would want anyone to know about Sutpen's throwing her over (one of her obsessive subjects in chapter 1), Mr. Compson telescopes the family history from Miss Rosa's childhood to Bon's death. The focus of his account presently changes, though. In chapter 2, Mr. Compson's interest had been largely in recounting how the community viewed Sutpen and how information about him was disseminated. In discussing the Sutpen wedding, he now focuses more precisely on interpreting motivations himself, particularly the motivations of Miss Rosa, her vantage point on events familial, local, and national.

Several factors alert the reader to an alteration in perspective. Unlike the preceding chapter, in which conversation is punctuated in a conventional manner, the present one uses no quotation marks to identify Mr. Compson's narration, instead italicizing the tag lines identifying speakers at the beginning. Except for one brief interruption, the remainder of the chapter is an unbroken monologue.[1] Fewer references to the way information is transmitted lead the reader to suspect that Mr. Compson allows his own imagination a freer reign in filling in motivations and interpreting actions. On a couple of occasions he points out that he had learned things from his father (100, 101) or his mother (93); information is even attributed to the Sutpen Negroes (96). He also occasionally alludes to things Miss Rosa has told Quentin, a further indication that Quentin must have related much of what he heard earlier in the afternoon during an unrecorded part of the conversation with his father. But such occasional references to the way he has learned things are secondary to his imaginative reconstruction of events. He vividly visualizes the appearance of Sutpen, of Ellen and their children, on what would have almost certainly been paltry evidence from his parents. Though we have no reason to doubt the accuracy of his descriptions of the Sutpens, his visualizations of Ellen as she enters her "butterfly summer" (94) and later as she stares at the shambles of her life in blank incomprehension owe their power to Mr. Compson alone.

He brings to his recounting an artistry which provides as well a neatness of cause and effect. Unlike his later admitted lack of understanding of Bon, Henry, and Judith's relationships in chapter 4, Mr. Compson seems sure of himself when interpreting the actions of the older women in the story—Rosa, Ellen, and their aunt. Once again, Faulkner teases the reader by drawing parallels with relationships in *The Sound and the Fury,* which would explain the peculiar way Mr. Compson views the characters. At least two passages seem designed clearly to allude to the earlier novel; the reference to "mothers who . . . can almost make themselves the brides of their daughters' weddings" (90) recalls the flirtations between Mrs. Compson and Herbert Head which Quentin remembers in *The Sound and the Fury (TSTF,* 114–17).[2] A later passage contains even more forceful overtones: Henry and Judith are described as having "a relationship closer than the traditional loyalty of brother and sister even; a curious relationship: something of that fierce impersonal rivalry between two cadets in a crack regiment who eat from the same dish and sleep under the same blanket and chance the same destruction and who would risk death for one another . . . " (96–97). To Quentin, this description must have been rather painful to hear. We learn at the close of chapter 5 (describing a moment actually earlier in the same afternoon that he listens to his father) that his imagination could not pass the scene in which Henry accosts Judith after killing her fiancé. Though Quentin does not interrupt his father at this point and the narrative persona never intrudes to describe his reaction, we must imagine his father's picture precipitated considerable emotional turmoil.

Such references clearly invite the reader to examine other facets of Mr. Compson's narration in view of what we know about him from *The Sound and the Fury,* and such an examination yields some interesting suggestions. Clearly his misogyny is evident in both books. Chapter 2 presents Ellen's aunt as a nearly hysterical harpy; Mr. Compson now emphasizes her sexual frustration, her attempt to revenge herself on all men for the "male principle . . . which had left the aunt a virgin at thirty-five" (71), and her ruthless desire to pass her bitterness along to Miss Rosa. Touching closer to home is his view of Ellen, which possibly owes a great deal to his attitude toward his own wife, Caroline Compson. Mr. Compson sees Ellen as essentially vacuous, concerned with her position in the community, with making an appropriate social match for her daughter, and as withdrawing into stunned incomprehension when catastrophe destroys her dreams—qualities not unlike those of his wife. His strangely ambivalent, at times even contradictory statements about Mr. Coldfield reflect paradoxes in Mr. Compson's own nature. On the one hand, Mr. Coldfield is a reasonable advocate of the Union, but his reaction to events he cannot control is eccentric in the extreme. He praises Coldfield's "coming into a new country with a small stock of goods and supporting five people out of it in comfort and security at least" (100)—a contradiction of his statement seven pages earlier that "his stock which had begun as a collection of the crudest necessities . . . apparently could not even feed himself and his daughter from its own shelves . . . " (93). The lack of condemnation of Mr. Coldfield's behavior results from the similarities in the old man's handling of vicissitudes and Mr. Compson's own. Both tend to withdraw—Coldfield into what Quentin's father calls "the dead and consistent impassivity of a cold and inflexible disapproval" (102), Compson into his aloof cynicism, underscored by his reading of Latin poets and his drinking.[3]

For readers familiar with *The Sound and the Fury* there is a pitiful sadness in Mr. Compson's justification of Coldfield's withdrawal: "He was not a coward. He was a man of uncompromising moral strength . . . " (100). Still he realizes how different had been Miss Rosa's view of her father. He maintains that she had hated him without realizing it, attributing her hatred to the agency of the departed aunt's repercussive influence. Yet he does not fail to remark the significance of Miss Rosa's beginning her first ode to the soldiers of the Lost Cause "in the first year of her father's voluntary incarceration and dated at two oclock in the morning" (101). Her method of rebellion is typical of Rosa; she asserts her independence apparently after bringing her father his meal during the night. And she is persistent: General Compson attests that her portfolio had contained "a thousand or more" tributes in 1885, as though the sheer number in some way compensated for the denial of her own sexuality for which she blamed her father.

More directly affected by Mr. Compson's concerns as reflected in *The Sound and the Fury* is his characterization of Judith, who had removed herself

> into that transition stage between childhood and womanhood where . . . though still visible, young girls appear as though seen through glass and where even the voice cannot reach them; where they exist (this the hoyden who could—and did—outrun and outclimb, and ride and fight both with and beside her brother) in a pearly lambence without shadows and themselves partaking of it; in nebulous suspension held, strange and unpredictable, even their very shapes fluid and delicate and without substance. . . . (80)

He could as well be describing his daughter Caddy (who both outruns and outclimbs Quentin in the first section of *The Sound and the Fury*), and once again, Quentin must also be aware of the similarities.

That Caddy is never alluded to directly in *Absalom, Absalom!*, never named, does not indicate that Faulkner expects the reader to be unaware of the parallels between her and Judith in Mr. Compson's description. Nor is Faulkner attempting to play a game with his readers or to trick them. Rather, the lack of direct reference to her is consistent with the author's practice throughout this most demanding of his novels.[4] We are constantly forced to accept things which are not presented in the text itself. An obvious instance would be the conversations in which General Compson tells his son about Sutpen, scenes which would allow a clearer interpretation of how information about Sutpen accrues, but many other examples exist. We do not hear the conversation between Quentin and his father after Quentin has met Henry, and there is considerable doubt concerning whether the conversation between Quentin and Henry is itself fully reported. Further, there are references to several pieces of information Quentin had acquired from Miss Rosa, but which do not appear in any passages attributed to her, as the preceding section illustrates. In short, we are called upon to fill in several gaps with material vital to understanding events and characters' reactions to them. In light of such demands, the unique device of avoiding mention of an important character in the earlier novel does not appear so unlikely.

Continuing attitudes revealed in the preceding chapter, Mr. Compson stresses the idea that fate is responsible for the Sutpen tragedy. He suggests that in Mr. Coldfield's death Miss Rosa saw "fate itself supplying her with the opportunity to observe her sister's dying request" (72). He sees fate "crowding the normal Indian summer" of Ellen's life (82) and Sutpen's relationship to the community as playing to an audience, while "behind him fate, destiny, retribution, irony—the stage manager, call him what you will—was already striking the set and dragging on the . . . next one" (87–88).

Compson's emphasis on fate recalls Miss Rosa's contention that there was a curse on the entire family, and both ideas are reinforced by the numerous classical allusions in his conversation.[5] His use of such references is commensurate with his character in *The Sound and the Fury*, and he has little trouble in transforming the players in the Sutpen tragedy into classical prototypes. Miss Rosa's childhood is "a Cassandra-like listening beyond closed doors" (72); the faces encountered in her childhood are like masks "in Greek tragedy interchangeable not only from scene to scene but from actor to actor" (74); to Ellen's family she disappears into "a shadowy miasmic region something like the bitter purlieus of Styx" (84); Bon appears "almost phoenix-like" (90). He also adds several references to shades and shadows, extending a pattern of imagery introduced by Miss Rosa's conversation in chapter 1. These references illustrate the importance to Mr. Compson of making his story aesthetically as well as psychologically satisfying. The imagery he summons is often powerful and gripping, as in his picture of the family moving toward the catastrophe which was their doom:

> Because the time now approached . . . when the destiny of Sutpen's family which for twenty years now had been like a lake welling from quiet springs into a quiet valley and spreading, rising almost imperceptibly and in which the four members of it floated in sunny suspension, felt the first subterranean movement toward the outlet, the gorge which would be the land's catastrophe too, and the four peaceful swimmers turning suddenly to face one another, not yet with alarm or distrust but just alert, feeling the dark set, none of them yet at that point where man looks about at his companions in disaster and thinks *When will I stop trying to save them and save only myself?* and not even aware that that point was approaching. (89)

Nowhere does Mr. Compson demonstrate greater dramatic skill in relating the story to Quentin. He manages to provide a memorable and accurate image to make his point while being consistent in both his resigned cynicism and in his terminology.

Mr. Compson's classical bent is so strong as actually to influence his interpretation of the characters. He interrupts his narration to speculate on Sutpen's naming of Clytie: "Yes. He named Clytie as he named them all, the one before Clytie and Henry and Judith even, with that same robust and sardonic temerity . . . " (73–74). Quentin's father suggests that Sutpen had made an error and that he had intended to name his daughter Cassandra, "prompted by some pure dramatic economy not only to beget but to designate the presiding augur of his own disaster . . . " (74). Obviously Mr. Compson has absolutely no evidence to support this theory; it merely fits well with his view of characters and events. It makes good dramatic sense. In the larger context of the novel, however, it makes thematic sense as well by linking Clytie with Miss Rosa, who is also twice compared to Cassandra by Compson. (Rosa will link herself with Clytie through the touch of flesh with flesh in chapter 5.) Both women's lives have been profoundly affected by Sutpen, and both will play vital parts in the final catastrophe.

Mr. Compson's reference to "the one [child of Sutpen's] before Clytie and Henry and Judith even" (73) has led some critics to conclude that at this point Mr. Compson is aware of Charles's true identity.[6] The structure of the novel, however, works against such an assumption. If Mr. Compson had believed that Charles was Sutpen's son, he certainly would not have offered Bon's octoroon mistress as the objection to marriage with Judith, as he does in chapter 4. Indeed, a great deal of what Mr. Compson finds mystifying in the relationship between the Sutpen children and Bon would have been clear to him. More likely, Mr. Compson is merely assuming that Sutpen would have named the child of his West Indian wife, about whom he knows because of his conversations with General Compson. (Quentin tells Shreve about this conversation, which descended from Sutpen to General Compson to Quentin's father to Quentin himself, in chapter 7, 331–32.) Cleanth Brooks argues that if Mr. Compson had known the identity of this child, he would have called him by name at this point.[7]

Mr. Compson's purpose in chapter 3 goes beyond bringing his particular prejudices and points of view to bear on events; he advances his son's knowledge in significant ways. By analyzing Miss Rosa's attitudes and the causes of them, he alerts the reader as well as Quentin to be wary of uncritical acceptance of her interpretations. He projects the story to the point of Bon's death, but by having Mr. Compson focus on Miss Rosa's view of the events, Faulkner manages to keep hidden several important details as well as some important questions. Still, the outline remains, and by the end of the chapter, with the introduction of Charles Bon and Clytie, all the important figures in the drama have made their appearance. More importantly, the focus on Rosa's personality and the manner of its development is strategically placed midway between her impassioned speech to Quentin in the first chapter and her lengthy (no less impassioned) monologue in chapter 5.

According to Mr. Compson, the major influence on Rosa's life had been her aunt. She had grown up in a "closed masonry of females" (71). The irrational resentment and fear of Sutpen Miss Rosa had apparently felt from birth was her inheritance from the aunt, who "seems to have invested her with [it] at birth along with the swaddling clothes" (72). Her resentment was perhaps part of the reason she did not move to Sutpen's Hundred immediately after her father's death. Instead, she had waited until summoned after Bon's murder. In an attempt to explain her reluctance, Mr. Compson traces her knowledge of her brother-in-law from Rosa's earliest memories, perhaps drawing upon what Quentin has told him about her comments to him earlier in the day. She has covered much of the same ground. With typical misogynist feeling, Mr. Compson imagines a sort of assault by the women—Ellen, Rosa, and their aunt—against Sutpen and Coldfield on the occasions when the Coldfields visited Sutpen's Hundred. (That Judith is not included is curious and perhaps results from Compson and Rosa's shared view that she remained in a world of her own, one more closely aligned with her father than her mother, as reflected in her behavior as a child in chapter 1.) Mr. Coldfield has resigned from the contest. Indeed, according to Rosa, he began this process in his conversation with Ellen at Sutpen's Hundred the Sunday Judith had refused to ride in the phaeton. Sutpen, on the other hand, is oblivious to the attitudes of the women; he is not even present on the occasions of the visits and declines to eat with the Coldfields on the days the Sutpens come to visit in town. Typically, the aunt refuses to believe Sutpen's perfectly plausible explanation that he preferred the company of the men at the Holston House on the rare occasions of his trips. His explanation seems even more plausible considering the momentous political developments of the 1850s. Dinner at the Holston House would provide Sutpen more than relaxation; it would give him an opportunity to learn the most recent developments and to gauge his fellow planters' reactions to events.

So Miss Rosa would have the opportunity to judge Sutpen's character only on the infrequent occasions when he would be present at his own dining table at Sutpen's Hundred after the aunt's elopement. Since Ellen had retreated into her butterfly summer, Miss Rosa was left to battle the unwitting Sutpen alone. Mr. Compson's picture of her gawking at the face across the table is both comical and pathetic, but he acknowledges that even such opportunities for observation would be few, since Mr. Coldfield soon quit going to visit the plantation. Rosa, then, had been forced to observe from a distance what Compson calls Ellen's transformation, Henry's entering into adulthood, and most significantly, Judith's growing maturity and courtship, which Miss Rosa vicariously shares.

The ostensible occasion for Mr. Compson's discussion is to explain the reason for Rosa's repudiation of Sutpen and her return to Jefferson (a topic which is not completely explored until the conversation between Quentin and Shreve in chapter 6). First, however, he must return to a subject introduced by Rosa herself in chapter 1—why, given the view of him instilled by her aunt, she had agreed to marry him in the first place. Mr. Compson's explanation is simpler than her own: the cause lies in the war: "Now the period began which ended in the catastrophe which caused a reversal so complete in Miss Rosa as to permit her to agree to marry the man whom she had grown up to look upon as an ogre" (81). Miss Rosa's view of Sutpen and of the conflict he had fought in is complicated by her ambivalent attitude toward her father. On one hand, Sutpen represents for her the negative impact of the southern system which the war would destroy—the waste which her puritanical father could not countenance. On the other, the soldiers themselves represent to her a romantic dream in which resides her own incipient sexual need. Hence, she feeds her father in the attic and composes odes to the gallant soldiers defending a lost cause. Her changed attitude toward Sutpen arises from the fact that "the ogre of her childhood made one and (he brought home with him a citation for valor in Lee's own hand) a good one" (81–82). In her monologue (chapter 5), Rosa explains to Quentin the role her vicarious participation in Judith's courtship with Bon had played in her acceptance of Sutpen's proposal, but nothing there conflicts with Mr. Compson's essential conception of her motives, a fact which could suggest that Compson is drawing in part on Quentin's account of Miss Rosa's conversation.

The initial question of Rosa's refusal of Sutpen gives way to other topics as the chapter progresses. The essential facts of Bon's relationship with Henry and Judith are outlined, to be fleshed out by Mr. Compson in the following section. Here we learn only that Henry had brought Bon home with him for Christmas and later to spend about a week at the end of the spring term before returning home to New Orleans. Almost as an aside, Mr. Compson mentions that during that summer Sutpen had also made a trip to New Orleans, a journey remarked neither by Ellen nor by Rosa, whose viewpoints are Mr. Compson's focus for the present. When Rosa learns of the intended nuptials from her sister, she offers the only gift in her means: to teach Judith the few domestic arts she commands. Ellen's shrieks of ridicule estrange Rosa from both sister and niece, further removing her from Sutpen's purlieu. Neither does she have any contact with Henry, whom she merely sees as he rides through town. As she later explains, the limited contact with her family had driven Rosa further into her own world, one in which she is forced to seek vicarious fulfillment. The events of this period acquire a mystical significance for her because they represent her closest approach to the realization of her frustrated dreams of being pursued and won; to Quentin she will call this her "summer of wistaria" (178).

Her concern with Ellen and the children and her limited contact with Sutpen result in his being less significant to her, though during this period he assumes an important position in the community—"He was the biggest single landowner and cotton-planter in the county now, which state he had attained by the same tactics with which he had built his house—" (86). Obviously, Mr. Compson's current view of Sutpen reflects Sutpen's altered position in the area. In chapter 2, Compson had seemed largely to agree with Miss Rosa's opinion of Sutpen as an outlaw, desperately concerned with acquiring and maintaining a sense of respectablity. His material prosperity and long-standing relationship with Jefferson had apparently lent him a sense of comfort, though rumors were still rife about the means of his acquiring his wealth and his ability to force his crops to such a high yield. But Sutpen had come a long way from the period of his marriage: " . . . he was accepted; he obviously had too much money now to be rejected or even seriously annoyed any more" (87). His overseer is the son of the sheriff who had arrested him years before, clear evidence of the security of his social and economic standing in the community, though he continues to hold himself aloof from it.

Mr. Compson cynically (and rather typically) suggests that this standing is the reason for Ellen's blossoming into what he calls her "butterfly summer." She seems to thrive in her role as "chatelaine to the largest, wife to the wealthiest, mother of the most fortunate" (83). But it is also this blossoming that leads directly to Rosa's alienation from her and the rest of the family. Ellen's role as social peacock and matriarch is totally foreign both to Rosa's interests and her means.

Similarly, Bon is foreign, not only to Rosa, but to all the Sutpen family. Mr. Compson's initial description of him ironically underlines his similarities to Sutpen. Like Sutpen, Bon was "a personage who in the remote Mississippi of that time must have appeared almost phoenix-like, fullsprung from no childhood, born of no woman and impervious to time . . . " (90). To Ellen, Bon represents the crowning glory of her new-found social position. He would complete the family circle, both as husband to Judith and as mentor to Henry, bringing to Sutpen's Hundred an elegance and sophistication which mahogany and crystal chandeliers were not sufficient to deliver.[8]

Rosa sees Bon in a very different light. Her reaction to Ellen's descriptions of him reflects Quentin's manner of listening to Miss Rosa's account earlier in the afternoon. Like Quentin, Rosa had not been listening to Ellen, for she "had got the picture from the first word, perhaps from the name, Charles Bon; the spinster doomed for life at sixteen, sitting beneath this bright glitter of delusion . . . " (91). (Rosa's monologue confirms Mr. Compson's theory, especially regarding the symbolic value she assigns to Charles's name: "*Charles Bon, Charles Good, Charles Husband-soon-to-be*" [184].) To Ellen, Charles's appearance had the effect of a fairy tale, but Mr. Compson maintains that "to Miss Rosa it must have been authentic, not only plausible but justified" (92).

The significance this courtship held for Miss Rosa is indicated in the fact that she sets about making Judith a trousseau. (The origin of this information is unclear, though it probably was related by Mr. Compson's mother, to whom Miss Rosa may have confided it. It seems unlikely that Miss Rosa would have revealed her intentions to Ellen given their current estrangement, and the garments she may have made were certainly never delivered to Judith.) Like so many of Miss Rosa's actions, this one combines elements of pathos and comedy. Given her poor knowledge of sewing and the meager materials she had at hand, she could not have managed garments of a very high quality. And she could hardly be unaware of

Ellen's ability to provide Judith with whatever she needed from the most fashionable shops, not just of Jefferson but of Memphis or New Orleans. The fervor with which she dedicates herself to the task—Mr. Compson believes that she had actually stolen the fabric from her father's store—suggests her private motives. These motives are symbolically defined by Mrs. Compson's acknowledgment that Miss Rosa did not know how to count money, that "she knew the progression of the coins in theory but that apparently she had never had the actual cash to see, touch, experiment and prove with" (93). Miss Rosa's lack of experience with money is emblematic of her larger inexperience with emotional matters. She is obliged by withdrawal to force such elemental passions as love and hope of fulfillment into abstract patterns, like the progression of coins, and doomed never to have any actual proof of the validity of her assumptions or conclusions. In both areas, the blame seems to rest largely with her father, whose rigid puritanism cuts Rosa off from fully realized experience. The result, as Mr. Compson reveals, is that while the nation had prepared for the great conflict, Miss Rosa had stitched tediously "on a garment which she would never wear and never remove for a man whom she was not even to see alive" (95).

National events in Rosa's perception provide a mere backdrop to developments in the Sutpen house. Lincoln's election and the fall of Sumter[9] pale beside the quarrel between Henry and his father, which forces the son to repudiate his birthright and leave Sutpen's Hundred with Bon on Christmas Eve. Given her estangement from Ellen at this point, though, Rosa is forced to get information about the argument the same way the rest of the town does—secondhand from gossip of the Sutpen blacks. Ellen is prostrated by the result and retires to her bed in shock. As in the preceding chapter, Mr. Compson focuses on how the town had perceived the events. Rosa and the rest of Jefferson had believed that the fight was a misunderstanding, or an altercation resulting from "the fiery nature of youth, let alone a Sutpen, and that time would cure it" (96). Mr. Compson conjectures that Rosa did not even inform her father of the episode and that she had continued to work on Judith's trousseau. He pictures her dedicated to that pathetic attempt to make her dreams materialize while Jefferson prepared for the inevitable conflict.

Mr. Compson describes Sutpen's departure as second in command to Sartoris of the regiment organized in Jefferson; he also jumps ahead to hint of Sutpen's decline after the war, when the paunchy stomach came upon him following Miss Rosa's return to Jefferson to live. But Rosa had not witnessed Sutpen's departure for battle, nor that of any of the other soldiers. She is prevented by her father, whom she blames for much of the frustration and lack of fulfillment in her life. Mr. Coldfield rages at the departing troops, quoting from the Old Testament. (Significantly, Mr. Compson digresses to mention Miss Rosa's recording of the deaths of Ellen, her father, Bon, and Sutpen in the Bible from which Mr. Coldfield declaims at the departing troops. Sutpen's entry is justified by his marriage to Ellen, but Miss Rosa's inclusion of Bon is remarkable, since he is not a member of the family. It provides a further reflection of his importance in Rosa's spurious emotional life.) The final blow to Mr. Coldfield occurs when soldiers, encouraged by the townspeople, loot his store, and he retreats in outrage to his attic.

Miss Rosa now occupies herself with sustaining her life and that of Mr. Coldfield until his death. Apparently, her odes to the southern soldiers begin to replace her work on wedding garments as an emotional outlet. Her father and sister dead, her aunt departed, Miss Rosa would naturally be expected to go to live with her niece at Sutpen's Hundred, since in doing so she would in part be fulfilling her dying sister's request that she protect Judith, though she was four years Judith's junior. She does not do so, perhaps in part because of the association in her mind of the Sutpen house with Sutpen himself. It seemed to embody his demonic presence, even before Ellen's death:

> As though his presence alone compelled that house to accept and retain human life; as though houses actually possess a sentience, a personality and character acquired not from the people who breathe or have breathed in them so much as rather inherent in the wood and brick or begotten upon the wood and brick by the man or men who conceived and built them—in this one an incontrovertible affirmation for emptiness, desertion; an insurmountable resistance to occupancy save when sanctioned and protected by the ruthless and the strong. (103–4)

This description functions on several levels, as do most of the novel's images. It links the original presentation of the Sutpen mansion in chapter 2 with haunting scenes of the book's final chapters. Further, it contributes to the suspense which begins to heighten at the end of chapter 5, in which Rosa asserts that something is living in the house. The reader is thus reminded that Quentin and his father are talking during the interval between Rosa's monologue and Quentin's departure to take her to discover the house's secret occupant.

The emphasis on the emptiness of the house also provides a capsule summary of conditions as the end of the war approached: Supten was away fighting; Ellen had died; Henry and Bon had vanished; Judith and Clytie struggled to stay alive with what little help Wash Jones provided. But Rosa seems still to be convinced that Henry and Bon would return, although she had no way of knowing that they were serving in the company organized by the university. Mr. Compson insists that Judith must have been apprised of their whereabouts, though she probably did not tell Rosa. (Mr. Compson does not speculate on Judith's reasons for withholding the information.) Thus Rosa, convinced that Bon would return to Judith, is free to pursue her dream of vicarious consummation until the moment Jones appears in front of her house to announce Bon's death and Henry's disappearance.

Originally, Faulkner had intended for Wash to reveal the reason for his summons at this point in the novel. Gerald Langford's transcription indicates that at the end of chapter 3 in the manuscript, Jones ascertains Rosa's identity and then says, "'Then you better come on out yon. Henry has done shot that durn French fellow. Kilt him dead as a beef.'"[10] Faulkner then eliminated the revelation in preparing the typescript, which ends with Wash telling her "'I reckon you better hurry'" (*TS*, 119). At some point in the preparation of the setting copy, Faulkner then added the revelation of the murder in a manuscript insertion, which he also apparently cancelled, appending in manuscript the line as it appears in the novel: "whereupon he lowered his voice somewhat, though not much. 'Air you Rosie Coldfield?' he said" (107).[11] In order to heighten suspense, Faulkner postpones Wash Jones's revelation until the end of the following section. Mr. Compson's monologue thus ends rather inconclusively, preparing for his more complete analysis of the relationship between Henry, Judith, and Bon when his conversation with Quentin resumes in chapter 4.

4

"Victims of a different circumstance": Mr. Compson's Explanation

When Mr. Compson resumes his narration in chapter 4 he covers essentially the same period of the Sutpen history which had occupied him in the preceding section: the years from Henry's meeting Bon and bringing him home to Bon's murder at the gates of Sutpen's Hundred. His focus shifts yet again, however; chapter 3 considers the events as perceived by Rosa and dwells on her reactions to them. Now, Mr. Compson virtually ignores Rosa to ruminate on the Sutpen children and, particularly, on Charles Bon. Most of what he says is pure conjecture. Indeed, he frequently punctuates his interpretation with the phrase "I can imagine. . . ." Not surprisingly, his own peculiar voice and attitudes are very much present. He insists on seeing the characters as manipulated by fate or destiny, as he has throughout, and his portrait of Charles Bon, the figure he finds himself most attracted to and fascinated by, owes a great deal to his own personality and world view. Donald M. Kartiganer explains Mr. Compson's narrative task as "to account for Bon's last action in such a way as to keep intact his own fundamental attitude toward life, his insistence that action and commitment are impossible to the thinking aware man."[1]

His conversation with Quentin is now directed toward his son's understanding of the letter which Bon ostensibly wrote to Judith at the close of the war and which she presented to Quentin's grandmother. A close examination of Mr. Compson's interpretation of the characters reveals that it is significantly influenced by the letter itself, along with what Mrs. Compson had apparently told him about Judith. From the letter Compson gleans the idea of the durance, the period in which Henry supposedly prevents communication between Bon and his sister in hopes that the war itself would settle the problem by removing either suitor or brother. It is also from the letter that Mr. Compson takes his clue in advancing fate as a character in the drama; Bon writes that he and Judith are "*strangely enough, included among those who are doomed to live*" (163). Finally, from the letter Mr. Compson may have developed his view of Henry and Bon as representatives of differing cultures—the puritan and the Latin—since Bon writes of the end of the great conflict in terms of the opposing mercantile society of New England, which produces the stove polish, and the genteel world of the vanished and vanquished South, represented by the paper bearing the best French watermarks.

Though Miss Rosa is not a significant presence in Mr. Compson's narration now, chapter 4 follows a section which focuses on her knowledge of the story and precedes her own testimony, delivered in the long monologue of chapter 5. The introductory passage by the narrative persona reminds the reader that Quentin is still waiting to escort her out to Sutpen's Hundred when evening arrives. Appropriately, the narrator emphasizes the encroaching darkness, which sets the atmosphere for the darker events to be related by Mr. Compson: "It was still not dark enough for Quentin to start, not yet dark enough to suit Miss Coldfield at least . . . " (108). Extending patterns of imagery introduced in the first chapter, Faulkner pictures Quentin as brooding, conjuring in his imagination a picture of Miss Rosa as she waits for the proper time in the darkness of her heat-sealed house. He knows she will take her umbrella, though her reasoning seems absurd: there is no sun to need protection from, and the evening will be "without even dew" (109). (Quentin does not anticipate her use of the umbrella to conceal a hatchet and flashlight.) The barren dryness, like the heat and the darkness, adds yet another element to the oppressive mood created by the setting.

Mr. Compson's first comments underline anew his cynicism and explain in part his attempt to categorize the motivations of Judith, Bon, and Henry, to fit them into neat compartments which would make their experiences more easily comprehensible in terms of his own. The electric light on the porch would be too bright for these people, he explains: "'Yes, for them: of that day and time, of a dead time; people too as we are and victims too as we are, but victims of a different circumstance, simpler and therefore, integer for integer, larger, more heroic and the figures therefore more heroic too . . . '" (109–10). This view of the figures of the past should warn us to beware of Compson's assertions about the Sutpen children. Later, he too seems dissatisfied with his own explanation of events, based upon his notion that neither Sutpen's objection to Bon and Judith's marriage nor the consequences of that objection are elucidated by the facts: "'It's just incredible. It just does not explain. Or perhaps that's it: they dont explain and we are not supposed to know'" (124).

The juxtaposition of these two comments reveals a great deal about Mr. Compson as narrator. Uncomfortable in the present and riddled with doubts about the value of his own experience, he is at a loss to interpret the lives of others and feels more comfortable in viewing them and the problems they faced as simpler than his own. For Compson, the difficulty lies not in the lack of concrete evidence to support his hypotheses but in his reluctance to grant the actors the ambiguities and complexities which have led to his own frustrations and relative defeats.

Nevertheless, he offers Quentin a detailed account of the relationship between Henry, Bon, and Judith, allowing Quentin access to the letter only when his analysis is complete. In a sense he seems to be preparing Quentin to interpret the letter according to Mr. Compson's own ideas, in much the same fashion as he imagines Bon's manipulating Henry to dispose him to accept the octoroon mistress in New Orleans. Indeed, the first word of his story expresses causality— "'Because Henry loved Bon'" (110). Typical of his structure of the novel as a whole, Mr. Compson begins by telescoping all the events he will discuss into a brief capsule, as though he is summarizing what Quentin already knows: how Henry had repudiated his birthright and left with Bon on Christmas Eve, 1860, the reason being that Bon had been an "intending bigamist" (110), a fact revealed to Henry by his father; how Henry had defended his friend, knowing his father spoke the truth and therefore imposing a period of waiting which had ended only when Henry killed Bon and left Judith to discover on his body the photograph of his octoroon mistress and their child.

Immediately, however, Compson begins to dress the characters with imaginary emotions. He emphasizes the conflict within Henry, who, intuitively knowing that his father's information is correct, nevertheless is unable to ask Bon to renounce his mistress and child in favor of Judith. Though he has given up everything for Bon and might reasonably expect a comparable sacrifice, Henry "'could not say to his friend, *I did that for love of you; do this for love of me'*" (112).

Mr. Compson concludes that Henry's response to this dilemma had been the probation, an idea Compson must have derived from the line "*We have waited long enough*" (162) in Bon's letter. He supplements this reading with insight apparently gleaned from the community's general store of knowledge, acquired at the time and distilled over the years. Henry and Bon had gone to New Orleans after Henry quarreled with his father. When the students at the university organized a company to serve in the war, Henry and Bon had joined, though they remained largely out of sight until the company had actually departed. Henry remained a private, and Bon was promoted to lieutenant. Henry had carried the wounded Bon to safety at Pittsburg Landing. From these meager facts—none of which are attacked elsewhere in the novel, despite Shreve's fanciful shifting of wounded and rescuer at Shiloh—Compson fashions an involved story of passion predicated on opposing cultures and conflicting loyalties.

Given the limitations of Mr. Compson's knowledge at this time, his story is plausible enough up to a point, though he ignores various other possible interpretations of events. Bon's phrase "*We have waited long enough*," for instance, might refer simply to the hardships imposed by the war itself, by Bon's fears for his own (or Judith's) survival, as the closing would seem to indicate. No evidence that Henry imposed any restrictions exists, nor does Bon allude to them or to Henry in his letter at all. Thus, Mr. Compson is forced to look for extraneous motivations, such as the difference in backgrounds between Bon and the Sutpens, to supplement his arguments.

He begins with the probation, assuming that Henry had communicated with

Judith about it, and that she had agreed without understanding the need for such a delay, until she discovered the photograph on Bon's body. He assumes that Judith would have acquiesced, but only up to a point, and that when that ill-defined point had been reached, she would have fought her brother as vehemently as he had fought their father.

Compson posits not only Judith's ignorance of the events but Bon's as well. Sure that Henry would not have related the conversation with his father in the library, Compson maintains that Bon would have had to arrive at the issue intuitively, which explains his conclusion that Bon had discovered the reason for Sutpen's trip to New Orleans the previous summer. How else could Bon have understood what would otherwise appear to him inexplicable behavior on his friend's part?

Drawing upon his earlier descriptions of Sutpen and (to a lesser extent) Mr. Coldfield, Compson envisions Bon as a passive spectator of this family disruption, a cynical and jaded man whose entrance into this provincial community had been as strange and unprecedented as that of Thomas Sutpen: "'He is the curious one to me. He came into that isolated puritan country household almost like Sutpen himself came into Jefferson: apparently complete, without background or past or childhood—a man a little older than his actual years and enclosed and surrounded by a sort of Scythian glitter, who seems to have seduced the country brother and sister without any effort or particular desire to do so . . . '" (114). At this point, Mr. Compson is unaware of the significance of Bon's similarity to Sutpen. However, knowing Sutpen's history in the West Indies, he perhaps remarks certain tenuous bonds of shared cultural experience and groups the participants accordingly. Thus Sutpen and Judith, who most resembles him, maintain closer ties with Bon's own cultural background, which Compson labels Latin. Henry, on the other hand, more closely resembles the Coldfields in his rigid adherence to the puritan codes of honor and morality. Bon then sees in "'Sutpen's action and Henry's reaction [to Bon's mistress] a fetish-ridden moral blundering which did not deserve to be called thinking'" (115). Despite closer links with Sutpen, Bon would relegate him as well into that group composed of "'people . . . who have not quite yet emerged from barbarism, who two thousand years hence will still be throwing triumphantly off the yoke of Latin culture and intelligence of which they were never in any great permanent danger to begin with'" (116). Here we see functioning Mr. Compson's desire to categorize the actors in the drama, to pin them down so that their behavior makes sense to him. We see too how this need forces him into improbable speculations and simplistic assumptions.

His next theory recalls his initial one, that Henry had loved Bon, even beginning with the same causative conjunction: "'Because he [Bon] loved Judith'" (116). Mr. Compson's draws Judith as a passionate woman, one who loves Bon and is capable of taking whatever action necessary to enable that love to flourish. As Elisabeth Muhlenfeld explains, "Everything we know about the adult Judith testifies to her devotion to duty as she sees it, and her conception of duty is neither meaningless nor rigid."[2] Compson emphasizes the incremental progression of time since Henry and Bon had left Sutpen's Hundred, the time during which Judith lives alone. She cares for her mother, who responds to the breach in her family by taking to her room, where she waits to die. Then Judith and Clytie endure the struggle to survive, working the fields themselves, aided only by Wash Jones, who occupies the abandoned fishing camp with his daughter and infant granddaughter. She remains a picture of endurance and of proper attention to duty, even appearing with her father in town within a week of Henry and Bon's departure.

The years of loneliness and privation take their toll; Mr. Compson imagines "'the same impenetrable and serene face, only a little older now, a little thinner now'" (155). Her sense of duty encompasses working with the wounded soldiers in Jefferson, where she must also listen to the women talk of the fates of their men, while Judith must content herself with anguished waiting, not even sure what she waits for. She learns only upon receiving the letter, and, indicative of the depth and sincerity of her belief, she and Clytie begin immediately to fashion the wedding dress. Mr. Compson speculates that her fortitude is shaken only when Bon is actually killed, and she discovers on his body the picture of his New Orleans mistress and child. He theorizes that she may have destroyed the earlier love letters at this point, though she carries Bon's last letter as a sort of testament, which she entrusts to Mrs. Compson's care.

Compson's narration ranges freely between Henry and Judith as he prepares Quentin to read this letter for himself. Having postulated the love of Henry for Bon and of Bon for Judith, he backs up to reconstruct and fill in the events which had culminated in Wash Jones's summons of Rosa the day Bon is killed, the episode which links the endings of chapters 3 and 4 to the opening of Rosa's monologue. He begins with the courtship between Judith and Bon, which according to Compson must have resulted from Henry's almost idolatrous attitude toward the older man, the world-weary aesthete. Henry would have been fascinated from the first encounter, perhaps when he saw Bon riding on the campus, or even presented to Bon "'reclining in a flowered, almost feminised gown'" (117)—a man too old, both in years and in experience, to be a student. Clearly Mr. Compson is again projecting his own defeated nihilism, though it is easy to imagine the attraction such a figure as Bon from such a city as New Orleans would hold for a Henry Sutpen, reared in relative isolation: Henry Sutpen was hardly the last young man who went away to college in search of more than an academic education, and who better to guide him than a sophisticated older cosmopolite? What too could be more natural than that Henry would carry stories of his new friend home to his sister, whose interest would quite naturally be piqued?

But Mr. Compson's musings carry him further to suggest that perhaps Henry's interest in Bon may have reflected a subsconscious attraction to Judith herself, that to an extent, Henry may have actually been courting his sister through Bon:

> "Henry was the provincial, the clown almost, given to instinctive and violent action rather than to thinking, ratiocination, who may have been conscious that his fierce provincial's pride in his sister's virginity was a false quantity which must incorporate in itself an inability to endure in order to be precious, to exist, and so must depend upon its loss, absence, to have existed at all. In fact, perhaps this is the pure and perfect incest: the brother realizing that the sister's virginity must be destroyed in order to have existed at all, taking that virginity in the person of the brother-in-law, the man whom he would be if he could become, metamorphose into, the lover, the husband; by whom he would be despoiled, choose for despoiler, if he could become, metamorphose into the sister, the mistress, the bride." (118–19)

Compson thus suggests Henry's possible sexual interest in both his sister and his friend. The homosexual overtones of the passage are reinforced later, when Compson postulates that " 'Bon not only loved Judith after his fashion but he loved Henry too and I believe in a deeper sense than merely after his fashion' " (133). The hints make a lasting impression upon Quentin, for in later chapters they reappear in his and Shreve's reconstructions of the story.[3] Indeed, this entire passage must have affected Quentin profoundly, since it strikes so near to his own experience as described in *The Sound and the Fury*. For the reader familiar with the earlier novel, the discussion here takes on even darker overtones because of the pain which Mr. Compson is unwittingly inflicting upon his son by exploring the relationship between Judith and Henry Sutpen, a relationship which shares so much in common with that between Quentin and Caddy Compson.[4]

The narrator does not intrude to describe Quentin's reaction to his father's suggestions; the chronology of the first five chapters of the novel, however, reveals, as we have seen, that this discussion follows his afternoon with Rosa, during which he is deeply shaken by the image of Henry and Judith meeting briefly together after Bon's murder. In this conversation with his father, though, Quentin almost certainly is both fascinated by the similarity between his own situation and Henry Sutpen's and indicted by the extreme contrast in the way the two young men approach the problem of a threat to their sisters' virtue. He doubtlessly views Henry as having forcefully and nobly defended the principle of family honor, of having taken the only action available to him, despite the pain the action must have inflicted. Quentin must recognize that Henry had succeeded against Bon in a way which underlines Quentin's miserable failure in *The Sound and the Fury* with Dalton Ames.

Seemingly unaware of his son's special interest in the story (or perhaps having a didactic purpose in mind if he does sense Quentin's obsessions), Mr. Compson continues to outline the courtship, if indeed, as he seems to wonder, courtship is the correct word. Bon and Judith could have managed to be together only a total of twelve days.[5] During this time, Bon would have had to pay obeisance to Ellen as well as indulge in the plantation pastimes with Henry, so occasions for private trysts would have been rare indeed. For all his powers of dramatic creation, Mr. Compson cannot even imagine the two lovers together; to him they are "'two shades pacing, serene and untroubled by flesh, in a summer garden'" (120). (The image of the pacing shades continues the development of the ghostly presence of the characters introduced in chapter 1.) Naturally he concludes that it had been Henry who "seduced" Judith, not Bon at all.

Still, he finds even this explanation problematic; none of the "ingredients" fits: Henry repudiates home and inheritance in defense of a marriage he will murder to prevent; Bon is a seemingly passive suitor, accepting both Sutpen's anathema and Henry's durance without protest, yet he forces Henry to murder him four years later to prevent his marrying Judith; Judith herself accepts the departure of brother and lover in the same spirit of resignation and goes four years without word from Bon, yet when his letter arrives, she begins fashioning her wedding dress. The situation is unfathomable to Compson: "'Yes, Judith, Bon, Henry, Sutpen: all of them. They are there, yet something is missing . . . '" (124).

As if in yet another tedious effort to recombine the elements in such a way as to make sense of them, Mr. Compson continues to recite the events as he sees them, now adding the supposition that Sutpen had made his journey to New Orleans almost by accident and there had discovered the mistress and child who would be the reason for his objection to Bon. (That Mr. Compson could consider this a valid objection is perhaps indicative of his desperate need to grasp at any straw to explain what is otherwise inexplicable. He himself seems aware that this is the weak point of his argument, suggesting that it had been Henry's puritan objection to the *ceremony* which had motivated him.) Again Compson arrives at the conclusion that Bon had merely acquiesced to the engagement, that he had not even been a fully realized being: "'Yes, shadowy: a myth, a phantom: something which they engendered and created whole themselves; some effluvium of Sutpen blood and character, as though as a man he did not exist at all'" (128). (Miss Rosa shares Mr. Compson's doubts about Bon's physical presence in the following chapter.)

The testament of Bon's very real body contradicts this fanciful interpretation, though Mr. Compson is incorrect in saying that Miss Rosa actually saw the corpse. More importantly, the fact that the engagement did exist, that it had been the factor which had led directly to the murder, indicates that Bon had been a very real presence. The same fact would lead us to question Mr. Compson's view of Bon as a sardonic, sated man of the world who watches the developments passively, if a little incredulously. Indeed, Compson himself acknowledges that Bon at least took an active role in corresponding with Judith, both during the summer while he was in New Orleans and during the next year, the last year of calm and quiet before the twin catastrophes—familial and national—would forever change the lives of all involved.

Mr. Compson ruminates as well on Sutpen's motives, questioning his reason for waiting till Christmas before confronting Henry with what he had learned as much as six months earlier. Perhaps, sure that Bon would learn of his visit and of his discovery, Sutpen had hoped Bon would realize he had been "caught" and would not return to the university. But what would have prohibited Sutpen from informing Henry of what he had uncovered during the fall term, even by letter? Mr. Compson suggests that one reason might have been the relationship between father and son. Henry had perhaps developed in maturity some of the rebellious nature typical of young men—Sutpen is made to acknowledge elsewhere that Bon had completely "corrupted" Henry, if not Judith—and his father may have understood that part of Henry's violent reaction would be precipitated by the fact that his father himself had delivered the news, had enjoined the prohibition.

In the tale Mr. Compson relates, Henry rides that Christmas morning racked by conflict—torn between his desire to believe in Bon and his certainty that his father has told him the truth. Together the young men go to New Orleans. Though Mr. Compson offers no proof for this assertion—like so many others it is quite logical—he spins a complicated and detailed account of how Bon, aware of the essential nature of the argument between father and son and fully knowledgeable of the ojections to him which had precipitated it, would introduce his young friend to the world of New Orleans. Now Bon would corrupt Henry indeed, carefully, both for love of Henry, leading to understanding and acceptance, and for love of Judith, removing, in Henry's eyes at least, the objection by explaining it away. Mr. Compson is amazed that Henry had gone to the very place where he could not help but prove the truth of his father's statement, which he had called a lie. In Mr. Compson's analysis, he goes as a provincial, a primitive yokel compared to Bon, the suave sophisticate. Bon's awareness of the differences in background between the two youths is his primary means of corrupting Henry.

The youth's "mysticism and that ability to be ashamed of ignorance and inexperience" (134) are the clues Bon uses to discover, first, Henry's objection to the mistress and child, and second, his method of obviating that objection by acquainting his friend with the peculiar institution as practiced in New Orleans. In Compson's account, because of Henry's puritan background, Bon assumes that " " "it would be the fact of the ceremony . . . that Henry would balk at" ' " (135). Moreover, Henry, the provincial, is unaware of the special position granted to the women courted at the quadroon balls. In the world he had known from Sutpen's Hundred, women were divided into three castes: the chaste virgins, the courtesans in the cities, and the slaves. Necessarily, Henry's experience would have been limited to the third class, since he would turn to the first only when considering marriage and the second would be unapproachable because of money and distance. Thus, Bon views Henry's objection only as a sort of misunderstanding, or rather an ignorance of the city's more urbane way of handling the demands of male sexuality in an era of rigid prohibitions.

With tortuous reasoning, similar to that used in analyzing the plans for Sutpen's wedding in chapter 2, Mr. Compson once again delights in allowing his mind to play delicately over a puzzling example of human behavior—in this case the prospect of the urbane Bon corrupting the provincial Henry. Compson offers the image of a man preparing a field for a crop as an initial analogy for Bon's actions, but he immediately substitutes the comparison of a photographer carefully manipulating a negative to retain the impression he desires. Bon sets about preparing Henry for his first meeting with the octoroon and the child. He begins by showing Henry the mere exterior, the architecture itself, the rich carriages and fancy dress, all " 'a little femininely flamboyant and therefore to Henry opulent, sensuous, sinful' " (136). (Mr. Compson even suggests later that Bon would have ordered an elegant coat especially for Henry on his first visit.) Postulating the situation of one man of the world conversing with another, Bon then hints of the delights to be had among the kept women. Finally, he suggests the value they possess in the eyes of the elegant, trim (and to Henry, goatlike) young men by a brief visit to the duelling ground and an elaboration upon the procedures followed in the defense of one's honor. Henry's diffident question, " ' "What would you—they be fighting for?" ' " (140), acknowledges the cultural differences between the two men and betrays his lack of understanding of what is to him an alien society.

Throughout, Mr. Compson paints Henry as torn between his almost obsessive desire to believe in Bon and his fierce inborn repugnance for the foreign city and its manner of doing things. Compson views Bon as cunning and clever, manipulating Henry deftly, counting always on the youth's fear that he will betray innocence or disapproval. Throughout, Bon remains a little aloof, a little condescending. Compson even imagines his making a joke in French with the gatekeeper of the duelling ground, who mistakes Henry for the young man's opponent; Bon corrects the doorman's mistake: " ' "He is a guest; I would have to let him choose weapons and I decline to fight with axes" ' " (139).

In order to make his story more effective, more colorful and dramatic, Mr. Compson surely exaggerates Henry's ignorance of New Orleans customs. We find it difficult to believe that Sutpen had not told Henry a good deal, since Sutpen's apparent insistence that Henry witness the fights in the barn would indicate his intention to raise his son in an aggressively masculine way. It would seem that even Sutpen's design itself would require considerable schooling of Henry in at least the sexual mores upon which the planter class based its ideal of feminine virtue and honor. Sutpen surely subscribed to these mores, if the supposition that tainted blood had been his reason for putting away his first wife is correct, and it would seem natural that he would want to educate his son so that he could avoid similar mistakes. Finally, part of Henry's fascination with Bon from the beginning had apparently been his admiration of the older man's sophistication, his suave manner. It seems unlikely, then, that what had so appealed to Henry in Bon at Oxford and Sutpen's Hundred would suddenly become repugnant in New Orleans. Rather, Mr. Compson's views of the two men would appear to derive from his own outlooks and his need to simplify the characters into abstractions. Reducing Henry to the avatar of Anglo-Saxon protestant morality provides a plausible explanation for the facts as Mr. Compson understands them at this point. To see Henry as a more mature and worldly young man would further complicate the picture, adding to the confusion and ambiguities of behavior of which Compson complains earlier in the chapter.

Another possible origin of Mr. Compson's view of Henry involves the fact that Quentin is the audience for his analysis. Mr. Compson's description of Henry in 1860 has a great deal in common with Quentin's outlook in 1909–10 as described in *The Sound and the Fury*: both are fearful of sexuality and shocked by what they perceive as affronts to standards of morality. And in both cases their disapproval is seen in the context of the preservation of the honor of their families in general and of their sisters in particular. Once again Mr. Compson can be seen as providing a specific lesson for his troubled son through the story of Thomas Sutpen and his children.

Mr. Compson next imagines Bon presenting his mistress and her son to Henry. Henry views her with compassion, perhaps indicating that Bon's careful planning for the moment has been less than totally successful. To Henry, she is " 'a woman with a face like a tragic magnolia, the eternal female, the eternal Who-suffers; the child, the boy, sleeping in silk and lace to be sure yet complete chattel of him who, begetting him, owned him body and soul to sell (if he chose) like a calf or puppy or sheep' " (141). Even Bon cannot tell whether he has been successful. He must return to his rooms wondering, " '*Have I won or lost?*' " (142). Henry's reaction follows predictably from the notion that the ceremony had been the point of contention: " ' "But a bought woman. A whore" ' " (142). Bon corrects him a bit more sternly, offering Mr. Compson an opportunity to project upon Bon another of his long speeches generally critical of human nature, specifically attacking Southern society and traditions.

Bon explains that they are not whores, at least not to the thousand men who support the institution and would attack Henry for so insulting them:

> " 'Not whores. And not whores because of us, the thousand. We—the thousand, the white men—made them, created and produced them; we even made the laws which declare that one eighth of a specified kind of blood shall outweigh seven eights of another kind. I admit that. But that same white race would have made them slaves too, laborers, cooks, maybe even field hands, if it were not for this thousand, these few men like myself without principles or honor either, perhaps you will say.' " (142)

Bon goes on to cast God in the image of the effete, jaded watcher of human suffering, a role similar to that which Mr. Compson envisions for Bon himself. God does not require that any of these creatures be saved, and Bon does not suggest noble motives in attempting to justify the institution. Yet the few women are saved from the more horrible manifestations of chattel slavery, a condition which Bon suggests is tolerated by God, even perhaps conceived by him " ' "in the hot equatorial groin of the world" ' " (144). Again, Bon contrasts the morality of the octoroons and their "white sisters," (144) who flee from them (and their frank, unashamed emphasis on pleasure) in "moral and outraged horror" and who in defense place sexuality on an economic basis. As opposed to this reaction, the octoroons are both more chaste and honest in sexual matters and more valuable according to the very system of economic worth established by their white counterparts. They are " ' "raised and trained to fulfill a woman's sole end and purpose: to love, to be beautiful, to divert; never to see a man's face hardly until brought to the ball and offered to and chosen by some man who in return, not can and not will but *must*, supply her with the surroundings proper in which to love and be beautiful and divert, and who must usually risk his life or at least his blood for that privilege" ' " (145). Moreover, he sees them as more loyal and pure than their white counterparts, remaining " ' "true and faithful to that man not merely until he dies or frees them, but until they die" ' " (145).[6]

When Henry objects to the ceremony, Bon replies that it had been merely morganatic, meaningless in the white society. But Henry is unmoved by this argument, and Bon is forced to play his trump card—the ceremony had been between a white man and a woman of mixed blood: " ' "Have you forgot that this woman, this child, are niggers? You, Henry Sutpen of Sutpen's Hundred in Mississippi?" ' " (146). The trump card is a cultural taboo, significantly the same one offered by Shreve and Quentin as the basis for Sutpen's actual objection to Bon. (Also, significantly, Sutpen himself uses the exact term in describing his options to General Compson in chapter 7; he dreads being " ' "forced to play my last trump card" ' " [341–42].) That Mr. Compson imagines Bon's making this point to Henry indicates Compson's ignorance of Bon's identity at this point; the next day after Quentin's return from his trip with Miss Rosa to Sutpen's Hundred, Mr. Compson presumably will learn that Bon too had been a "nigger."

The basic elements of the conflict established, the basic unchanging personalities of the participants outlined, Mr. Compson suggests that the climax, the murder itself, could have occurred the next day. Bon knows that Henry will not change his mind about the ceremony, though Mr. Compson imagines that Henry's conflicting emotions would perhaps even support the marriage if not for his sense of personal honor in needing to oppose it. Likewise, Henry knows immediately that Bon will not renounce that marriage. Thus, the intervention of the war is greeted by them both almost with relief, since the removal of either man would eliminate the problem. Surely, however, Mr. Compson is mistaken in seeing Judith as playing a comparatively insignificant role in the conflict. He relegates her to the status of a passive vessel: "it was not Judith who was the object of Bon's love or of Henry's solicitude. She was just the blank shape, the empty vessel in which each of them strove to preserve, not the illusion of himself nor his illusion of the other but what each conceived the other to believe him to be . . . '" (148). Such an interpretation is very much in keeping with Mr. Compson's attitudes: he sees several participants in the tragedy as passive victims. But his view of Judith (and later Quentin's) seems at odds with the passionate young woman who faithfully waits for her beloved, who later will summon his mistress and care for their child. Indeed, Mr. Compson's comment contradicts his earlier assertion that when the moment came, Judith would marry Bon in opposition to both Henry and her father.

Just as Mr. Compson has framed the opposition between the two men in terms of cultural differences, he describes the conflict between Henry and Judith in terms of the characteristics inherited from the two sides of their families.[7] Judith shares more in common with Sutpen, who follows the " 'code of taking what it wanted provided it were strong enough' " as opposed to Henry, burdened with " 'the Coldfield cluttering of morality and rules of right and wrong' " (149).[8] Judith remains in the dark about what had happened, since she would not have asked her father, and Henry would not have told her.[9] Mr. Compson assumes she undergoes the durance, not because of stubbornness or defiance of parental authority, but for love. Her pride enables her to withstand the incomprehension, to go on treating her father in the same way, unquestioningly. Yet the pride is also the defense of the love she feels; she says to herself " '*I love, I will accept no substitute; something has happened between him and my father; if my father was right, I will never see him again, if wrong he will come or send for me; if happy I can be I will, if suffer I must I can*' " (150). Compson guesses that Henry had told Judith his and Bon's whereabouts, so she may have known about their having joined the company formed at the university, though none of them participate in the rites of preparation for war, the balls and marches and passing of tokens of remembrance between the departing soldier and the lover who stays behind.

She remains alone, waiting while Bon, now a lieutenant, and Henry depart, while Henry rescues the wounded Bon at Pittsburg Landing, though Mr. Compson asserts that she had not lived in solitude but worked to keep life in her mother, Clytie, and herself. Despite Mr. Compson's emphasis upon her passivity, Judith emerges as a towering example of endurance, doing what she can to alleviate the suffering first of her mother and later of Rosa, after Mr. Coldfield's death, not to mention that of the wounded soldiers in Jefferson. Throughout adversity, her love remains constant, as does her belief in Bon's return. She and Clytie fashion the wedding dress, and her hopes die only with Bon's death.

Much of what Mr. Compson knows or imagines about Judith must derive from what his mother's impressions of her had been.[10] We can perhaps trust that the essentials of Judith's comments to Mrs. Compson have been preserved, though the poetic imagery attributed to her perhaps owes something to Mr. Compson himself. She offers Bon's letter as a sort of testament to his love and to her devotion to him, a mere gesture which she makes in an attempt to fix their emotions permanently against the vicissitudes of the times. Her use of the loom image is gripping and precise in a way she can hardly understand, since she is presumed to be unaware of the extent to which her love for Bon is at cross purposes with her father's design. What seems to bother her most is that human life is so ephemeral, what we leave behind so meaningless. She seems to be groping to make sense of her feelings in light of Bon's death (and her discovery of the picture on his body). Her gesture has meaning because it is performed by a living hand; it is an assertion of existence in the present:

> " 'And so maybe if you could go to someone, the stranger the better, and give them something—a scrap of paper—something, anything, it not to mean anything in itself and them not even to read it or keep it, not even bother to throw it away or destroy it, at least it would be something just because it would have happened, be remembered even if only from passing from one hand to another, one mind to another, and it would be at least a scratch, something, something that might make a mark on something that *was* once for the reason that it can die someday, while the block of stone cant be *is* because it never can become *was* because it cant ever die or perish. . . .' " (158)[11]

Stephen M. Ross explains the logic of her action:

> By "scratching" a mark on another's consciousness, Judith would guarantee significance not . . . by the permanence of the mark but by its "erasability." Only that can be remembered which can become *was*; only those can remember who can someday die. *Was* is necessary for *is*. A legitimate memorial is not something exempt from time's law but something that can be called forth (re-called) from time to time.[12]

Her language, reminiscent of Bon's in the letter itself, hints of suicide to Mrs. Compson, but Judith demurs, and her tone becomes more resigned, almost bitter. Cynically, she denies love as a motivation for suicide and, true to her nature, acknowledges her duty to Clytie and her father, who will be returning soon, " " "since they have begun to shoot one another now" " " (158), apparently a disillusioned reference to Bon's death. Besides, with death filled with departed shades, what rest would be available for her there?

To Mr. Compson, the gesture is a token of love, and he asserts as much to Quentin in giving the letter to him. As Elisabeth Muhlenfeld has pointed out, the letter does not reveal a nature "gentle sardonic whimsical and incurably pessimistic," as the narrative voice, reflecting Mr. Compson's attitudes, suggests (160). Rather, it preserves the feelings of a man of good humor, a strong man who has endured a great deal yet is aware that his lover has endured nearly as much herself.[13] Most of all, it asserts that love between them did exist, however improbable. That the two of them are *"included among those who are doomed to live"* (163) means that Bon and Judith will make the most of whatever opportunities for life the new order will offer. Clearly, Bon is dubious of that new order and uncertain even of when he will arrive to begin their life together. Yet there is no doubt of her faithfulness, her desire to have him, nor any apparent fear of obstacles. He mentions neither Henry nor her father, and, as suggested earlier, the reference to their waiting could point to circumstances other than those offered by Mr. Compson.

Quentin's father brings his narration to a close by reconstructing the scene of the two men returning to Sutpen's Hundred. The conflict between them remains as rigid and inflexible as when it had assumed its final form in New Orleans: "'the one calm and undeviating, perhaps unresisting even, the fatalist to the last; the other remorseless with implacable and unalterable grief and despair'" (164). Compson does not describe the actual shooting but merely imagines the two riding up to the gate. He then switches to the scene which closes chapter 3, that of Wash Jones calling to Rosa from the street. This time, however, he provides more information about Jones's mission: "'"Air you Rosie Coldfield? Then you better come on out yon. Henry has done shot that durn French feller. Kilt him dead as a beef"'" (165).

As chapter 4 draws to a close, Faulkner shifts the emphasis by having the narrative voice focus more directly on Quentin's response to his father's story and to the letter. We are twice told that Quentin heard his father's voice "without having to listen" (160). Instead, while his father talks, Quentin creates his own images, particularly those of Bon and Henry as they approach the gate of Sutpen's Hundred. At the end of chapter 5, he will imagine the point immediately after the murder, when Henry accosts Judith; now, however, he focuses on the second of the killing itself:

> They faced one another on the two gaunt horses, two men, young, not yet in the world, not yet breathed over long enough, to be old but with old eyes, with unkempt hair and faces gaunt and weathered as if cast by some spartan and even niggard hand from bronze, in worn and patched gray weathered now to the color of dead leaves, the one with the tarnished braid of an officer, the other plain of cuff, the pistol lying yet across the saddle bow unaimed, the two faces calm, the voices not even raised: *Dont you pass the shadow of this post, this branch, Charles*; and *I am going to pass it, Henry.* (164–65)

Quentin here is imagining the scene in terms of his own experience. His conversation with his father about the Sutpens occurs in September 1909 in the summer following his sister's affair with Dalton Ames and Quentin's own confrontation with him. In *The Sound and the Fury*, Quentin recalls that Dalton Ames had "looked like he was made out of bronze" (*TSTF*, 197), and his own showdown, in which he enjoins Ames to leave town by sunset and in which Ames offers him a pistol to enforce his will, had occurred only about a month before his interview with Miss Rosa.

In his August 1909 conversation with his father about the value of human experience, Quentin attempts to justify suicide as escape from the pain he feels and from the fear that that pain is ephemeral, that, as his father maintains, " 'nothing is even worth the changing of it' " (*TSTF*, 96). In this talk, recorded at the end of his monologue in *The Sound and the Fury*, his father does not seem to take Quentin's suicide threat very seriously, though he suggests that his son might take a vacation in Maine before school in the fall. Despite the lack of overt references to the earlier discussion in *Absalom, Absalom!*, many of the concerns in the two episodes are the same. Judith's apparent inability to make sense of her life or to give her experience some feeling of permanence must remind Mr. Compson of his son's dilemma. It would appear unlikely that Mr. Compson was aware of the confrontation with Dalton Ames, but Quentin would have to recognize the tremendous contrast between Henry's actions to protect his sister's virtue and Quentin's pitiful attempt to remove Ames as a threat. If Mr. Compson had hoped to provide some relief for his son's obsessions in reconstructing the story of Judith, Henry, and Bon, he would be sadly disappointed. If Quentin sees Henry's actions as an indictment of his own, as a meaningful attempt to preserve something of lasting value, the events later in the evening at Sutpen's Hundred will prove him tragically mistaken.

5

"A time altered to fit the dream":
Rosa's Monologue

Miss Rosa's monologue covers all but the last page of chapter 5. It occupies an important place in the structure of the novel, and it does a great deal to deepen its tone of tragedy and despair. The poetry of the chapter represents what Hugh Ruppersburg calls "translated character narration," like the language in the monologues that make up *As I Lay Dying*.[1] That is, the language does not necessarily reflect the exact words spoken by Miss Rosa or heard by Quentin (if he were listening). On the contrary, the rich, baroque prose, almost like an ornate fugue, reveals the personality of the speaker through language heightened by the narrative voice and reflected through Quentin's own perception. The richness of the chapter leads Estella Schoenberg to suggest that Miss Rosa "may have been a good poet,"[2] though given the description of her poetry in chapter 1, this would seem unlikely. But good poet or mediocre, Miss Rosa is a fine character, and the monologue assigned to her is a masterpiece, revealing her warped personality and her obsessive concerns.

The monologue's central position serves as the climax of what might be called the book's first "movement"—the outlining of the basic events in the lives of Sutpen and his family and the delineation of the characters themselves. It also provides a break, leading to the novel's second movement—the reconstruction of those events with emphasis upon motivation and interpretation of action by Shreve and Quentin at Harvard, precipitated by the arrival of Mr. Compson's letter announcing Miss Rosa's death. That the chapter details Rosa's views is indeed significant, for this narration by the novel's most biased, perhaps least reliable source reminds the reader to beware of accepting what she says wholeheartedly. Her lack of reliability is in itself ironic, for she is the only character/narrator who knew the main participants in the story firsthand. The peculiar view she has of them, however, renders much of what she says worthless in unravelling the essential truth (or even the necessary facts to approach that truth) in the Sutpen history.

Miss Rosa accurately characterizes her approach to the story she relates:

> You see? There are some things which happen to us which the intelligence and the senses refuse just as the stomach sometimes refuses what the palate has accepted but which digestion cannot compass—occurrences which stop us dead as though by some impalpable intervention, like a sheet of glass through which we watch all subsequent events transpire as though in a soundless vacuum, and fade, vanish; are gone, leaving us immobile, impotent, helpless; fixed, until we can die. That was I. (188–89)

Rosa here answers the question posed by the narrative voice on the novel's first page. There she is described as sitting in her enclosed house, dressed "in the eternal black, whether for sister, father, or nothusband none knew . . . " (3). We discover as the monologue unwinds that she mourns the blighting of her hopes, first as represented by Charles Bon, who becomes the symbol of her stunted sexuality during what she calls her "summer of wistaria" and later as manifest in Thomas Sutpen himself, whose proposal offers an opportunity for fulfillment, at least of a sort, and whose insult drives her back to her barren house in Jefferson, where she mourns for forty-three years, until she unburdens herself to Quentin on a September afternoon in 1909.

Her long speech is an attempt to justify herself to Quentin, though at times she sounds as though she is trying to justify herself to herself. As Joseph W. Reed, Jr. has put it:

> Rosa is looking for vindication of her actions. In order to justify what she was and what she did, she must make Sutpen a demon and transform the rest of his family into the characters of a melodramatic fairy tale. . . . She is unable to get beyond the events which strike her dumb with outrage so that she may deal with the significant details which might make sense of the outrage.[3]

She is tremendously concerned with her own blighted life and with Sutpen's culpability. Thus, her primary emphasis is on her own perception of events, not upon the events themselves. Significantly, her monologue adds almost nothing to our knowledge of the characters (with the exception of Rosa herself) or of actions during the period she describes—basically from Bon's death to her return to town. She does set the stage for Sutpen's death, which Quentin describes in chapter 7, but she does not deal directly with it. She is mistaken about some of the things she herself claims to have known, such as what the photograph in the locket Judith found on Bon's body had actually depicted; Rosa assumes the picture had been of Judith herself. And, finally, Rosa's interpretation of events and of characters is sharply called into question in other parts of the book. She maintains, for instance, that Judith's lack of visible grief had indicated an absence of genuine feeling for Bon, despite the apparent evidence to the contrary provided by Judith's conversation with Mrs. Compson and her entrusting Bon's letter to her.

The poetic excess of the monologue should warn the reader to examine *what* Miss Rosa says very carefully. The first thirteen pages, for instance, record only the journey to Sutpen's Hundred with Jones and her entrance into the house.[4] She calls for Henry, is briefly stopped by Clytie, who calls her by her given name. Rosa responds, " *'Take your hand off me, nigger!'* " (173) and ascends the stairs to find Judith, who appears calm and resigned, though she clutches the metal case. Judith quietly instructs Clytie to plan on Rosa for dinner and accompanies her back downstairs to " *'speak to Mr Jones about some planks and nails'* " (187). The subject matter of these pages is very limited, but Rosa manages to invest them with the energy of her hatred of Sutpen and the bitterness resulting from her continual retreat from life. This very bitterness contributes to her inability to recognize a shocked, stunned grief in Judith's behavior—she still holds the photograph, though several hours would have passed in order for Jones to make the twenty-four-mile round trip journey to Jefferson with a weakened mule. An even stronger clue is provided by Judith's calculated reluctance to use the word *coffin* in speaking to Rosa.

Miss Rosa's bitterness is all the more potent because of her extreme egotism. She is concerned exclusively with herself, with her own reactions and ways of seeing things. Combined with her tendency to reduce emotions and the people who exhibit them to abstractions (a trait she shares with both Quentin and his father), Miss Rosa's persistent self-interest cuts her off from all other people, even those in her family. She admits to Quentin that she could not fathom Judith, and she had spurned Clytie from childhood. Living with them at Sutpen's Hundred after Bon's death, she still cannot manage any vital human connection.

Rosa's self-imposed isolation—she refers to herself as a *"self-mesmered fool"* (171)—explains and justifies the imagery which characterizes her tirade, much of it carried over from chapter 1, where her concerns are very much the same. Cleanth Brooks remarks "the metaphor of a reluctant and difficult birth [which] haunts Miss Rosa's account of her early life."[5] She had lived in *"some projection of the lightless womb itself . . . gestate and complete, not aged, just overdue because of some caesarean lack . . . "* (179). Thus, the paradoxical nature of her life and perception—at once both passionate in her desire and hatred and alienated from human emotion and need—is reflected in her language. She walks, for instance, into the *"thunderous silence of that brooding house"* (169). She regards facing Clytie at the bottom of the stairs, a scene which anticipates their confrontation in the same place in chapter 9, *"not as two faces but as two abstract contradictions"* (171). Her description of her altercation with Clytie embodies these contradictions. She remembers herself both in motion and frozen in a stasis which she associates with dream states: *"We just stood there—I motionless in the attitude and action of running, she rigid in that furious immobility, the two of us joined by that hand and arm which held us, like a fierce rigid umbilical cord, twin sistered to the fell darkness which had produced her"* (173).[6]

Developing her concerns in chapter 1, Rosa presents Sutpen as an ogre, a demon whose presence pervades the house completely.[7] To her, it is not Clytie who attempts to block her entry, but the force of Sutpen present in the house itself.

Similarly, Judith represents her absent father, who inhabits the house like a ghost, a shade (again contributing to a pattern of imagery introduced in chapter 1 and reinforced by Mr. Compson's view of Bon). When she speaks to Clytie, Miss Rosa defines the origin of the voice: "*It said one word: 'Clytie.' like that, that cold, that still: not Judith, but the house itself speaking again, though it was Judith's voice*" (176). Such comments virtually personify the house, so closely is it identified in her mind with Sutpen's destructive power. But they also provide a basis for Quentin's sense of dread, heightening the drama when she reveals at the end of the chapter her belief that someone other than Clytie is living hidden there.

Rosa sees herself as inhabiting a dream world, a world which acquires more terrors than reality itself, a world motivated by the evil inherent in Sutpen from the beginning. Another continuing pattern of imagery defines that world for her. The wagon driven by Jones is drawn "*not by mortal mule but by some chimaera-foal of nightmare's very self*" (175). She compares arriving at Sutpen's Hundred to being in a nightmare from which Henry would awaken her. She describes how she heard "*an echoed shot, ran up a nightmare flight of stairs*" (185). Eventually the dream Rosa inhabits becomes her reality; she retreats there as her father had fled into his attic:

> *I, the dreamer clinging yet to the dream as the patient clings to the last thin unbearable ecstatic instant of agony in order to sharpen the savor of the pain's surcease, waking into the reality, the more than reality, not to the unchanged and unaltered old time but into a time altered to fit the dream which, conjunctive with the dreamer, becomes immolated and apotheosized. . . .* (175)

Not surprisingly, Miss Rosa's monologue contains most of the obvious literary allusions in *Absalom, Absalom!*. Like Mr. Compson, she is fond of classical references. Clytie is "*the cold Cerberus*" of Sutpen's private hell (169); Rosa claims inheritance "*from all the unsistered Eves since the Snake*" (179); Sutpen returns from the war to face "*the Herculean task*" of rebuilding his plantation (196). Her imagination seems particularly moved by Macbeth's speech which provides the title for *The Sound and the Fury*. Her language echoes this passage in *Macbeth* on several occasions: Bon is referred to as a "*shadow*" (186). Rosa remembers the afternoon of her insult with the same despairing attitude with which Macbeth anticipates the future: "*—oh there was a fate in it: afternoon and afternoon and afternoon: do you see?*" (210). Most obvious is her reference to Sutpen: "*He was a walking shadow*" (214).

Yet another of her borrowings is certainly unintentional on Rosa's part but was quite possibly calculated by her creator to strike a responsive cord in the reader who knows *The Sound and the Fury*. Referring to Charles Bon's death, she says: "*Yes. One day he was not. Then he was. Then he was not*" (190). Rosa continues to expand her meaning: " . . . *he* [Bon] *was absent, and he was; he returned, and he was not; three women put something into the earth and covered it, and he had never been*" (190). In *The Sound and the Fury* Quentin uses a very similar expression, phrased in Latin, in anticipation of his own death: "A quarter hour yet. And then I'll not be. The peacefullest words. Peacefullest words. *Non fui. Sum. Fui. Nom sum.* Somewhere I heard bells once. Mississippi or Massachusetts. I was. I am not" (*TSTF,* 216). I do not mean to suggest that Faulkner intends a parallel between the deaths of Bon and Quentin; rather, he seems to be echoing the language of the earlier novel once again to remind the reader of the story's possible effect on Quentin. In this respect, the echoes function in a way similar to the allusions to *Macbeth*, which also reverberate throughout Quentin's monologue. The language Miss Rosa uses here also recalls that between what *was* and what *is* in both Bon's letter to Judith and in Judith's conversation with Mrs. Compson at the end of chapter 4. Miss Rosa cannot be aware of the similarity. Faulkner obviously is, and, I believe, expects the careful reader to be.

Throughout her harangue, the reader feels that Miss Rosa is consciously attempting to sway her listener, to persuade him to accept her interpretation of the Sutpen tragedy. She constantly makes assumptions about what Quentin has already been told and how he may have responded to that information. She begins with the words "*So they will have told you doubtless already*" (166), and she uses similar phrases throughout the monologue. At times she makes a denial, recants her denial, and proceeds to yet another assertion, as though responding to her listener's physical reactions to her story, as though no one could believe her. One instance is particularly instructive. Referring to her interest in the romance between Judith and Bon, Rosa states:

> There must have been some seed he left, to cause a child's vacant fairy-tale to come alive in that garden. Because I was not spying when I would follow her. I was not spying, though you will say I was. And even if it was spying, it was not jealousy, because I did not love him. (How could I have, when I had never seen him?) And even if I did, not as women love, as Judith loved him, or as we thought she did. (182)

This statement tacitly acknowledges what Rosa attempts to deny, that she would spy on her niece, that she thought herself in love with Bon, that she was jealous of Judith's relationship with him. Such passages represent occasions of Miss Rosa's being what she calls "self-mesmered," but they also show her carefully manipulating Quentin's understanding of the story. She herself becomes an artist, carefully fashioning her tale for maximum effect on her audience. Brooks has analyzed this aspect of Miss Rosa's character: "Miss Rosa is not without insight, nor, in spite of her inflamed rhetoric, does she lack literary flair. She is utterly sincere; she is carried away with her rhapsodic convictions; yet at the same time she manages to maintain something of the artist's detachment."[8]

Her seemingly incoherent rantings actually exhibit a carefully contrived sense of organization developed through association. (The same process will motivate Sutpen's account of his early life to General Compson in chapter 7; the smoking torches and the horses' faces during the hunt for the architect will remind him of his experiences in Haiti.) The point at which she chooses to begin links the monologue to the ending of the two preceding chapters, both of which had closed with Jones's arrival to escort Rosa to Sutpen's Hundred after Bon's death. She hints about one of her obsessive concerns by characterizing Wash as a *"brute who was not only to preside upon the various shapes and avatars of Thomas Sutpen's devil's fate but was to provide at the last the female flesh in which his name and lineage should be sepulchered . . ."* (167), an anticipation of Milly's supplanting her, *"if not in my sister's house at least in my sister's bed"* (166). On the trip, she learns only that Henry has killed Bon, though she imagines the confrontation between brother and sister, the point beyond which, the narrator informs us on the last page of the chapter, Quentin could not pass.

Rosa enters the house for the first time since Ellen's death to discover in it the undeniable presence of Sutpen. Miss Rosa associates Clytie most directly with the absent Sutpen, whose face she carries. Clytie becomes Sutpen's avatar, bent on preventing Miss Rosa from doing anything to alter his destructive design, even had there been anything Rosa could have done at that point. She sees Clytie as enforcing her father's will, as part and parcel of the demonic Sutpen presence which overwhelms the house itself in Rosa's imagination.

Clytie, then, is not only witness to events which Rosa has not seen but is also in some sense a fashioner of those events. She looks not at Rosa, but through her, listening to a presence Rosa is not supposed to hear—*"a brooding awareness and acceptance of the inexplicable unseen, inherited from an older and a purer race than mine . . . "* (171). Rosa acknowledges that Clytie merely represents the will of Thomas Sutpen himself, and she seems to blame Sutpen for Bon's death. Her reasons are purely selfish, and she cannot understand the ironic accuracy of her view. What she perceives Clytie as witnessing is the presence of Bon's dead body in an upstairs bedroom. She arrives, then, not in response to her dying sister's request—she seems almost totally unconcerned with Judith—but in order to salvage some token which could validate her vicarious romance with Bon though her niece.

Clytie stops Rosa only momentarily, and Rosa insists to Quentin that Clytie had been merely the "instrument" of Sutpen's will to bar her entry (172). She accosts Clytie for calling her by her Christian name; when Clytie touches her, she commands her to take her hand off, maintaining that she had not been speaking to Clytie, but to the presence which inhabited the house. The twin concerns of her monologue, hatred and love, are evoked when she considers the meaning of Clytie's touch: *"Because there is something in the touch of flesh with flesh which abrogates, cuts sharp and straight across the devious intricate channels of decorous ordering, which enemies as well as lovers know because it makes them both—"* (173). This miraculous touch is what Rosa has been denied in her life; her only contact, enemy or lover, has been through the mind, hence her tendency toward abstraction, hence too her retreat into the dreams which she details later in the chapter.

Rosa's remembrance of the closeness between Judith and Clytie provides the reader with a clue to interpret Clytie's action. She apparently wishes to prevent Rosa's intrusion upon Judith's grief. As children they had occupied the same room, often had slept together either on Clytie's pallet or even in Judith's bed. Rosa remembers the account of how Judith had witnessed her father's fighting bouts with his slaves, and there too Clytie had been present. Clytie's concern now is to protect her half-sister from Rosa's furious assault. Judith's voice breaks Clytie's hold, and Rosa rushes up the stairs to find "*no grieving widowed bride but Judith standing before the closed door to that chamber . . . and if there had been grief or anguish she had put them too away, complete or not complete I do not know, along with that unfinished wedding dress*" (176).

Rosa's insistence that Judith had not been bereaved stands in stark contrast to Mr. Compson's earlier assertion that she had loved Bon. The reader, aware by now of the nature of Miss Rosa's warped, manic perception of events, doubts her interpretation, especially since Rosa seems aware of what she will find even before she arrives. Judith appears to be in shock, a fact which her aunt does not understand, even though Rosa attempts to rouse herself from the dream state in which she had apparently existed since the summer when she was fourteen, the summer during which Judith and Bon had seriously begun their courtship: "*Ay, wake up, Rosa; wake up—not from what was, what used to be, but from what had not, could not have ever, been; wake, Rosa—not to what should, what might have been, but to what cannot, what must not, be; wake, Rosa, from the hoping, who did believe in a seemliness to bereavement even though grief be absent . . .*" (175). Rosa finds herself lost because her dream is destroyed. She awakes from what had not been, implying that Judith and Bon had not loved, that perhaps Judith's view of Bon had contained no more of substance than Rosa's own, an idea she returns to later in remarking that neither woman had cried when Bon was buried. Since Rosa's own romance had lived only through her niece, her perception that Judith does not suffer from Bon's death forces her to admit to the sterility of her own ridiculous romantic attachment. John T. Matthews demonstrates how Rosa fills her romantic need by creating a personal image of Bon which occupies her until his death destroys the image, forcing her to seek elsewhere. She substitutes Sutpen for Bon until his insult and death deprive her again.[9]

The metaphor of the arras-veil which Rosa chooses to describe her insulation from reality is a revealing indication of her perception of Bon's death and Judith's grief. She maintains that the future is available to those brave enough to tear through it. Wisdom is not required, perhaps not even courage. She wonders if all that is needed is the acknowledgment of the dichotomy between the physical and the spiritual natures, that the dream is the prisoner of the body. When the dream manages to free itself from the physical ties—to escape the body completely and thus to transcend reality itself—the world is created. Thus, Rosa explains her peculiar view of events and defines her own relation to the dream she had fashioned and found destroyed: "*but is that true wisdom which can comprehend that there is a might-have-been which is more true than truth, from which the dreamer, waking, says not 'Did I but dream?' but rather says, indicts high heaven's very self with: 'Why did I wake since waking I shall never sleep again?'*" (177–78).

The explanation of the nature of Rosa's dream provides the spark which recalls to her the summer during which it had been conceived. It had been "*a summer of wistaria*" (178), echoing the opening line of chapter 2: "It was a summer of wistaria. The twilight was full of it . . . " (34). Her mind operates on two levels at this point. Her memory of the wisteria comprises the fabric of dream which she associates with the flower, and thus she begins to explain her view of Charles Bon. On another level perhaps this passage harkens back to Quentin's concern in chapter 1 with why Rosa wants to tell the story to him. It would seem likely that the present summer of wisteria recalls that of Rosa's youth, and that recollection provokes a need to re-experience those events in yet another attempt to make sense of them. This interpretation is reinforced by her comments on the nature of remembrance; the "*substance of remembering*" (178) is in the senses, not in some quality of intellect. She cites the examples of the sleeper's hand, either burned or soothed by contact with real objects; the sleeping mind, however, translates these sensations into dream, refusing consideration of the reality from which the experience arises. She concludes with a point which would have special significance for Quentin had he been listening: "*Ay, grief goes, fades; we know that—but ask the tear ducts if they have forgotten how to weep*" (178). The reality of the senses, as represented by the capacity to weep when moved, outlasts the experience of the mind, the abstraction of grief. This seems a curious, almost a paradoxical view for Rosa to take, since her entire life has been wasted in an effort to fix an abstraction—her hatred of Sutpen.

The summer of wisteria had been the time when Rosa's sexuality developed. She is aware that she had not been attractive. Using the analogy of the growing wisteria itself, she does not compare herself to the bloom, nor does she even exhibit the growing leaves. Rather, she is the root, which she associates with the urge to flower, the urge which needs only some tenderness, some evidence of caring in order to grow. The absence of that caring has both stunted and warped her, forcing her to live through the period "*not as a woman, a girl, but rather as the man which I perhaps should have been*" (179). She summons images of incomplete birth and of the subterranean fish which does not miss the sense of sight because it has never had it; sight becomes only a memory without the physical sense to trigger it. Significantly, however, she describes her emotions during that summer not in terms of her own feelings, but in terms of Judith's "*moment which only virgins know: when the entire delicate spirit's bent is one anonymous climaxless epicene and unravished nuptial"* (180).

It had been the summer of 1860, when Rosa had gone to stay at Sutpen's Hundred because her father and Sutpen had both been absent.[10] Though Rosa had never seen Bon, he had been in her house the previous New Year's, and her arrival at the location which she associates with the courtship between him and Judith sparks her romantic reveries. Identifying herself with the male sexual role, yet maintaining the image of the root and urge of the female, she *"became all polymath love's androgynous advocate"* (182). Eventually, though, her association of Bon's features with Ellen's garrulous ramblings about him invites Rosa to identify with the beloved more directly, to see in her niece's beau her own vicarious fulfillment. She sneaks stealthy views of Bon's photograph on Judith's dressing table and creates her own lover from the image; she walks the garden path and chooses her own bowered tryst while imagining how the garden had witnessed the lovers. Yet she maintains that she had not been jealous of Judith, not in love with Bon.

The fact that Rosa creates such a dream for herself absolves her of the need of jealousy or of love. She inhabits a realm halfway between childhood and womanhood which is itself metaphorical of Rosa's hovering between her dreams and reality. Her yearning convinces her of her understanding of love, like Emily Dickinson's "Success is counted sweetest / By those who ne'er succeed."[11] She imagines that instead of listening to Judith tell of love while the two lie in bed together, she would say " *'Dont talk to me of love but let me tell you, who know already more of love than you will ever know or need'* " (185). She gives her love, not to Bon, but to Judith, for her to add to her own, though Rosa realizes that *"that penny's modicum which is the donor's all"* will add *"nothing to the substance of the loved"* (185).

When Rosa returns to her story, she again stresses Judith's lack of grief, as though her attitude reflects Bon's nonexistence, denying to Rosa *"all the dreamy panoply of surrender which was my surrender, who had so little to surrender . . . "* (186). Though the dream had died with Bon, Rosa insists that love and faith had remained to give hope, to provide some purpose for continuing to exist.

Having explained the substance of her dream and the circumstances leading to its dissolution, Rosa's narrative now takes on a more direct tone, moving through events at a more rapid pace as she recalls the preparations for Bon's burial and the interment itself.[12] In a scene reminiscent of *As I Lay Dying*, she describes her outrage that Jones and another man constructed the coffin so near the house, though Judith seems unaware. Rosa remarks that Judith had helped prepare the meal, and she sees her niece gathering eggs later in the barnyard. She becomes fixated on the idea that Judith's usual demeanor reflects the fact that Bon had never existed, had never been there to grieve for. She goes so far as to attempt to take the full weight of his coffin on her own shoulder as he is carried to his grave. Judith manages to keep her composure throughout, even asking if anyone knows how to conduct a Catholic funeral. Instead, Theophilus McCaslin offers his own Confederate ritual—a modified and rather inappropriate battle cry.[13] The women return to the house, prepare supper, and retire, never weeping, Rosa never even inquiring about Henry.

Nowhere is Rosa's selfish abstraction more in evidence than in her remarkable lack of curiosity regarding the background for these events. Obviously Rosa has no way of knowing about the durance. She has not been to Sutpen's Hundred since Ellen's death, and she had learned only what the town had learned concerning the events of Christmas 1860, only what filtered back through the slaves. Though it is possible that she has questioned Judith on the occasions her niece had visited her in town, Judith herself ostensibly has no understanding of the nature of the objection her father and Henry have toward Bon. Rosa can hardly have the faintest inkling. Still, she never alludes to the question which dominates the reflections of the book's other characters/narrators. She accepts that Henry has killed Bon and vanished; that she never even wonders *why* indicates two things—the degree to which she ascribes the family's disaster to Sutpen's demonic influence and the extent to which she is incapable of interest in anything which does not relate to her directly.

Rosa's account now turns to the mundane matters of life at Sutpen's Hundred during the relatively long (and unexplained—again Rosa seems uninterested in the delay) period before Sutpen himself returns from the war in January 1866. In the same way she justifies herself in chapter 1, Rosa considers all the reasons she would have had for remaining with Judith, yet she discards them all. She asserts simply, "*I stayed there and waited for Thomas Sutpen to come home*" (191). Aware of the local gossip, she suspects that Quentin thinks she may have planned to marry him from that time, but she denies this, maintaining that she had waited for him because he was all that she and Judith had had. The fact that Rosa and Judith would be needed in restoring Sutpen's Hundred had been their only purpose in continuing to exist. Sutpen had needed them, though they had not needed him. Their existence had been barren, valueless, aided only by the occasional contribution of Wash Jones. The women had worked like men in an attempt to survive. Rosa now acknowledges almost a grudging respect for Clytie, though she sees Clytie and Judith's attempts to feed the returning soldiers as heedless and unjustified magnanimity. Her respect does not ripen into anything more, however. Rosa cements her continued hatred of Clytie, along with her continued lack of understanding of Judith. In the evenings the women talk of the war, of Sutpen's return, of Henry's whereabouts, but never do they mention Charles Bon. Curiously, though Miss Rosa denies that Judith had felt bereaved, she asserts that twice in the fall Judith had gone to clear his grave of falling leaves.

For Rosa, the most terrifying result of this fearful and bizarre time was her consent to marry Sutpen. In rationalizing this to Quentin (this is another area she had covered in some detail in chapter 1), she insists on claiming an active role in the courtship as an indication of the way town legend had painted her. The facts themselves are indeed very different. Sutpen returns scarred and tattered, though he correctly anticipates what has happened in his absence. There is clearly an understanding between him and Judith, as his truncated questions and her brief answers indicate. Rosa is astonished at this point only by Judith's tears, though the reader can easily understand the reason for them. She realizes that Bon's death is the culmination of what had begun at Christmas 1860, of events which her father had set in motion. Still, she is the dutiful daughter, and having managed the plantation as well as she could in her father's absence, having fulfilled her duty to him as best she knew how, she is now free to let her emotion manifest itself more visibly. Her action is both understandable and laudatory; her father certainly does not question it nor seem surprised by it.

Sutpen's behavior in accepting his new position and his heroic attempts to restore his property are viewed positively by Rosa, though she recoils from the monomania with which he sets himself this goal. He seems constantly focused on his plans, covering in his mind the hundred square miles, talking not to the women present but to the house itself and to the land he would not wait even one day to begin to restore. He spends no time regretting the war, never even alludes to it; rather he seems to live under the necessity of reaching his goal before old age and death overtake him, concerned—Miss Rosa insists on the word—that he might not have time to succeed. He works constantly, aided only by Wash and another man, works while others attempt to regain their honor and to restrain the social and political changes manifest in their defeat by forming groups of nightriders. Miss Rosa's admiration of Sutpen reaches its zenith in her account of his answer to these men who attempt to force Sutpen to join their numbers: " . . . *their spokesman delivered his ultimatum: 'This may be war, Sutpen,' and [he] answered, 'I am used to it'* " (202). The episode illustrates Rosa's sharp observation of character: she remarks the level tone of Sutpen's voice, his fearlessness in outlining his body in the doorway, his caution in holding his lamp above his head so as to free his vision if he should be attacked. Still, she sees Sutpen's desire as vanity. The reader cannot help but admire his attempt to fight not only old age and the dissolution of his plantation, but the "*ponderable weight of the changed new time itself*" (202). For Rosa, admiration has given way to present disdain. She justifies her earlier attitude as resulting only from her youth and inexperience, which she still defines in terms of incomplete gestation: "*living in that womb-like corridor where the world came not even as living echo but as dead incomprehensible shadow . . .* " (202).

This state is her ultimate justification for becoming engaged to Sutpen. While preparing an okra bed in April, Rosa notices Sutpen looking at her, a fact she remarks primarily because he is usually absent, seeing to the restoration of his lands. She becomes entranced, not even aware of finishing the preparation of the ground and observing no change in Sutpen at dinner. But there is a definite change in her, an acquiesence which, typically, she couches in sexual terms: *"There is a metabolism of the spirit as well as of the entrails, in which the stored accumulations of long time burn, generate, create and break some maidenhead of the ravening meat . . ."* (204). Later in Judith's room, he proposes not by asking Rosa to marry him, but by pointing out to her that he would make no worse a husband for her than for her sister. Her changed attitude will allow her to accept him.

She does not admit her vicarious love and loss of Bon as motivating factors, but the structure of her monologue suggests their impact upon her. She refers to her courtship, remarks that she had not even responded yes. She had heard Sutpen bid Judith fetch her mother's wedding band and had accepted it when he placed it on her finger. Her feelings are different now from those of her summer of "wistaria," during which the urges of her physical being had demanded response; it is now her spirit which she attends to, *"as Ellen must have listened in her own spirit's April thirty years ago"* (205). She embraces marriage as an abstraction, a balm to help heal the wounds of her earlier blighted love as well as to join with Sutpen in attempting to restore something of the health and dignity of the vanquished land. When she listens to his speech, she discovers that he is not addressing her at all, but talking *"to the very dark forces of fate which he had evoked and dared, out of that wild braggart dream where [existed] an intact Sutpen's Hundred . . ."* (205–6). She views Sutpen as mad, yet she abets him in madness, asserting that her salvation would later arise from the complete sacrifice of her nature, what she calls being *"free of all excuse of the surprised importunate traitorous flesh . . ."* (206).

Sutpen uses Rosa only as a tool toward re-establishment of his dynasty, a fact she seems aware of from the beginning. She remarks that after her engagement he had relegated her to the same oblivion which had characterized his view of her for twenty years. She creates the analogy of the man lost in the jungle who approaches the sun not for any joy in its warmth but because it represents for him the lack of the oppressive swamp and suggests that one of the reasons for his ignoring her was how busy he had been, that even his madness had a pragmatic angle: *"If he was mad, it was only his compelling dream which was insane and not his methods . . ."* (207). She rationalizes her new attitude toward Sutpen, telescoping her family's entire history with him and concluding with her altered perception; the ogre had *". . . vanished, consumed somewhere in flame and sulphur-reek perhaps among the lonely craggy peaks of my childhood's solitary remembering—or forgetting . . ."* (209). Though she dreams still of love, she knows that Sutpen had not, that to him she had represented only a tool, a vessel, or, to borrow the image Rosa herself employs, a patch of firm ground after the dark and treacherous swamp.

She accepts him, fully aware of the limitations of his emotional involvement, and precisely up to the moment when he forces her to recognize that there is no love, no real commitment at all, that he is planning to use her in the same way he would use Wash or Clytie to accomplish a task required in the restoration of his plantation and lineage. On the afternoon when he learns that, as one of the victims of the new order, he can keep only about one square mile from his original hundred—the rest will be one of the spoils of the victors—he realizes his need for haste; in desperation he knows he has no time at all for further mistakes. His proposal to Rosa, the result of his desperation, outrages her not necessarily for any reasons of virtue or honor, but because it blasts her completely from her dream, which until then she had been capable of extending to allow her acceptance of him, as she verbalizes in an imaginary encounter: *"'O furious mad old man, I hold no substance that will fit your dream but I can give you airy space and scope for your delirium'"* (210).

The extent of her outrage is conveyed by the fact that she does not even repeat the exact proposal, at least in the monologue itself. (Quentin and Shreve later make reference to several things Quentin had supposedly learned from Rosa which are not in the monologue. Rather than assuming that Quentin had made them up and ascribed them to her, it is reasonable to suppose that the novel simply does not record the entirety of her tirade, and that the wording of Sutpen's proposal as repeated by Shreve in the following chapter is essentially accurate.) She explains her reluctance to Quentin:

> *I will tell you what he did and let you be the judge. (Or try to tell you, because there are some things for which three words are three too many, and three thousand words that many words too less, and this is one of them. It can be told; I could take that many sentences, repeat the bold blank naked and outrageous words just as he spoke them, and bequeath you only that same aghast and outraged unbelief I knew when I comprehended what he meant; or take three thousand sentences and leave you only that Why? Why? and Why? that I have asked and listened to for almost fifty years.)* (208)

At this point Rosa returns to seeing herself through the eyes of the town: *"They will have told you how I came back home"* (210). She has become the object of old-maid ridicule. Once again, she describes Sutpen as a demon, above being harmed by the war, and, demon or not, her only chance at marriage. Yet the townspeople would be kind, at least in their acknowledgment that she had been right in hating her father, since his death had led indirectly to her insult. Only to Rosa, being right is not enough; she is one of those women *"who had rather be wrong than just that who want the man who was wrong to admit it"* (212). Thus, Sutpen's final insult to her is his dying before she had forced him to acknowledge the outrage.

She had returned to town, where she had foraged for food from neighbors' gardens and brooded upon her insult. Her attitude toward Sutpen remains marked by inconsistencies. She tells Quentin that she had been outraged by the fact that Sutpen had been considering his proposal for a day, a week, a month. Earlier, though, she had maintained that Sutpen had not thought of the idea until he broached it to her, because he would not have hesitated a moment to propose it aloud once it had occurred to him (207). A more startling contradiction is her assertion that she had forgiven him because he had never been hers. By her reasoning, if no commitment had ever existed, no insult could have taken place. Her demonizing includes a catalogue of those women Sutpen had detroyed by clinging to them to stave off the dark forces opposed to his design: first Ellen, then Rosa herself, finally Wash Jones's granddaughter. (That she does not mention Sutpen's Haitian wife confirms her complete ignorance of this part of his life.)

Rosa ends her monologue by her apostrophe to Sutpen when a neighbor informs her of his death: " '*Dead?' I cried. 'Dead? . . . you're not dead; heaven cannot, and hell dare not, have you!'* " (215). Her view of Sutpen the demon is here complete. As a demon he can find no refuge in heaven; but the potency of his demonic personality makes him a threat to Satan himself.[14] In a more personal sense, Sutpen has not died because she preserves him as an object of hatred in her own imagination. The result is that she becomes a grotesque figure, blighted by her unfulfilled dreams.

The final page of chapter 5 departs from Rosa's monologue to represent Quentin's reaction to a part of her story. The reader is told that Quentin has not been listening, having become fixated on the confrontation between Judith and Henry after Bon's death. The narrative voice describes the image which Quentin conjures, the picture of Judith and Clytie at work on the wedding dress when Henry breaks in to announce that he has prevented the marriage by killing the groom. The passage is problematical for a couple of reasons. Most significant, perhaps, is the question of whose creation the scene actually is. Rosa's monologue brushes past the confrontation itself, though she provides the unlikely suggestion that Judith and Clytie were at work on the wedding dress. The conversation between Henry and Judith appears in italics, possibly indicating that Rosa at some other point had provided it.[15] The descriptions of Judith and Henry themselves would seem to owe most to Quentin's imagination. Who is responsible for assigning speech to the characters is immaterial, though, for Rosa did not witness the scene and informs Quentin that she did not even ask Judith how Henry had looked. So the conversation is a fanciful construction in any case.[16]

Ultimately, what is at issue is not the source of the scene, but our understanding of its effect upon Quentin. Here once again the reader of *Absalom, Absalom!* who is unacquainted with *The Sound and the Fury* will fail to comprehend its impact. As we have seen, conflation of the chronology of the two novels reminds us that Quentin endures Rosa's monologue only a few weeks after his ineffectual confrontation with Dalton Ames, an episode which turns out badly for Quentin, who refuses Ames's offer of a pistol and even faints. His actions thus provide a sharp contrast to those of the brother who murders his sister's lover. We must also bear in mind that the scene Quentin could not "pass" provides the context of his discussion with his father, who in chapters 3 and 4 also focuses on the significance of the murder and the relationship between Judith and Henry.

At any rate, Miss Rosa forces Quentin to attend to her at the close of the chapter. She asserts that something has been " 'for four years, living hidden in that house' " (216). Neither Rosa nor the narrator explains how she arrives at her intuition that someone inhabits the rotting mansion. Cleanth Brooks wonders whether the frightening of a family traveling through the area, apparently reported in Jefferson (267), had been Rosa's reason for being so precise in dating the entrance of "something" into Sutpen's house.[17] For the first time the reader understands the reference in chapter 1 to the fact that "it would be three hours yet before he would learn why she had sent for him" (9). Her reason, as Mr. Compson had guessed (10), is to have someone to accompany her to the house and investigate. Chapter 5's ending, like that of the two preceding ones, links this section of the narration with the rest of the novel, answering questions posed in earlier chapters and looking forward to the descriptions of that trip in later ones.

6

"Tell about the South":
Quentin and Shreve's Reconstruction

The narrative challenges presented by chapter 6 of *Absalom, Absalom!* are formidable, perhaps the most complex in the entire novel. Hugh Ruppersburg points out that the difficulties of the section result from "Faulkner's use of the narrative structure as a metaphor of Quentin's state of mind—in constant flux between past and present. . . ."[1] But another reason lies in the structural demands placed upon the material. With this chapter, the second "movement" of the novel begins, the part which Cleanth Brooks calls "an attempt at interpretation."[2] The setting shifts from Mississippi to Quentin and Shreve's sitting room at Harvard. By this time, Quentin knows all he ever will about Sutpen and his family, though the reader still has a great deal to learn. The final four chapters reveal what—to Quentin at least—are the clues which explain Henry's murder of Bon, which Quentin sees as the seminal event in the Sutpen tragedy.

Though the setting of the last four chapters is different and we find Quentin discussing the story with a new character, the central themes and questions still remain unresolved. Indeed, they become considerably more intense. This renewed intensity builds until the final episode and provides one of the central unifying devices in the book. Toward that unity, Faulkner very carefully provides links between this chapter and both those preceding and those to follow. Shreve makes his first apprearance, delivering Mr. Compson's letter announcing Miss Rosa Coldfield's death. The news is dramatic, particularly since the reader has just witnessed her frenzied peroration in chapter 5. Its arrival provides an occasion for Shreve to ask about the South, and his question, involving Miss Rosa's relationship to Quentin, provides a transition to the memory of the evening in the previous September when Quentin had accompanied her to Sutpen's Hundred to discover the presence living in the house.

This material picks up almost immediately a thread left hanging at the end of chapter 5, a reference which itself is carried over from the opening pages of the novel. Quentin's memories of that night in September also anticipate the book's climax in chapter 9, when Quentin is forced to recall his meeting with Henry Sutpen. But Quentin's account breaks off inconclusively for the present, heightening suspense by recording merely his extreme reluctance to discover whatever remains hidden in the rotting mansion. Shreve intrudes to recapitulate all he knows about the Sutpen story, and the reader, bombarded with a plethora of sometimes contradictory information he can hardly remember, much less assimilate, is grateful for this telescoping of the story.

Using Miss Rosa as his focus, as Mr. Compson had in chapter 3, Shreve summarizes the facts from Sutpen's arrival in Jefferson until his death at the hands of Wash Jones, and his recital adds to the reader's store of knowledge, particularly regarding events following Rosa's return to Jefferson in the summer of 1866. (To a degree, then, for the reader, the story advances chronologically, since the primary accounting in this chapter by both Mr. Compson and Shreve will cover the postwar years, just as Miss Rosa's main concern in the second half of her monologue had been with the years of the war itself and its immediate aftermath.)

Shreve's comment that Judith had spent the money from the sale of her father's country store for a tombstone prepares for a long interpolation, related in part by the narrative persona, in part by Mr. Compson, which details the visit to Bon's grave by his octoroon mistress and son and Judith's attempts to raise that son after his mother's death. Mention of the tombstone recalls to Shreve an account Quentin had provided earlier of a conversation with his father in the Sutpen family cemetery when a birdhunt had been interrupted by rain. The portion of the story advances to Judith's death and Miss Rosa's commanding her headstone from Judge Benbow.

For the remainder of the chapter, Shreve recalls what Quentin has told him—relating the tales of ghosts inhabiting the house, the terror of the young boys when approaching it and seeing Clytie and Jim Bond, the mentally deficient grandson of Charles and the octoroon. Thus, by the end, Shreve has come full circle, back to the point which spurred his account—Quentin's visit with Rosa to Sutpen's Hundred. Typically adhering to the structural demands of the novel, however, Shreve postpones revealing the identity of the inhabitant, and the chapter closes, as does chapter 7, with Shreve's demand for more information. In the latter instance, Quentin provides that information immediately—Milly Jones's child by Sutpen had been a girl, thus provoking Sutpen's insult and his murder by Wash. The identity of the person living in Sutpen's house, however, remains a mystery until the closing pages of the novel.

The sparsity of description of Shreve is perhaps yet another invitation to draw upon *The Sound and the Fury* in interpreting *Absalom, Absalom!*.[3] We know almost nothing about Shreve as chapter 6 opens except for what may be remembered of his characterization in the earlier novel. This lack of information stands in sharp contrast to the way Miss Rosa is dealt with in the first chapter, in which she is described in grotesque detail and in which her distant relationship with Quentin is carefully delineated. Faulkner does describe Shreve physically, and he shows that Shreve is well adjusted to the cold of New England, which Quentin seems to find so alien. But the apparently close relationship between the two roommates in *The Sound and the Fury* is hinted at only obliquely and develops gradually as the novel progresses. Knowledge of the loyalty Shreve exhibits in supporting Quentin after his abortive fight with Gerald Bland—he seems even to guess his roommate's destructive plans on June 2, 1910—makes the intense conversation between the two youths in *Absalom, Absalom!* easier to accept and to understand.

At first, Shreve seems almost totally unaware of the impact the story has upon Quentin. He badgers him about Rosa's relationship with him after the letter arrives, and he deliberately forces recognition of his own ignorance of the Southern way of life. Cleanth Brooks suggests that Faulkner includes Shreve as an exponent of "the modern 'liberal,' twentieth-century reader, who is basically rational, skeptical, without any special concern for history, and pretty well emancipated from the ties of family, race, or section."[4] As Shreve learns more about the story, he is himself moved by it, and he seems at times to sense intuitively the extent of Quentin's involvement. He points out in chapter 9 that he is not trying to be funny or smart (450), and when he can no longer ignore the effect of the story upon his roommate, when Quentin begins shaking uncontrollably after the two finally go to bed, he offers to cover him with the overcoats. A part of the mystery of the entire affair for Shreve is its impact on Quentin, which he never fully comprehends, in part because of his distance geographically, in part because of his greater adjustment to life.[5] In the Genealogy appended to the novel, the contrast between the two roommates is unmistakable: though his suicide is not mentioned, Quentin is recorded as having died in Cambridge in 1910; Shreve, on the other hand, has served in the First World War and is "now a practising surgeon" in Canada (477).

Throughout the final four chapters, the differing reactions of the two young men to the tale they reconstruct (or create) is as remarkable as their respective fates (to borrow Mr. Compson's word). With the exception of chapter 7, which Quentin narrates almost entirely using information his grandfather had learned about Sutpen's early life and death, frequent intrusions by the narrative voice throughout the novel's second movement underline the pain that hearing the story causes the young Southerner. (Such interpolations are less frequent in the seventh chapter, though they are still present.) Significantly, the materials of chapter 7 are those with which Quentin is least emotionally involved, and they are the only ones which he tells directly in the entire novel. Shreve, on the other hand, approaches what he hears as if he is reading a hard-boiled detective novel. He readily assimilates the points of view of the other characters and approaches the entire matter irreverently. Miss Rosa is for him " 'this old dame' " (221), and he goes Rosa herself one better when he describes Sutpen as " 'this Faustus, this demon, this Beelzebub' " (223). Mr. Compson's view of the fate which destines the lives of the characters is transformed by Shreve into the "Creditor" (223) who waits patiently to deliver to Sutpen the retribution he so much deserves.

At the University of Virginia in 1957 Faulkner stated what he had intended as Shreve's role in *Absalom, Absalom!*: "Well, the story was told by Quentin to Shreve. Shreve was the commentator that held the thing to something of reality. If Quentin had been let alone to tell it, it would have become something completely unreal. It had to have a solvent to keep it real, keep it believable, creditable, otherwise it would have vanished into smoke and fury" (*FIU*, 75). Though this statement is hardly a truthful characterization of Shreve's role in the entire novel—in chapter 8 he fashions events and characters quite fancifully in order to make the story sensible—it defines pretty well the way Faulkner uses him in chapter 6. He provides a sense of ironic detachment which Quentin knows he lacks. Considering the occasion of Sutpen's bringing the gravestones to the plantation, the narrative voice comments that Quentin "could see it; he might even have been there. Then he thought *No. If I had been there I could not have seen it this plain*" (238). To Shreve's recounting of events, Quentin offers only the word *yes* (221, 223, 225, 227, 232, 269, 270), indicating his assent to the summation on one level, perhaps hinting on another at his reluctance to correct the account because of the suffering he must endure in hearing the story over once again.

The various passages in which the narrative persona interrupts the account to focus on Quentin's reactions were added to the novel after the completion of the manuscript.[6] The first of these links Shreve's account to Mr. Compson's:

> "Yes," Quentin said. *He sounds just like Father* he thought, glancing (his face quiet, reposed, curiously almost sullen) for a moment at Shreve leaning forward into the lamp, his naked torso pink-gleaming and baby-smooth, cherubic, almost hairless, the twin moons of his spectacles glinting against his moonlike rubicund face, smelling (Quentin) the cigar and the wistaria, seeing the fireflies blowing and winking in the September dusk. *Just exactly like Father if Father had known as much about it the night before I went out there as he did the day after I came back.* . . . (227)[7]

Later additions to Faulkner's original conception focus on Quentin's having to hear the tale once more: "*Yes. I have heard too much, I have been told too much; I have had to listen to too much, too long* thinking *Yes, almost exactly like Father* . . . " (259–60). The phrase "too much, too long" appears twice more (263, 264), becoming a refrain which keeps Quentin's psychological involvement present in the reader's mind.

Quentin's identification of Shreve's comments with his father's arises because he recognizes that neither narrator is as involved as he is; neither has a personal stake in the telling (unless Mr. Compson has a didactic purpose in mind, in which case he makes some very curious assertions, as we have seen). Thus, the first two additions involve descriptions of the Mississippi setting on the Compson porch, emphasizing the smoke and the wistaria. And all the added passages imply the presence of Shreve himself, for it is Shreve who obliges Quentin to listen to the story against his will. The few descriptions of Shreve's appearance thereby acquire added symbolic import. He becomes a mirror in which Quentin sees reflected his own despair. Shreve's glasses and face look like moons; his youth and optimism are underlined, as opposed to the world-weariness which Quentin has acquired by the age of twenty. His baby-like pink body signals his ignorance of the depth of the tragedy his friend cannot understand or escape. His nakedness is a continual reminder that he is at home, accustomed to the New England cold, but it also looks forward to the hints of a homosexual attraction between the two youths as their intimacy grows during their shared creation of the conflict between Henry and Bon. Though Shreve does not always hold the story to reality, he serves as an effective foil for his obsessed, effete roommate.

The letter Shreve delivers is yet another linking device, since the reader must wait until chapter 9 to find the conclusion of it. Like Shreve's talking, the letter reminds Quentin of his conversation with Mr. Compson in September, and the images which become recurrent motifs in the remaining chapters are introduced: "that dead summer twilight—the wistaria, the cigar-smell, the fire-flies—attenuated up from Mississippi and into this strange room, across this strange iron New England snow" (217). The subject of Mr. Compson's letter is death, and he cannot resist the opportunity to comment on it philosophically, suggesting that it must be "*a brief and likewise peculiar state*" of the subject as well as of survivors (218). He doubts if death would bring comfort to Miss Rosa and bemoans the constant awareness of mortality as one of the painful realities of the human condition. (His reference to an idiot having escaped this realization is curious and seems indelicate in Benjy's father. Apparently Faulkner did not consider Benjy in defining Mr. Compson's character as revealed in the letter. Nor does Shreve seem aware that Quentin has an idiot brother at the end of the book when referring to Jim Bond. Neither Shreve nor Mr. Compson would be so insensitive about a matter which would occasion considerable embarrassment in 1910, as indeed it would among many people today.)

Mr. Compson's characteristic voice in the letter sets the stage for his part of the narration later in the chapter. For the present, the reading of it breaks off as Quentin explains to Shreve (to whom he apparently reads the letter) who Miss Rosa was. Apparently at this stage Quentin also takes some time to inform Shreve of her part in the tragedy and of her own attitudes toward Sutpen, since Shreve seems unaware of her identity on page 218, yet he understands her peculiar attitudes toward Sutpen a couple of pages later. Extending a pattern of interrogation begun with Quentin's arrival at Cambridge, Shreve taunts him about Miss Rosa, hinting at his somber, even perhaps morose personality and stating one of the novel's most pervasive themes—the meaning of human experience: "*Tell about the South. What's it like there. What do they do there. Why do they live there. Why do they live at all . . .* " (218).

Quentin's attention remains fixed on the memories evoked by the letter of his trip to Sutpen's Hundred with Miss Rosa. Once again we are reminded of the point which he could not "pass," though now the narrator suggests that the image of Henry's confrontation with his sister after Bon's murder had kept Quentin transfixed not only through Miss Rosa's speech but through his father's conversation as well. His memory of the trip itself focuses on the darkness, the heat, and especially the dust, which becomes a personified entity summarizing Quentin's own attitude toward what he is to discover: *"you will find no destination but will merely abrupt gently onto a plateau and a panorama of harmless and inscrutable night and there will be nothing for you to do but return and so I would advise you not to go, to turn back now and let what is, be"* (220).

Shreve's interruption suggests that Quentin has explained something about Miss Rosa to his friend in the interim while his mind has been occupied with his reminiscence. Shreve starts his recounting with Miss Rosa's coercion of Quentin into going to Sutpen's Hundred. But he soon backs up to demonstrate considerable knowledge of events and of the personalities that had set them into motion. He assumes that Rosa had hated her father, her aunt, and Sutpen, and that her strongest desire had been for vindication of this hatred. This viewpoint is very similar to Rosa's own comment that *"being right, is not enough for women . . . who want the man who was wrong to admit it"* (212). If Shreve is drawing here on something which Quentin has told him, then he must have been listening to Miss Rosa with at least some part of his mind. This is a logical conclusion, since on several occasions Shreve's interpretations reflect comments made by either Rosa or Mr. Compson.

The first new information provided by Shreve is the exact nature of Sutpen's proposal, which had so outraged Rosa: "'that they breed together for test and sample and if it was a boy they would marry . . . '" (222). We must assume that at some time not recorded in her monologue Miss Rosa gave this information to Quentin, who has passed it along to Shreve. Shreve does not seem at all tentative in stating it, nor does Quentin disagree. We might notice, however, that Shreve's interpretation of Rosa's consent to marry Sutpen—that she had been "'betrayed by the old meat'" (222)—hardly sounds at all like something he has heard from Quentin, who manifests an extreme reluctance to ascribe any motivation to physical desire or need throughout the novel.

Shreve suggests that the outrage had been compounded by Sutpen's almost immediate choice of Wash's granddaughter, whom Rosa would have considered absolutely beneath her, and by the fact that Sutpen's death would forever absolve him from having to admit his fault. Shreve's description of the power of the scythe as a phallic symbol that jeers at Rosa draws a sharp distinction between his own viewpoint and Quentin's. This flippancy in dealing with sexual matters is a far cry from Quentin's hypersensitivity about the subject. Shreve is badgering his roommate, and Quentin's simple "Yes" as a rejoinder should not necessarily be interpreted as a confirmation of Shreve's opinion. Rather it may represent merely a reluctance to become more involved.

The presence of both Miss Rosa and Mr. Compson is felt in Shreve's summation of Sutpen's career in Jefferson until the Civil War. He accepts (as does Quentin, apparently) the idea Rosa advances that Sutpen had arrived in Jefferson in need of a place to hide and that his early career represented his attempt to cloak himself in respectablity, a notion to which Mr. Compson has assented. The metaphor of the Creditor, who keeps a running tab of Sutpen's transgressions with the threat of punishment, recalls Mr. Compson's fascination with sin and retribution, but the monetary emphasis is reminiscent of Mr. Coldfield's attempts to balance his spiritual books and discover himself solvent, as well as Shreve's later invention of the lawyer who follows the accumulation of Sutpen's wealth so as to be able to make maximum use of Charles in blackmailing him out of that wealth.

Shreve's mask of cynicism becomes more evident in his discussion of Sutpen's behavior after the war. His suggestion that Sutpen could have been consciously attempting to get Miss Rosa to leave his house, attempting on a larger scale to achieve freedom from his family entirely, is completely without substantiation in the earlier narrative. Finding his family destroyed and having escaped marriage twice (once through the death of his wife, once through insult of his fianceé), Sutpen, Shreve suggests, may have then decided that freedom was not right for him and so began courting Milly.

Part of Shreve's personality is reflected in his tendency, shared by Mr. Compson, to pause in his account to make a more generally encompassing statement about human nature. As with Quentin's father's comments, these statements usually reflect his misogyny or his need to see a pattern or evidence of destiny in events. Shreve is more given to seemingly cynical pronouncements about sexual behavior, though they too have a misogynist cast. Thus Sutpen's insult is applauded by Shreve as an attempt to invent " 'with fiendish cunning the thing which husbands and fiancés have been trying to invent for ten million years: the thing that without harming her or giving her grounds for civil or tribal action would not only blast the little dream-woman out of the dovecote but leave her irrevocably husbanded . . . with the abstract carcass of outrage and revenge' " (226). (This interpretation of Sutpen's action also provides a foreshadowing of Shreve's picture of Sutpen's first wife in chapter 8.)

These comments prepare for Quentin's observation that Shreve sounds "*just like Father*" (227). The narrator describes Shreve's appearance, and Quentin gives the first hint that he had forced a complete reinterpretation of events by what he had learned at Sutpen's Hundred. The participle *thinking* links Quentin's observation with Shreve's continuing summation, which now appears in italics.[8] Shreve examines the fate of the Sutpen children: Henry vanished and doomed—Shreve speculates—to continue his life under another name; Judith condemned to a hollow spinsterhood. He accepts Rosa's notion that Judith did not grieve for Bon, another idea he has gleaned from Quentin, who cannot see love at all between Bon and Judith, despite the considerable evidence of its existence.

Shreve's account of Sutpen after the war emphasizes the once great man's degeneration accurately enough, though Shreve makes some mistakes, like his calling Jones Sutpen's "partner" in the store (229). Quentin allows these to stand without comment, and Shreve develops his story of Sutpen's seduction of Milly and his drinking bouts with Wash. The picture of the two men together foreshadows the concern with class distinctions which is a major theme of chapter 7.[9] Wash is presented as the loyal retainer, agreeing with Sutpen, supporting his vanity, commandeering a passing wagon to take him to his house and seeing him to bed. (This would seem another misapprehension; given the probable sparsity of wagons going through what had been the Sutpen plantation, one wonders how long Jones would have had to wait to hail one. Once again, Quentin offers no correction.) Sutpen's history is significantly advanced by Shreve's elaborating upon the period when Sutpen had seen that it would be impossible to regain the point he had lost in 1861, *"that the task* [of restoring the plantation] *was hopeless"* (231). Wash, however, continues to view Sutpen through the glorified eyes of the past.

The account of Sutpen's declining years seems to reflect both Mr. Compson and Shreve; perhaps the italics represent a blending of the two speakers in Quentin's mind. The romantic image of Wash and Sutpen in the beyond probably owes more to Shreve's youthful fancy, though its suggestion that the tragic divisions between the two in life had been essentially meaningless—that they had not really mattered—is characteristic of Mr. Compson. Sutpen's death is wrought with irony which Shreve recognizes and underlines. He refers to the "son" of Sutpen's stallion, born of its "wife" Penelope (232), instead of using the terms *colt* and *dam* (perhaps another indication of differing backgrounds.) After Sutpen's death, Judith borrows two mules to take his body to town for the funeral—recalling her pleasure in riding fast behind horses to church—but when they bolt and the coffin is thrown, she returns to bury her father and conduct the service herself, something she had not done for Charles Bon. Then she works on the farm and runs the store with only Clytie's help until she sells the store to purchase Bon's tombstone.

The mention of the tombstone triggers a question about a quail-hunting expedition Quentin has told his friend about. The question, addressed in second person, provides the transition to an extended interruption, nearly forty pages, of Shreve's summation of the Sutpen story. The interpolation, combining Quentin's thoughts with remembered conversation with Mr. Compson and descriptions by the narrative voice, is set in the Sutpen family graveyard and essentially concerns Judith's life after her father's death, especially her attempts to rear Charles Bon's son, Charles Etienne Saint-Valery Bon.

When rain interrupts the hunt, Mr. Compson and Quentin seek shelter beneath the cedars in the cemetery, leaving Luster to find a crossing of a flooded ditch with the horses.[10] The rich poetic description sets the tone of the discussion dealing with the puny monuments of human mortality. The graveyard is dark, lessened only by "the faint light which the raindrops brought particle by particle into the gloom and released" (236). A reference to a small animal, descendent of the original ones which had entered the grave for food, comments on the ignominious ends to which all human actions and strivings eventually lead. The setting is obviously designed as the perfect backdrop for Mr. Compson's musings on the significance of life and death.

Quentin remarks that Sutpen's gravestone betrays neither the place nor date of his birth, prefiguring the uncertainties of Sutpen's early life outlined in the following chapter. He also notices that Ellen's stone, which Sutpen himself had had carved, offers no sentimental remembrances of love: "thinking *Not beloved wife of. No. Ellen Coldfield Sutpen*" (236). But he questions his father only about how the marble had been acquired in 1869. The question introduces Mr. Compson's comments, supplemented occasionally by the narrative voice, which describes other aspects of the setting and presents Quentin's reactions. Compson sees Sutpen's ability to get two huge marble slabs shipped during the war—" 'the best, the finest to be had' " (236)—as evidence of his almost superhuman ability, as well as of his confidence that he would survive to install them. Quentin imagines in detail how the marble stones ran the blockade and were hauled around by Sutpen before he could bring them to Sutpen's Hundred in the fall of 1864, desperate days indeed for a Southern officer to be engaged in so personal and frivolous a mission. The narrator suggests that there had been some truth in the town's view of Miss Rosa's motives in going out to live with Judith; she would daily see Sutpen's own stone, set up in the hall, "possibly (maybe doubtless here too) reading among the lettering more of maiden hope and virgin expectation than she ever told Quentin about . . . " (238).

Mr. Compson uses Quentin's question about the other three headstones as an occasion to train him in interpreting human motivation. He asks who would have paid for them and watches his son carefully as he formulates his response. Quentin correctly identifies Judith as purchaser of Bon's stone, using the money from the sale of the store (a fact Shreve is aware of, since his allusion to it introduces the entire interpolation). The second headstone, that of Bon's son, Charles Etienne, baffles him though, since the date is the same as Judith's own and the money from the store sold in 1870 would have been long gone in 1884. He thinks too "how it would have been terrible for her sure enough if she had wanted to put *Beloved Husband of* " (239) on Bon's stone. This idea indicates that Quentin's active imagination had been set on the Judith-Bon-Henry relationship some time before Miss Rosa's summons causes him to re-examine the story in detail. Drawing upon information about the weather emphasized in creating the imagery of dryness and dust during Quentin and Rosa's trip to Sutpen's Hundred, Cleanth Brooks demonstrates that the hunting trip could not have occurred in the fall of 1909 because of the rain, so it probably is supposed to have taken place in either 1907 or 1908.[11] Quentin's remark, then, indicates that he has learned a good deal about Judith and Bon by this time, and that his thinking indicates that Judith had not really loved Bon: it would have been terrible *if* she had wanted to have had the inscription carved. The scene suggests that Quentin brings to his hearing in 1909 ideas established much earlier, providing at least a partial explanation of his reluctance to accept his father's notion that love had existed and of his easy acquiescence to Rosa's assertion that Judith had not mourned.

In explaining that Judith had put up the money for that stone, curiously bringing it and the inscription to General Compson while Clytie was in New Orleans fetching the boy,[12] Mr. Compson makes a generalization which does a great deal to illuminate his view of all the women in the novel: "'They lead beautiful lives—women. Lives not only divorced from, but irrevocably excommunicated from, all reality. That's why their deaths . . . are of no importance to them . . . yet to them their funerals and graves, the little puny affirmations of spurious immortality set above their slumber, are of incalculable importance'" (240). His illustration concerning an aunt of Quentin's provides one of the novel's brief moments of humor, but he quickly turns his attention to the octoroon's visit to Bon's grave.

References to Wilde and Beardsley underline Mr. Compson's *fin de siècle* outlook as he paints the sentimental picture related to him by his father. To Compson, the entire scene seems spurious, like a stage set, in which the emotions have no weight or depth. He calls the picture a "ceremonial," and—contradicting the passage in which he imagines Bon describing the fidelity of these women in chapter 4—presents the octoroon in terms he had earlier used to describe Ellen: "'changing from phase to phase as the butterfly changes once the cocoon is cleared, carrying nothing of what was into what is . . . '" (246).

Mention of Judith as she observes the scene provides the occasion for Quentin's again asserting that Judith "*not bereaved, did not need to mourn*" (243) and for yet another expression of the pain the memories cause him.[13] The descriptions of Judith during this episode are reminiscent of Miss Rosa's view of her reactions to Bon's death and burial, yet the very fact that Judith would go to the trouble to discover the woman's identity, inform her of Bon's death, and invite her to visit his grave indicates a continuing love of some kind. Surely she would not have done so if she had been indifferent to him at the time of his death. A remote possibility, not suggested by any of the characters, is that Judith had been aware that Bon was her half-brother. Mr. Compson assumes that Sutpen would have told her nothing and that she would not have asked him. He hypothesizes also that Henry would have confined his communication to his and Bon's whereabouts and welfare, though in both instances Mr. Compson is making suppositions without concrete evidence. It is certainly not impossible that Judith may have been aware at some point after Christmas 1860 that Bon was Sutpen's son. Indeed, such an interpretation would explain a great deal about her reaction to his death, which so puzzled Rosa, and Sutpen's reaction to the news when he returned from the war. Here a mutual understanding certainly seems to exist. Though they would have to be reassessed, the statements Judith makes to Mrs. Compson when she presents the letter could also support such an interpretation. The letter itself, then, would bear testimony that Bon was unaware of his own identity, or at the very least, that he had had no inkling that Judith knew who he really was.

The idea that Judith may have known Bon's true identity—another possibility is that Henry informed her after the fact to justify his action in killing Bon[14]—would also provide an explanation of her treatment of Bon's son. Mr. Compson offers a detailed account of how Clytie had gone to New Orleans after the boy had become an orphan and had brought him back at the age of about twelve. He assumes, completely without substantiation, that Clytie would have treated the boy harshly, and that Judith had reacted to him by maintaining a cool distance, an interpretation which, as Elisabeth Muhlenfeld has pointed out, "seems unlikely in view of her other responses throughout the novel."[15] Mr. Compson fashions his story of Charles Etienne along lines similar to Gavin Stevens's interpretation of Joe Christmas's problem of reconciling his supposed mixed blood in *Light in August*. Charles Etienne's anomalous position in the society of the time is symbolized by where he sleeps, on a trundle bed between Judith's bed and Clytie's pallet on the floor—that is, between the station and role of the white owner and the black servant.[16] He finds himself caught between Judith's cold distantness and Clytie's "'curious blend of savageness and pity, of yearning and hatred'" (248). Compson even imagines an unspoken communication between the women and the boy:

> *"You are not up here in this bed with me, where through no fault nor willing of your own you should be, and you are not down here on this pallet floor with me, where through no fault nor willing of your own you must and will be, not through any fault or willing of our own who would not what we cannot just as we will and wait for what must be."* (248–49)

This would seem an unusual remark from two women who had already flouted social convention to the point of entertaining and serving Bon's octoroon mistress and fetching the boy to live at Sutpen's Hundred, fully aware of his mixed blood.

General Compson had speculated about who had altered the boy's original circumstances, moving him out of Judith's room and informing him that he would have to be a black, relegated to a subservient position which his rearing and background had left him completely unprepared for. He assumes that Clytie had likewise moved into the hall, though the boy's cot had remained elevated above hers until he took a place in the attic. Clytie had maintained her jealous guardianship, refusing to allow the boy to associate with either whites or blacks. The town, not knowing as much as General Compson, took the presence of the boy as an explanation of why Henry had killed Bon, assuming that the boy was Bon's illegitimate son, conceived with Judith out of wedlock, "'believing now that it had been a widow who had buried Bon even though she had no paper to show for it . . .'" (252). Before associating the boy with the child of the octoroon, General Compson had even entertained the notion that the child was Clytie's, begot by Sutpen himself, though he is disabused when he makes the connection.

Naturally, Judith would turn to General Compson for help when the boy began getting into the trouble Mr. Compson would certainly expect as the result of his treatment at Sutpen's Hundred. The trouble had arisen from a fight started by Charles Etienne at a Negro ball, as if the youth were inviting punishment, eliciting it as retribution for the unnamed sin which had so altered his circumstances. General Compson had sensed another reason: "'the presence of that furious protest, that indictment of heaven's ordering, that gage flung into the face of what is with a furious and indomitable desperation which the demon himself might have shown . . . '" (254).[17] Indeed, the protest is very similar to that which his grandfather, Thomas Sutpen, had made after his insult at the plantation door. Far from reacting with indifference to his plight, however, Judith had been desperately concerned, though Mr. Compson would perhaps suspect that her concern had been for her own position in fostering such a man rather than care for his welfare.

General Compson bursts into the court just in time to prevent a rather serious breach of society's handling of justice among the blacks. The presiding magistrate assumes that Charles Etienne is a white man, and twice calls him that before Compson can reach him. But Compson's behavior is the only hint the judge needs to suspect the truth, and he demands, "'*What are you? Who and where did you come from?*'" (255). The wording of the questions indicates the same fear of the blacks which had motivated the nightriders who had threatened Sutpen. Mixed blood relegates Charles Etienne to a subhuman position, a "what." The ambiguity concerning his parentage makes appropriate the query of "who" they had been.

Public acknowledgment of the fracas and of his mixed blood means that Charles Etienne could not remain with Judith, at least not for the present. General Compson advises him to go away and offers him money. Anticipating what Isaac McCaslin tells Roth's octoroon mistress at the end of "Delta Autumn,"[18] General Compson says, "'Whatever you are, once you are among strangers, people who dont know you, you can be whatever you will'" (255). He seems strangely confused about the youth's relationship with Judith, however. He declines to refer to her as "'Miss Judith, since that would postulate the blood more than ever. Then he thought *I dont even know whether he wants to hide it or not.* So he said Miss Sutpen'" (255–56). Mr. Compson has already pointed out that his father had made the correlation between Charles Etienne and the boy he had seen with the octoroon. And even if he had yet to make the association, a man in his position in the 1870s would hardly recognize Judith as kin to a man of mixed blood, conceived in incestuous miscegenation, which the shocked General Compson had once suspected the boy to be.

The general seems unable to read Judith's signs of concern, though. He fails to see the worry she exhibits, both in summoning him to Charles Etienne's trial and in inquiring about his welfare when General Compson arrives to tell her that he has sent the youth away. As he offers his words of comfort, he thinks to himself, "*'Better that he were dead, better that he had never lived'*" (256), and even postulates that Judith has said the same thing to herself, "'changing only the person and the number'" (256)—that is, wishing that she too, like Charles Etienne, were dead or had never lived. Her behavior throughout her relationship with him, even the manner of her death, shows how absolutely wrong General Compson is in interpreting her character.

Charles Etienne returns some years later with "'a coal black and ape-like woman and an authentic wedding license'" (257), still refusing to conform either to the world of the blacks or that of the whites. His son is born about a year later, but Charles Etienne himself continues to move violently in both worlds, apparently suspended in a state of confusion imposed by Clytie during his early adolescence. No one knew what Judith's reaction to his return had been, though Mr. Compson imagines a compelling scene in which she attempts to cement a kinship between them. Mr. Compson resorts to the idea of the love Judith had felt for Bon as rationale for the conversation he imagines. The mention of love provokes a predictable response in Quentin, who again thinks that he has had to listen "*to too much, too long*" (259–60). The imagined scene itself uses the same technique Faulkner had used earlier when Quentin had remarked that Shreve sounds just like his father (227): he remembers his father's version and translates it through his own imagination. (We must bear in mind that he could also be remembering what his father had said at the same time that Shreve was covering essentially the same ground.) Mr. Compson speculates that though she remains cold, Judith tries a different approach with Charles Etienne, inviting him to put away his wife and child and live as a white man. Magnanimously she even offers to raise the child herself, suggesting that he go to one of the northern cities (an even closer anticipation of Isaac McCaslin's advice). She agrees to acknowledge him as Henry's son, making the proposal quietly, tentatively, fearfully. When he refuses, she even tells him to call her "Aunt Judith," though neither Mr. Compson nor Quentin when he first hears this story could realize the irony of this.

In a final romantic flight of fancy, Mr. Compson describes Charles Etienne's refusal as an attempt to achieve some sort of salvation through suffering, "'treading the thorny and flint-paved path toward the Gethsemane which he had decreed and created for himself, where he had crucified himself and come down from his cross for a moment and now returned to it'" (261–62). Whatever his motivation, however, a change takes place in him. He begins to farm on shares from Judith, associating with neither race, appearing rarely in Jefferson to drink and brawl, for four years until he contracts yellow fever and dies.[19] Nowhere does Judith exhibit greater caring or self-sacrifice than in taking Charles Etienne into her own house and nursing him. Indeed, she finally gives her life in a futile attempt to restore his.

Judith's death focuses attention once more on the gravestones; her grave is at the other end of the enclosure. Quentin's misunderstanding of Judith is demonstrated by his imagining that she herself had roused from her fever to give instructions and an inscription to Clytie, an idea which likely derives from his father, but which is nonetheless without evidence and rather absurd. The inscription itself bears the unmistakable mark of Miss Rosa's malice toward Sutpen: *"Judith Coldfield Sutpen. Daughter of Ellen Coldfield. Born October 3, 1841. Suffered the Indignities and Travails of this World for 42 Years, 4 Months, 9 Days, and went to Rest at Last February 12, 1884. Pause, Mortal; Remember Vanity and Folly and Beware"* (264). Mr. Compson continues his musing about women begun on page 240 in explaining how Miss Rosa had caused Judith's stone to be erected: *"Beautiful lives—women do. In very breathing they draw meat and drink from some beautiful attenuation of unreality in which the shades and shapes of facts . . . move with the substanceless decorum of lawn party charades, perfect in gesture and without significance or any ability to hurt"* (264). Though ostensibly describing Miss Rosa, that he can make such a statement in view of the unmistakable evidence of Judith's sense of duty and self-sacrifice indicates the extent to which Mr. Compson is capable of coloring his interpretation of character with his own bitterness and cynicism.

His description of Miss Rosa indicates that she had indeed lived divorced from reality after Judith's death, ordering her headstone from Judge Benbow and accepting the anonymous gifts of food made by neighbors.[20] (The comment supports Rosa's own view of her existence as being a dream state, distant from reality in chapter 5.) It is ironic that the daughter of a man who saw his state of spiritual health in terms of a ledger sheet should be supported by a judge who uses the winnings from betting on horse races (and an amount equal to each loss) to care for her. This is one irony, at least, of which Mr. Compson seems fully aware.

That Mr. Compson's narration gives way to Shreve's without a change of italics or quotation marks suggests that the italicized portions of the chapter are a sort of fused narrative, a notion supported by Quentin's frequent observation that Shreve sounds like his father. Beginning on page 266, though, Shreve's voice becomes once again unmistakable, addressing Quentin directly: *"But you were not listening, because you knew it all already. . . ."* (266). He refers to the conversation in the cemetery, though it seems unlikely that Quentin would have known all this in the fall of 1907 or 1908. Shreve's summation concludes as it had begun, with Shreve talking and Quentin periodically offering monosyllabic assent. The material describes Quentin's visits to the Sutpen house, his glimpse of Charles

Etienne's idiot son, Jim Bond, and his flight from Clytie, who speaks with a voice which Quentin remarks had sounded *"almost like a white woman's"* (268). Like Mr. Compson, Shreve accepts the theory of degeneration and conflict arising from the mixed blood itself; Jim Bond " 'had inherited what he was from his mother and only what he could never have been from his father' " (269).

Shreve concludes at the moment when Miss Rosa and Quentin discover something living in the house, after describing Bond's mental incapacity and Clytie, whose " 'body just grew smaller and smaller like something being shrunk in a furnace . . . ' " (270). Shreve does not recognize the irony that the mulatto idiot was Sutpen's last surviving heir (though he may indeed be aware of it from earlier conversations). Acknowledgment of that fact is postponed until the novel's final pages, where it emerges dramatically after the revelation that Henry is the hidden inhabitant of the abandoned mansion.

"So he told Grandfather": Sutpen's Design

When a questioner at the University of Virginia asked Faulkner who the central character of *Absalom, Absalom!* is, he replied, "The central character is Sutpen, yes. The story of a man who wanted a son and got too many, got so many that they destroyed him. It's incidentally the story of Quentin Compson's hatred of the bad qualities in the country he loves. But the central character is Sutpen, the story of a man who wanted sons" (*FIU,* 71). One can argue, as indeed many critics have, about the relative importance of Quentin's role in the novel, and it would appear that Faulkner's answer tended to misrepresent the nature of Quentin's involvement with the Sutpen story. The comment provides an accurate view of the major concerns of chapter 7, though, for it is the only unit in the novel which deals almost exclusively with Sutpen himself, rather than with his wife or children or with another character's biased perception of him, as in Miss Rosa's sections. Of course, all the accounts of his family relate at least indirectly to Sutpen, even Rosa's tirade in 1909 about her blighted life. But only in chapter 7 is an attempt made to understand Sutpen directly, apart from his impact on other members of his family or the community.

That Sutpen is the central focus on the chapter, however, is not to say that Quentin and Shreve retreat entirely into the background. On the contrary, frequent references throughout remind the reader of their presence; descriptions of the setting in their dormitory room open the chapter, and their comments close it. Still, less emphasis is placed on Quentin's pain in hearing the story; on only a single occasion does his thinking turn to his own involvement.[1] At one of the points when Shreve interrupts him, Quentin thinks: *"Am I going to have to hear it all again . . . I am going to have to hear it all over again I am already hearing it all over again I am listening to it all over again I shall have to never listen to anything else but this again forever . . . "* (345). Significantly, this interruption comes when Quentin is beginning to focus once more on the Sutpen *children* and how they are destroyed by his design. This is the portion of the story which most moves Quentin, in which he finds his imagination most directly involved because of his personal concerns.

His narration of the events of Sutpen's life, inherited from General Compson through his father, does not hold any particular emotional commitment for him, and he tells the story for the most part straightforwardly, limiting his own interpretation to a minimum, transmitting faithfully the theories developed by both his father and grandfather.

It comes as no surprise to discover that the Sutpen history is linked in Quentin's mind with the relationship between fathers and sons. Over forty acknowledgments in the chapter to things "Grandfather said" point to General Compson as the sole source of information about Sutpen's early life before his arrival in Jefferson. Similarly, Quentin cites his father as informant over a dozen times in relating the story of Sutpen's death at the hands of Wash Jones. He understands that he is not the first Compson to be fascinated by the tragedy of the Sutpen family: his grandfather had witnessed several important events, including a confrontation between Jones and Sutpen over Milly (as well as scenes involving Judith after Sutpen's death, recorded in the preceding chapter), and Sutpen had told him about others. General Compson begins the process of interpreting Sutpen's behavior and attempting to make sense out of his life.

Quentin's father, as we have seen, is interested in the story for different reasons. His involvement is not personal, as his father's had been. Rather he looks to the Sutpen history for confirmation of his own ideas regarding the nature and meaning of human life. He forces Sutpen's degeneration and death into a pattern of sin and retribution, especially prominent in passages during which Quentin considers Sutpen's death. We are told, for instance, that Sutpen himself had not called the failure of his design retribution, " 'no sins of the father come home to roost; not even calling it bad luck, but just a mistake. . . . Not moral retribution you see: just an old mistake in fact . . .' " (333–34). Clearly the idea of moral retribution belongs either to General Compson or to his son. Quentin does not identify its author, but its tone corresponds closely with Mr. Compson's interpretation in chapters 2 through 4.

What Quentin has learned from the input of both his father and grandfather forces him to confront directly one of the novel's major themes—the impact of the past upon the present. He states this theme in chapter 7's longest projection of Quentin's thinking:

> *Yes. Maybe we are both Father. Maybe nothing happens once and is finished. Maybe happen is never once but like ripples maybe on water after the pebble sinks, the ripples moving on, spreading, the pool attached by a narrow umbilical water-cord to the next pool which the first pool feeds, has fed, did feed, let this second pool contain a different temperature of water, a different molecularity of having seen, felt, remembered, reflect in a different tone the infinite unchanging sky, it doesn't matter: that pebble's watery echo whose fall it did not even see moves across its surface too at the original ripple-space, to the old ineradicable rhythm* thinking *Yes, we are both Father. Or maybe Father and I are both Shreve, maybe it took Father and me both to make Shreve or Shreve and me both to make Father or maybe Thomas Sutpen to make all of us.*
> (326–27)

Like his later cry of despair at having to hear the story over again, this comment is elicited by Shreve's asking how the design had affected Sutpen's children. Apparently both passages were incorporated into the novel while Faulkner was preparing the typescript. Neither appears in the holograph manuscript, indicating that in Faulkner's earliest conception during the book's composition, the story of Thomas Sutpen was the exclusive subject of chapter 7. The additions give Quentin and Shreve a larger role, highlighting the increasing anguish Quentin feels as the evening wears on.[2]

Shreve's part in chapter 7 is less important than in the other units of the novel's second movement. Essentially his purpose is to provide a listener for Quentin. He interrupts with relative frequency, adding flippant remarks which the narrative voice describes at one point as "just that protective coloring of levity behind which the youthful shame of being moved hid itself, out of which Quentin also spoke . . . " (349). At the beginning, he badgers Quentin about the South as he had earlier badgered him about Miss Rosa's kinship: " 'Jesus, the South is fine, isn't it. It's better than the theatre, isn't it. It's better than Ben Hur, isn't it. No wonder you have to come away now and then, isn't it' " (271). He corrects Quentin's mistake that Sutpen had been born in West Virginia (275) and hits a sensitive spot with Quentin by suggesting that Sutpen's architect may have fled because he had wanted a girl (273). When Quentin mentions the shadow which had passed Sutpen during the Haitian siege, Shreve assumes it is a girl and commands Quentin to continue. He asks for explanation of the affair with Mr. Coldfield, for more information about the design, and for an analysis of how it had affected the Sutpen children.

On several occasions Shreve interrupts to describe Sutpen with Miss Rosa's term "demon." At the end of the chapter he is confused about Wash's reason for killing Sutpen, questioning at three points (357, 360, 364–65) why Sutpen had reacted the way he did to the birth of a son until Quentin informs him that Milly's child had been a girl. Shreve's questions on this issue seem a rather artificial device for creating suspense, since the tenor of Quentin's narration itself should make clear that the child had not been useful in advancing Sutpen's design. At an earlier stage, though, Shreve's questions strike to the heart of one of the novel's central puzzles—how Quentin had acquired his information about Charles Bon's identity. When he remarks that Mr. Compson had " 'got an awful lot of delayed information awful quick' " (332), Quentin explains that he had provided that information the day after he and Miss Rosa had visited Sutpen's Hundred. Later, Shreve underlines both Mr. Compson's and his father's lack of understanding: " 'When your grandfather was telling this to him [Mr. Compson], he didn't know any more what your grandfather was talking about than your grandfather knew what the demon was talking about when the demon told it to him, did he? And when your old man told it to you, you wouldn't have known what anybody was talking about if you hadn't been out there and seen Clytie' " (342).

These comments are crucial to evaluating Quentin's account.[3] They imply that at this point Shreve knows more than the reader does, that he has already heard the story of Quentin's visit to Sutpen's Hundred which was begun in chapter 6 but will be completed only in chapter 9. They clearly reveal that Quentin had learned something significant, though they do not reveal what, or how. Shreve brings them up in order to stress Quentin's knowledge of Bon's parentage, not the reason for the murder, which is not considered at length in the present chapter. It is never made clear whether Bon's trace of black blood is a conjecture or something else that Quentin supposedly had discovered on his visit with Miss Rosa.

Chapter 7 provides the key which Mr. Compson had requested in chapter 4 to unravel the puzzle that did not make sense to him—that Bon had been Sutpen's son by his first wife. However, Quentin does not explain how this knowledge forces re-evaluation of the characters and events leading up to Charles's murder, for him still the central action to be accounted for. Even for Quentin important questions remain, such as whether or not *Bon* had known who his father was. It falls to Shreve in chapter 8 to weave a new explanation of the murder using his awareness of Bon's parentage and the possible conjecture of his tainted blood.

A couple of deleted passages in Faulkner's manuscript indicate that his original conception had been to provide more tangible evidence of Bon's mixed blood. At one point when Quentin considers the extent of his grandfather's knowledge (corresponding to pp. 339–40 of the corrected text), Faulkner had intended General Compson to be considerably better informed: "and so he (Grandfather) believed that he knew all that Sutpen could know knew [sic]: that Bon might decide at any moment to defy Henry and come to Judith, and that when he did so Judith would marry him half brother or no."[4] A later alteration indicated that Sutpen had told General Compson what his trump card was to be, though the line was eliminated when Faulkner added the passage indicating Quentin's reluctance to hear the story again.[5] The reference to the trump card is given to Shreve in the revision. Finally, and perhaps most radically, Faulkner deleted a passage on the last page of the chapter which verified Bon's tainted blood; Quentin refers to Sutpen sitting in his grandfather's office in 1864 "and telling him about how he never found out until after Bon was born that the mother that they had told him was a Spaniard had some nigger blood."[6] It would be safe to assume that Faulkner cancelled these passages at the same time he added material hinting about the significance of what Quentin had learned at Sutpen's Hundred. The effect is to emphasize the theme of the illusiveness of truth and to heighten the suspense as the reader waits to discover what the problem with Bon's mother had actually been. (Even in the manuscript Faulkner remained true to his technique of withholding the information until the last moment; the reader would have learned of the taint only on the final page of the chapter.)

Concern with Bon in chapter 7 is limited to how he would have been viewed by Sutpen, who dominates the telling almost exclusively. The placement of

Sutpen's background so late in the novel is a brilliant structural gambit, one that Faulkner had attempted with less success in *Sanctuary,* in which Popeye's background is sketched near the end of the book. Unlike the earlier instance, Sutpen's history forces the reader to once again re-evaluate everything he knows about the man. It repeats the process used earlier when Mr. Compson humanizes Sutpen (chapters 2 and 3) after he has been presented as an almost supernatural demon by Miss Rosa (chapter 1). Chapters 5 and 6 had dealt primarily with the aftermath of the tragedies Sutpen is largely held responsible for, so the reader is faced with a considerable challenge when asked to see him in a different and more positive light.

Quentin's account of Sutpen's life to the time when he abjured his first wife and child is almost entirely sympathetic. Several factors contribute to that sympathy, including the fact that all the information arises from Sutpen himself. We could hardly expect Sutpen to be biased against his own position, but some of his confessions, such as his virginity, his ignorance of the world, his naiveté regarding the truth contained in books, are hardly those a man would reveal in an attempt to impress his listener. General Compson also seems to have been a largely sympathetic audience; though he expresses incredulity at times, he does not pass harsh judgments, allowing Sutpen to develop his story at his own pace, not even questioning him about areas that are unclear, such as how he had arrived in Haiti, how he had come to a position of responsibility on the sugar plantation, how he had subdued the rebellion. Further, much of this part of the story would obviously appeal to Mr. Compson, who relays what his father has told him to his son. Sutpen's early innocence (General Compson's term) would probably appear refreshing to a man of Mr. Compson's cynicism. And he could no doubt admire Sutpen's resolution and strength, qualities which Mr. Compson does not possess in abundance, as the portrait of him in *The Sound and the Fury* makes clear.

Despite the sympathy exhibited by the narrating characters, the reader must not be betrayed into accepting whatever they say at face value. Under no circumstances could Sutpen's account of his early life be considered objective; like Rosa, he too is attempting to persuade his listener (as, indeed, any speech arguably attempts to do). Further, Quentin is relating information first communicated in some cases nearly eighty years before and descended through several tellings: Sutpen to General Compson; General Compson to Quentin's father; Mr. Compson to Quentin; Quentin to Shreve. Obviously the possibilities for error are multiplied with each transmission.

We must also assume that each speaker has brought his own interpretation to the telling. General Compson devises the theory of Sutpen's innocence; Mr. Compson probably adds the notion that the destruction of Sutpen's design is justly deserved; one of the speakers has most likely fashioned the long speech attributed to Sutpen in which he explains his design (329–30) from a mere kernel of remembered dialogue. Finally, the internal debate the boy Sutpen carries on concerning how to handle the insult he has endured at Pettibone's front door hardly sounds typical of a man who would plunge into the unknown by going to sea or walk out and subdue a violent slave revolt, and it contrasts rather strongly with much of what we know of Sutpen's behavior after his arrival in Jefferson. It sounds a great deal like the kind of moral debate Mr. Compson seems to relish, and, indeed, it seems to have even more in common with Quentin's habit of thought and action than with what we know of Sutpen's. (It is reminiscent, for instance, of the two separate Quentins described as listening to Miss Rosa in chapter 1.) Likely, this passage too is the creation of one or more of the narrators.

Perhaps the strongest factor undercutting the sympathy accorded Sutpen in the account of his youth is the structure of chapter 7 itself. Sutpen tells General Compson most of the story while engaged in a hunt for his fugitive architect. This story is a testament to the indomitability of the human spirit, and it provides some of the best of the novel's rare humor. But the humor does not deny the fact that Sutpen treats his architect as a virtual slave, little different from the slaves used to trail him. In this respect the comedy functions in a manner similar to that in "Was," the first chapter of *Go Down, Moses,* in which Faulkner uses virtually the same situation to make a similar point; men in both cases are being treated as subhumans, hunted like animals. Rituals guide the hunt in both cases: Uncle Buck dons a tie to pursue Tommy's Turl, and when the slave is not caught in time, Buck is obliged to endure the hospitality offered by Hubert and Sophonsiba. Sutpen sends back for food, champagne, and whiskey to entertain his guests during the hunt.

The episode with the architect demonstrates the extent to which Sutpen's ruthless will sublimates everything to the completion of his design. He forces the Frenchman, whose clothing and demeanor mark him as a man of considerable culture and sophistication—the house itself reveals him to be a man of skill and talent—to live a spartan existence on the promise of pay (if Mr. Compson's account is to be trusted). When the architect attempts to escape, Sutpen hunts him down and forces him to return until the task is completed (an action which would seem to support Miss Rosa's view of the relationship between the two men). Sutpen is contrasted with General Compson in his treatment of the architect. As if to acknowledge a similar bond of civilization or culture (or perhaps even simple humanity) in which Sutpen does not participate, the architect bows specially to Compson before drinking the neat whiskey Compson offers him at the end of the chase. When the architect departs, Compson presents him with a hat to replace the one he had lost.

The essentially positive view of Sutpen at the beginning of chapter 7 is further undercut by the detailed description of his death at the end. Shreve provides the skeleton of the story in chapter 6, and Quentin's account is penetrated by ironies of which both young men seem completely aware. Sutpen, who bars the door on his son when he has achieved his goal of owning a mansion and vast plantation, is eventually cut down as a result of reducing people to pawns in his design. And he is destroyed by a man who represents the very class Sutpen himself had risen from. The reader can freely bestow tremendous sympathy on the boy unjustly turned away from the big house, but he must withhold it completely from the man who denies the mother of his child the comforts of his stable.

Chapter 7 begins with a reference to passing time and to the New England cold. Quentin thinks that the temperature has reached zero outside, yet Shreve remains shirtless. He smokes a pipe, and suddenly an hour has passed and the pipe "lay smoked out and overturned and cold, with a light sprinkling of ashes about it" (271). Shreve goads Quentin with the idea that Sutpen had merely wanted a grandson (perhaps another deliberate misstatement on Shreve's part) and ridicules this desire as an example of the weird exaggeration of the South, incomprehensible to the world outside. Quentin does not respond to the taunt (though in the manuscript he answers "Yes," as he had to Shreve's summation in the preceding chapter);[7] instead he justifies Sutpen's need for progeny by repeating what he knows of Sutpen's early life. Throughout his narration, Quentin remains languid, "his face lowered a little, brooding, almost sullen"(272), staring at the letter announcing Miss Rosa's death, the letter which in Quentin's mind links his conversation with Shreve to his earlier conversations with his father.

Quentin seems to relate the tale almost exactly as he had heard his father tell it. Mr. Compson had apparently relished the story for qualities other than what it reveals about Sutpen himself. It exhibits typical touches of exaggeration and humor which connect it to the southern oral tradition: Sutpen is not even aware that the architect has fled until sundown; the slaves have no idea what the architect's role is; his outfit is alien, " 'in his embroidered vest and Fauntleroy tie and a hat like a Baptist congressman' " (273). Thus, the architect is related to the tradition of the city slicker who runs rings around the country hicks, as indeed the architect does for two days. Quentin is apparently so bemused by the tragic elements of the story that he is completely unaware of the humor in the tale, nor does Shreve seem to respond to it. The participants in the hunt make quite a lark of it: " 'Grandfather said it was fine weather and the trail lay pretty good but Sutpen said it would have been fine if the architect had just waited until October or November' " (274). The easy sense of comradeship on the hunt stimulates a candor in Sutpen which is uncharacteristic of him.

General Compson fashions the idea that " 'his [Sutpen's] trouble was innocence' " (274), a concept drawn apparently much later from what he had learned in 1835 and in 1864, when Sutpen had explained something about his design. Cleanth Brooks has cautioned that General Compson does not define the word in a conventional sense, and to do so will mislead the reader.[8] Compson's definition, as Brooks points out, is that Sutpen " 'believed that all that was necessary [for the success of his design] was courage and shrewdness and the one he knew he had and the other he believed he could learn if it were to be taught . . .' " (305). Thus, Sutpen shares a common idea of innocence with other male characters in Faulkner, an abstraction which "amounts finally to a trust in rationality—an overweening confidence that plans work out, that life is simpler than it is."[9] Quentin's recounting of Sutpen's experience at the tidewater plantation house illustrates how the boy had arrived at his simplified view of the world. Quentin admits that at the time Sutpen had been completely ill-equipped to understand the world he found himself in: "'All of a sudden he discovered, not what he wanted to do but what he just had to do, had to do whether he wanted to or not . . .'" (275). Clearly this is a theory spun by General Compson or his son, based upon later knowledge of Sutpen's efforts to found a dynasty, but it fits well with the facts as the Compsons understand them. It is a naive notion, but one which Quentin asserts had been Sutpen's heritage from his mountain rearing. His childhood had not instilled in him a strong sense of family—he seems almost totally indifferent to his family except for the episode with his sister and the carriage—but the privation and isolation of the mountains had contributed to his simplistic approach to the world.

General Compson assumes that Sutpen's experience of hardship and isolation remains constant in his thinking, along with the other mountain traits of independence and judgment on the basis of ability rather than ownership. He imagines that Sutpen journeyed to the tidewater section of Virginia with a sense of alien amazement. The splendor of the plantations and the leisure of their owners would certainly be astonishing to a boy reared in the southern mountains in the early nineteenth century (or the early twentieth century for that matter). And Sutpen appears to have been a child peculiarly lacking in curiosity or imagination; he pays no attention to the stories he hears about low-country splendor, since he has had no experience to relate them to.[10] Quentin says that Sutpen "'did not even imagine that there was any such way to live or to want to live, or that there existed all the objects to be wanted which there were . . .'" (276).

Sutpen's father is not hindered like his son by ignorance of established society. His slovenliness prefigures that of Wash Jones, and his lack of regard for his family's welfare renders him an impotent role model for his son, who is obliged to look elsewhere for guidance, with disastrous effect.[11] Sutpen's father seems to have remained drunk for most of the journey out of the mountains, the journey itself periodically delayed while the family waited for him to be ejected from doggeries and saloons. Sutpen sees his first black man when one of the taverns employs as a bouncer "'a huge bull of a nigger . . . his . . . mouth loud with laughing and full of teeth like tombstones'" (281). Sutpen measures the increasing refinement of the civilized land by the manner of his father's ejections: "'That's the way he got it. He had learned the difference not only between white men and black ones, but he was learning that there was a difference between white men and white men . . .'" (282).

When settled, Sutpen continues to look at his new surroundings with amazement. He is particularly fascinated not by the differences in topography, but by the plantation owner who spends his afternoons in a hammock while a servant brings him drinks. Sutpen maintains to General Compson that he did not envy the man, though he envied his possessions, because he ascribed ownership to luck. His innocence is represented by his choice of an analogy to express his view of Pettibone: the fine rifle owned by the mountain man, the gun which might be fine indeed but which vested no greater worth in the individual *because* he owned it. Sutpen is ignorant of class and even racial distinctions because his thinking had not yet been forged by the experience of being turned away from the front door of the plantation house by the liveried servant, the "monkey nigger" (286).

With this insult, Sutpen comes up full against the reality of southern antebellum class and social distinctions. Until that point, he had been unaware of the look of his clothes, unaware that people existed who would judge him on his appearance, that the way he looked placed him in an identifiable and unmistakable social or economic category. When told to go around to the back—Faulkner typically withholds the exact nature of the repulse for some pages—Sutpen reviews the experiences that he had had since leaving the mountains, and suddenly they make sense in a new way. At least a part of his innocence is gone, or rather transformed.

He surveys the two years during which he had learned practically nothing about social structure and standards with a new eye, " 'like when you pass through a room fast and look at all the objects in it and you turn and go back through the room again and look at all the objects from the other side and you find out you had never seen them before . . .' " (287). He recalls the " 'speculative antagonism' " (287) with which the women in his family looked at the blacks, and the obsequious submission with which the blacks approached all the whites, even those whose circumstances were beneath their own. Two particular episodes remain seared in his memory: the occasion upon which his sister had been almost run down by a fine carriage carrying two women when she had refused to give way on the road and his father's joining a group of men who had assaulted one of Pettibone's slaves. When the boy had asked what the man had done, his father had replied, " ' "Hell fire, that goddam son of a bitch Pettibone's nigger" ' " (289).

In reviewing the previous two years, Sutpen senses that the carriages and the salves are not really substantial; rather they only mask the problem he wants to combat. He seeks the refuge of the woods to sort out his feelings. A product of the violent culture which had spawned him, he first thinks, " *'But I can shoot him'* " (292). He does not mean the salve, sensing immediately that the slave is merely the instrument of a larger force, much as Rosa had seen Clytie as the avatar of the absent Sutpen. The object of Sutpen's vengeance is beyond even Pettibone, and he realizes that shooting him would do no good. He imagines Pettibone watching him approach the door and laughing at him and his family from behind his Negro servant. Ironically, in visualizing this scene, Sutpen adopts Pettibone's own attitude. He cries convulsively at the thought of home, and as he approaches the house for supper, for the first time he recognizes its dilapidated poverty, the bovine appearance of his sisters and the brutish work they are engaged in.

In bed Sutpen continues to argue with himself about what his response should be until his true insignificance in the landed society explodes upon his consciousness: "*there aint any good or harm either in the living world that I can do to him* [Pettibone]'" (297). Awareness of his place within the social structure wipes away all the young Sutpen's moral debate, leaving of his thinking "'just a limitless flat plain with the severe shape of his intact innocence rising from it like a monument'" (297). He recognizes at last that Pettibone is not himself the issue, that the issue comprises all the forces that structure the society. As John T. Irwin explains, "Sutpen wants revenge not against the injustice of that mastery which the powerful have over the powerless, but against those 'artificial standards and circumstances' that determine who are the powerful and who are the powerless, against the artificial standard of inherited wealth and the circumstances of one's birth."[12] Reverting to his rifle analogy (the developing symbol of that innocence), he decides that the only way to combat a man with a fine rifle is to acquire one as much like it as possible. So he resolves to combat the injustice he had met in the only way he can imagine, by becoming, like Pettibone, a participant in the power structure. In the final analysis, as Richard Poirier has stated, Sutpen "justifies himself by an appeal not to any moral code which might have been violated at the plantation door, but to some inexplicable compulsion over which he apparently can exert no discipline."[13]

His innocence betrays him into thinking that the accumulation of similar possessions will open the doors of privilege for him. To an extent, he is correct, since fortunes were often made by enterprising (or merely ruthless) men during the first half of the nineteenth century. Though class and social distinctions were hardly rigid during the time, Sutpen discovers that the accumulation of wealth is not sufficient to meet his ends. Both Miss Rosa and Mr. Compson have commented on his need of respectability, a quality he can never fully achieve without a sense of past. His arrest after his engagement to Ellen and the reaction of Jefferson to his marriage are ample evidence of Sutpen's limitations in this area. (Faulkner provided some extratextual evidence as well when an editor questioned in the margin of the typescript setting copy whether knowledge of Sutpen's background would have really helped Sutpen win support among the townspeople. Faulkner responded, "It would in the South. If they had known who his father was more than Compson and Coldfield would have appeared to get him out of jail" [*TS*, 31].)

Sutpen's desire for sons is only tangentially related to his attempt to combat the system which had insulted him. He sees himself in a continuum of human descent, even if this continuum does not for him define a tradition or elevate family relationships to a rank of first importance. He needs a son, children, only as confirmation of his success when he has achieved his material goals. Of themselves, sons and grandsons would have no value; they would merely make more permanent his place in what Rosa calls *"the tradition in which Thomas Sutpen's ruthless will had carved a niche"* (194).

Quentin interrupts his account of Sutpen's early experiences to catch up the story of the architect, which serves as an ironic contrast to the tale Quentin is telling about Sutpen each time he returns to it. The architect devises an ingenious method of eluding his pursuers, who he must have guessed would trail him with dogs. Only hints are given as to how the architect had used his suspenders to vault from one tree to another, and one guesses that considerable exaggeration adds to the effectiveness of the account, since we are told that he could traverse " 'a gap to the next nearest tree that a flying squirrel could not have crossed' " (298). The point is that, forced to rely on his most natural talents, the architect uses his knowledge of physics to avoid capture, just as Sutpen must rely on what limited experience he has had to fashion his plan. Even the dogs which are sure the architect is in the first tree he climbed and which refuse to leave it point to the simplistic monomania of Sutpen's goals. The intervention of the architect at this juncture also provides a plausible excuse for a greater period of time during which Sutpen and Compson could talk. While the slaves search for the architect's trail, Sutpen tells more of his story.

Shreve's summation of Sutpen's life in chapter 6 reveals that he has perhaps heard much of the story before, and Quentin feels comfortable in jumping both forward and backward in time. Before relating Sutpen's experiences in Haiti, he moves ahead briefly to 1864, when Sutpen had told Quentin's grandfather about his design in the latter's office. Quentin disrupts the chronology in order to draw a comparison between Sutpen's bald statement " 'So I went to the West Indies' " (299) in 1835 and his similarly bald explanation of his reasons for repudiating his first wife: " ' "I found that she was not and could never be, through no fault of her own, adjunctive or incremental to the design which I had in mind, so I provided for her and put her aside" ' " (300). Presumably like his father and grandfather, Quentin sees the continuation of Sutpen's innocence in the similar way he delivers these two statements separated by nearly thirty years. General Compson is aware that Sutpen had achieved everything he had set out to do, as he had made clear while hunting for the architect: he had reached that point " 'where he can say *I did all that I set out to do and I could stop here if I wanted to and no man to chide me with sloth, not even myself'* " (299). Mr. Compson's hand is evident in the idea that this moment of hubris is " 'the instant which Fate always picks out to blackjack you' " (299). Despite the achievements, the accumulated wealth and family, Quentin suggests that Sutpen had not lost his innocence in the thirty years, that his outlook and his motivations had remained essentially unchanged. The projection in chronology allows the reader to learn about Sutpen's Haitian experiences after he has learned the eventual outcome of them—his rejection of the wife he had met there because she could not contribute to the design he had devised as a fourteen-year-old boy.

Using the rifle analogy, the young Sutpen sets his first goal: matching the fine weapon of the man he wishes to fight. He translates this to mean that he must acquire wealth, servants, and a great house. Once more he demonstrates the ignorance that constitutes a large portion of his innocence by choosing to go to the West Indies because he had heard in school that the islands were a place where fabulous fortunes could be made. Sutpen's response to school reveals his pragmatism: he declines to memorize sums or engage in repetitious exercises, but he listens when the teacher reads aloud, learning only what he thinks will someday be of use. He accepts without question the fact that the book from which his teacher reads about the islands records the truth. But since Sutpen recognizes the teacher to be less of a man than the youth himself, as well as a figure of minor authority in what to the boy is an unfamiliar locale, he accosts him to make sure he had not merely invented the tales. He acknowledges his naiveté at the time to General Compson: " ' "I was that green, that countrified, you see" ' " (303).

Once more the hunt for the escaped architect intrudes, and Quentin comments on the exultation the architect had felt, an exultation the dogs seemed to sense in the tree he had climbed to escape. The remark introduces what is perhaps the most heroic episode of Sutpen's life: his response to the slave uprising. When the other men on the hunt return to town, Compson remains because he has become interested in the story and wants to hear more, though after they find where the architect had returned to earth the chase resumes until a bit after dark. Once again, Quentin jumps ahead to contrast the Sutpen of the early Jefferson days with the Sutpen of the Civil War years. In both manifestations, General Compson finds that the man's destiny had fitted him like a suit of clothes, had conformed " 'to his innocence, his pristine aptitude for platform drama and childlike heroic simplicity' " (307).

When Sutpen resumes his tale, he does not pick up where he had left off; rather, reminded by the pine torches and the slaves on the hunt of the desperate situation some years earlier, he projects Compson into the besieged house. For the first time he mentions the girl who would become his first wife and whom he would put aside, as he explains to General Compson in 1864. Compson's reaction in 1835 mirrors Shreve's in the current telling; he asks Sutpen to back up, to provide more details about how the siege had come about. Despite the lack of coherence and the wildly improbable nature of much of the narrative, Compson does not question the objectivity or truth of the speaker: " 'He was not bragging about something he had done; he was just telling a story about something a man named Thomas Sutpen had experienced . . .' " (309). This explanation, however, does little to inspire the reader's confidence in the reliability of Sutpen's testimony. We should not forget that the circumstance is precisely that which gave rise to the tradition of the tall tale in the popular imagination, if not in actuality—men in the big woods swapping yarns while drinking whiskey around a campfire. Faulkner must have consciously intended the irony.

Though at Compson's insistence Sutpen backs up and fills in some of the details, they are "'not enough to clarify the story much'" (309). We learn that in the six years between his arrival on the island and the siege he had acquired something of the patois he had used to oversee the plantation and also some French. We discover too that his innocence had extended even to his sexuality, an assertion that Compson accepts as well. That Sutpen had been a virgin at the time of his marriage does not indicate a staunch puritanism regarding sexual mores, though puritanism is certainly a part of his makeup. (General Compson comments that as a youth "'he probably could not have believed in anything that was easy'" [305].) Rather, the obsessive drive that Sutpen calls his design descends upon him at about the same time as sexual curiosity, and all other motivations, physical and spiritual, are subsumed by it. Sutpen's virginity at the time of his marriage is an early indication of the destructive, life-denying impact of the design itself. (In fairness we might recognize that many more youths were virgins in their late teens and twenties during the nineteenth century than today; still, Sutpen himself seems slightly offended that Compson believes his assertion so readily.)

According to General Compson, Sutpen's innocence had prevented him from accurately gauging the desperate situation on the island. Compson categorizes Haiti as a halfway point between the dark inscrutable forces of primitive man represented by Africa on the one hand and those sometimes equally negative forces of civilization, symbolized by the chattel slavery of the American South on the other. The lush vegetation of the island, watered by suffering and blood in Compson's parable, becomes a symbol of the wealth and power based upon the economic exploitation of the blacks. That Sutpen is capable of erecting his own vast edifice on this foundation is indicated by his heroically simple handling of the slave uprising. He does not see the signs of the impending crisis—he takes the planter's fear as "gallic rage" (314) and must be told that the stains on the rag left as a threat are blood—but he handles it with exceptional bravery and at great personal risk.

Quentin's grandfather accepts much of what he hears because of Sutpen's unique treatment of his own slaves; Compson had witnessed the fights with the blacks Sutpen had persisted in engaging in for years after his children had been born. The description of the Haitian experience dramatizes what Sutpen would consider vital to maintenance of authority—physical supremacy. Having witnessed such scenes, Compson perhaps finds no mystery in Sutpen's failure to explain exactly how the siege had ended—after eight days he simply "'put the musket down and went out and subdued them'" (317). What amazes Compson is that at the end of the crisis Sutpen and the planter's daughter had become engaged. Sutpen offers only the explanation that it took him some time to recover.

The end of this anecdote concludes Sutpen's storytelling. The qualities of indomitability and personal strength in the tale he has related are again mirrored in the architect, who is caught the next day. Quentin tells the episode essentially as he had heard it, seemingly unaware of the humor it entails. Nor does he seem aware that it reflects Sutpen's own situation. The architect is seen

> "standing there, not scared worth a damn either, just panting a little and Grandfather said a little sick in the face where the niggers had mishandled his leg in the heat of the capture, and making them a speech in French, a long one and so fast that Grandfather said probably another Frenchman could not have understood all of it. But it sounded fine; Grandfather said even he—all of them—could tell that the architect was not apologizing; it was fine. . . . And Grandfather saw the eyes in the gaunt face, the eyes desperate and hopeless but indomitable too, invincible too, not beaten yet by a damn sight Grandfather said. . . . " (321)

Faulkner shifts the scene from the architect to a narrative, view of Shreve and Quentin which emphasizes their similar natures. Quentin breaks off the narrative, and for a brief period he responds to direct questions from Shreve, since Sutpen had not progressed with his story for thirty more years until the afternoon in 1864 when he had brought the tombstones for his and Ellen's graves. Shreve asks Quentin to explain what the business arrangement between Mr. Coldfield and Sutpen had been, but Quentin does not know and substitutes an analysis of Mr. Coldfield's moral outrage when he had discovered that whatever the shady deal had been was going to work. Shreve then directs attention to the design. Quentin proceeds by sketching Sutpen's situation at the outbreak of the war, wealth accumulated, children added, the boy barred from the door symbolically taken in. Shreve's taunting comment, " 'Dont say it's just me that sounds like your old man . . .' " (326), alludes to Quentin's thoughts (apparently verbalized) during Shreve's summary of the story in the preceding chapter (277, 260, 264). Quentin is momentarily sidetracked, spinning his analogy of the past as being like a pebble dropped into interconnecting pools, but he soon returns to focus on Sutpen and his children, who precipitate the destruction of his design.

When Sutpen takes up his story thirty years later, he justifies somewhat cryptically to General Compson his reasons for putting away his first wife and child. His rationalization confirms in General Compson's mind the nature of Sutpen's innocence, " 'which believed that the ingredients of morality were like the ingredients of pie or cake and once you had measured them and balanced them and mixed them and put them into the oven it was all finished and nothing but pie or cake could come out' " (328). The comparison indicates, as James Guetti has remarked, that Sutpen's innocence results from his need to define a system of order when his youthful understanding is destroyed by the insult; the lack of order in Sutpen's world becomes for him a kind of blackness which is personified in Bon's threat to his design.[14] Significantly, Sutpen does not define that flaw in his first wife which had rendered her unsuitable. Whereas thirty years earlier General

Compson had accepted what he had been told because Sutpen had not appeared to be bragging, he now accepts what he hears despite his lack of comprehension because Sutpen's tone indicates that Sutpen himself has decided he could never understand it. He is telling it perhaps in hope that General Compson's legal training would be able to point out his flaw.

The idea of moral responsibility is no part of the design itself: " ' "Whether it was a good or a bad design is beside the point; the question is, Where did I make the mistake in it, what did I do or misdo in it, whom or what injure by it to the extent which this would indicate" ' " (329). Without recognizing the fact, Sutpen points out the very flaw he is seeking, that he had not taken into account the human toll of his plan, not considered those who might be injured by it. What in the youth had been an idealistic attempt to combat a personal injury by hard work and application has become in the adult a rigid and unbending abstraction to which all other values and structures of meaning are forced to conform. In his eyes, the Haitian family had betrayed *him,* willfully, purposely: " ' "they deliberately withheld from me the one fact which I have reason to know they were aware would have caused me to decline the entire matter, otherwise they would not have withheld it from me . . ." ' " (329). He insists that he had behaved magnanimously toward his wife and child, providing for them when casting them aside, and he implies that his reasons had been accepted: " ' "and this was agreed to, mind; agreed to between the two parties" ' " (330).

Sutpen's emphasis on the fact that the arrangement had apparently been assented to by his first wife (and probably her father) could be cited as support for Shreve's view of her character as he outlines it in chapter 8. Sutpen seems amazed that a circumstance to which they had agreed could in some way damage his design at a later date. Perhaps he had encountered his first wife on his visit to New Orleans in the summer of 1860 and had been shocked to discover her resentment and desire for vengeance. Sutpen would seem to be pointing toward a recanting of the agreement when he is interrupted by General Compson. Unfortunately (or brilliantly, from the point of view of the author of the novel), he does not return to elaborate on the idea. General Compson's interruption seems to proceed from an understanding of the woman's outrage and desire for retribution. But like Sutpen's diverted line of thought, the General's comments are ultimately ambiguous, perhaps attributable to his own misogyny which, along with the Sutpen legends, will be the inheritance of his son.

However the first wife may have reacted or whatever the part she may have played, the result is the same: Bon, Sutpen's child by her, appears at Sutpen's Hundred and threatens the design. Shreve announces this crucial piece of evidence, which apparently had not been part of what Sutpen had explained to General Compson. Quentin repeats the theory, attributed to both his father and to his grandfather, that Sutpen would have named the child Charles Bon, refusing the boy either his own or his maternal grandfather's name. (Unless General Compson and his son had suggested theoretically that Sutpen would have named his first son, this passage would hint that the earlier narrators of the story were in possession of information which Faulkner takes care to point out later they did not know. It is curious that Quentin would credit his grandfather with the idea, since in chapter 3 the notion seems original with Mr. Compson [73].) Dialogue between the two roommates sidetracks Quentin's account to establish that he had conveyed this information to his father after his nighttime visit to the house with Miss Rosa. He does not, however, reveal *how* he learned what he knows.

Mr. Compson imagines Sutpen's feelings when he met Bon: " 'he must have felt and heard the design—house, position, posterity and all—come down like it had been built out of smoke, making no sound, creating no rush of displaced air and not even leaving any debris' " (333). Sutpen, they think, had believed his problem was that he had simply made a mistake, and that he could correct it, but that first he would have to determine what the mistake itself had been. Toward an explanation of this point, Quentin revises his father's theories about events recorded earlier in the novel: six months after he met Bon, Sutpen had gone to New Orleans, though no one knows whom he saw or what he accomplished (or failed to accomplish) there; after six more months, he had informed Henry of Bon's identity and then watched and waited for Henry to act as he knew he would. No one ever knew if Bon had been aware that he was Sutpen's son, though from Sutpen's point of view his knowledge would be inconsequential, since the design is threatened either way. Sutpen had probably known, Quentin thinks, where Henry and Bon had been during the war, that Henry had carried the wounded Bon to the rear at Shiloh. He had also predicted what Judith would do when Bon returned for her. Sutpen's actions (and those of his son) resulted from a far more serious objection than Bon's marriage to a woman of mixed blood, as Quentin now sees.

Mr. Compson and his father justify Sutpen's incredible behavior in spending his one afternoon of leave from the war in General Compson's office, to discuss his problem in order to isolate the mistake while it could still be corrected. The earlier man of action has now become " 'fogbound by his own private embattlement of personal morality: that picayune splitting of abstract hairs while (Grandfather said) Rome vanished and Jericho crumbled . . .' " (339). But the general is able to offer no help, largely because Sutpen declines to tell him all of the story. The two missing ingredients are Bon's identity and the factor which had tainted his mother in Sutpen's eyes. Sutpen's peculiar brand of morality, according to General Compson, would not allow him to impugn his first wife's reputation, either to Compson or to Henry, except as a last resort (what Sutpen calls his trump card), though there seems no doubt that Sutpen would have used that information without hesitating if he had found he needed to. This is the second choice which General Compson does not understand, though he accurately predicts that if it too fails, Sutpen will begin to build his design a third time.

Shreve interrupts again to verify that neither General Compson nor Quentin's father had understood what choice Sutpen was referring to until Quentin had told his father about Bon's identity. Shreve's analysis of Sutpen's choice is somewhat curious: " 'He chose. He chose lechery. So do I. But go on' " (343). Apparently he refers to Sutpen's final attempt to establish a dynasty by seducing Milly Jones, though Shreve certainly knows at this point what Sutpen's trump card had been, since later in the same evening he uses this knowledge in fashioning his reconstruction of events leading to Bon's murder. Quentin remains impassive, "his face still lowered, still brooding apparently on the open letter upon the open book between his hands" (343).

He relates how Sutpen had returned to the war and theorizes an understanding between Judith and her father, both aware of the other's position and what action they would take toward the proposed marriage. When Quentin records that Sutpen had spoken to Henry at General Compson's old regimental headquarters, Shreve attempts to jump ahead, but Quentin stifles him: " 'Wait, I tell you!' Quentin said, though still he did not move nor even raise his voice—that voice with its tense suffused restrained quality: 'I am telling' " (345). His anguish, recorded in italics, prefaces his account of how Sutpen returned to find Henry gone, Bon dead, and Judith still maintaining her stoic acceptance. Sutpen's need now is for haste; as General Compson had predicted, he is prepared to begin a third time to complete his design.

The narration shifts to an italicized passage recording Sutpen's behavior after the war and his engagement to Miss Rosa; Mr. Compson is ostensibly the speaker, though the italics indicate that Quentin is going over the conversation in his mind. He seems to revert to his father's narration at the point he finds most difficult to confront—Judith's feelings about her dead fiancé. (We are reminded that Quentin questions Caddy several times about her feelings for Dalton Ames in *The Sound and the Fury*.) Mr. Compson categorizes Sutpen's behavior during this period in terms of courage, will, and shrewdness. The now aging man demonstrates the first two traits by plunging into his third attempt to begin from scratch, the last by getting Miss Rosa to agree to marry him. In making his proposition to Rosa, though, his shrewdness had failed him: "*It broke down, it vanished into that old impotent logic and morality which had betrayed him before . . .*" (348). His logic had told him that if he failed to father a son by Rosa, he might not have sufficient time for another chance. Once again, in the heat of pursuing his design, he fails to take into account how his actions will affect those around him, who are themselves involved in the design without being aware of it. (Miss Rosa, for instance, questions the reasons for Sutpen's action by demanding "*Why? Why? and Why?*" in her monologue [208].)

Once again, Shreve attempts to intercede, describing the advent of Wash Jones into the design: " 'then the voice of the faithful grave-digger who opened the play and would close it, coming out of the wings like Shakespeare's very self . . . '" (349). The narrator identifies Shreve's levity and irreverence with Quentin's "sullen bemusement," as a youthful means of covering the extent to which the story had moved them, but he links their "logical" attempts to make sense of the story to Sutpen's idea of morality and to Miss Rosa's "demonizing," thus reminding the reader that the young men are merely constructing a possible interpretation that has no more authority than Sutpen's or Rosa's means of defining their experiences. Quentin understands the mask of cynical humor Shreve assumes, since "he did not even falter, taking Shreve up in stride without even comma or colon or paragraph:" (350).

The colon introduces the last concern of chapter 7, Sutpen's relations with Jones and his death. The imagery of Quentin's first line picks up that of the italicized portion ascribed to Mr. Compson, suggesting that Quentin has repeated his father's words to Shreve while he focused on his memory of them. Whereas his earlier references to his grandfather had identified him as the source of that part of the narrative, he now emphasizes his father as the author of the account, though he must have gotten the facts upon which he constructs the story from General Compson. Hugh Ruppersburg has pointed out that Mr. Compson has no evidence for his characterization of Wash Jones: "Mr. Compson likes to use parables; the tale of Wash offers a parable of the destruction of the landed upper class at the hands of a landless, subservient lower class. It neatly mirrors Sutpen's 1835 account of being turned away by the Negro servant of a Virginia plantation house . . . . Mr. Compson is thus able to bring Sutpen's rise and fall to an artistic, if artificial close."[15]

Wash's attitude toward Sutpen is based on his own notions of white supremacy. Forced to acknowledge, as the boy Sutpen had, that Sutpen's slaves were better housed and clothed, he rationalizes his own position as follows: Sutpen is a white man, and all white men are created equal, were equal in the eyes of God at least. Thus, he is able to elevate himself to Sutpen's level vicariously. Because of his worshipful attitude, he does not protest Sutpen's gifts to Milly for a long time, according to Mr. Compson's theory. But when the talk of the loungers in the store becomes too much to bear, he accosts Sutpen in the scene overheard by Quentin's grandfather.

Wash demands that Sutpen take responsibility for his actions and assumes that he will marry Milly if it becomes necessary (we are told that the child had been born a year from that day, so she is not yet pregnant): " ' "And I know that whatever your hands tech, whether hit's a regiment of men or a ignorant gal or just a hound dog, that you will make hit right" ' " (355). Wash is unaware of the ironic truth of his compounding his granddaughter with a regiment or a dog, since Sutpen makes no such moral distinctions. His comment prefigures Sutpen's equation of Milly with his mare Penelope. Sutpen does not respond to Wash, though the intensity of the confrontation is revealed by General Compson's assertion that he had called out several times but had not been answered.

Quickly Quentin rehearses the events of Sutpen's murder as his father had described them. What interests Mr. Compson is not the murder itself, but Wash's changed attitude toward Sutpen. He imagines Wash's obsequious image of Sutpen as he waits on the cabin gallery for his granddaughter to give birth: "*'He is bigger than all them Yankees that killed us and ourn, that killed his wife and widowed his daughter and druv his son from home, that stole his niggers and ruined his land; bigger than this whole county that he fit for and in payment for which has brung him to keeping a little country store for his bread and meat . . . '*" (358–59). Ironically in Mr. Compson's version of the story, by rejecting Milly and her child, Sutpen does show Wash what to do. Wash hears the exchange between Sutpen and the girl with disbelief while holding the reins of Sutpen's horse. His immediate response is grim and deadly: he cuts Sutpen down with the scythe he had borrowed two years before to cut the weeds from around the cabin.[16] We might expect Mr. Compson to expand upon the scythe as symbol of the inexorable encroachment of time, but he chooses instead to focus on Wash's thoughts as he awaits his death. He imagines the men of Sutpen's class preparing the posse which would come for him, seeing them as evidence of the overbearing domination of the planter class over Wash's own. Mr. Compson allows Wash a shred of tragic dignity by assuming that his refusal to run evolved from his perception that the men of Sutpen's class would expect a man such as Wash to do just that. Instead, he sits and finds justification for the South's defeat in the imposition of artifical differences between men, differences such as the class structure dictated. Not surprisingly, considering the author of the account, Wash's final conclusion is nihilistic: "*'Better if his kind and mine too had never drawn the breath of life on this earth. Better that all who remain of us be blasted from the face of it than that another Wash Jones should see his whole life shredded from him and shrivel away like a dried shuck thrown onto the fire'*" (362–63). When the posse arrives, Wash rushes at the entire group with the scythe after killing both his granddaughter and the infant. His action is a condemnation of Sutpen's class, though it is also indicative of his complete resignation. He comes at them in silence, posing no real threat, in Mr. Compson's view, offering only a symbolic one they cannot understand.

Appropriately, Quentin again violates chronology to conclude the chapter by picturing Sutpen in his prime attempting to justify his desire for a son. He corrects Shreve's misperception that Milly's child had been a boy. Shreve then resorts once more to a bluff and flippant rejoinder, betraying as he had earlier the extent to which he has been affected: "'——Come on. Let's get out of this damn icebox and go to bed'" (365). But they do not, and this line is echoed after more cold hours pass at the end of chapter 8, in which Shreve himself finally gets to play.

8

"Brothers to outrage and shame": Shreve's Version

Shreve McCannon resumes as the principal spokesman in chapter 8, as he had been for a large part of chapter 6, but there are some important differences between his narration in the two sections. In his earlier exposition of the Sutpen story, Shreve sticks relatively close to a "factual" recital of events as he has heard them from Quentin. That is, he accepts most of what he has listened to as accurate and provides a complete overview of events to which Quentin frequently responds in the affirmative. In chapter 8, Shreve exchanges his role as chronicler for that of interpreter as he seeks to analyze and to explain the motivations for what he and Quentin see as the central event in the downfall of the Sutpen family—Henry's murder of Bon.

As Faulkner revised the manuscript while preparing the setting copy, he added several passages which emphasize Shreve's spurious cynicism and misogyny, illustrating how carefully Shreve has attended to Quentin's accounts and how much he has absorbed from Mr. Compson's and Miss Rosa's views of the characters. He frequently alludes to things they have said as he elaborates upon and revises their theories. Shreve knows more of the story than either Mr. Compson or Rosa, and one might expect his account to make more sense. But he is hampered by his lack of understanding of the South (as we have seen) and perhaps even more so by a highly dramatic (and cogent) imagination.[1]

At the University of Virginia, Faulkner suggested that Shreve probably "had a much truer picture of Sutpen" than Quentin did (*FIU,* 274). However, it is difficult to credit Shreve's account as being more real, more believable than Quentin's, since his roommate is the source of all Shreve knows about Sutpen and his family. Here Shreve assumes the role of the novelist himself, creating characters to fit the needs of his plot (such as his fabricated lawyer in New Orleans) or altering circumstances to heighten the emotional drama (as in his reversal of which man had been wounded at Shiloh).[2] He imagines how the characters look, think, and feel, in a way similar to Mr. Compson's in chapter 4, and his narration covers essentially the same ground as had Compson's late one afternoon in the previous September.

The fact that Shreve has no substantial evidence for his conjectures hardly damages the verisimilitude of his account. He is capable of telling the story with great skill; his insight into the workings of narrative art easily rivals that of Mr. Compson or Quentin, who appear to be the joint authors of several of Shreve's interpretations. Stephen M. Ross has identified the technique of making conjectural scenes convincing as one of Faulkner's most important borrowings from Joseph Conrad.[3] Such imagined conversations at the end of chapter 8 between Henry and Sutpen and between Henry and Bon are both psychologically and aesthetically satisfying, as had been earlier fancifully conceived episodes like Bon and Henry's journey to New Orleans and Judith's moving interview with Charles Etienne.

The structure of chapter 8 makes absolute attributions of the conjectural scenes to either Shreve or Quentin practically impossible; they appear to be a combined effort. But their credibility has led to wide acceptance of the theory that Bon had Negro blood, which Donald M. Kartiganer has called "the great imaginative leap of the novel," suggesting that it is made possible by "what has been happening to Quentin and Shreve during the narration: [their] growing sense of communion. . . . "[4] It is easy to lose sight of the fact that the passages are imagined episodes by becoming caught up in their powerful emotional impact. Ultimately, though, they have no more authority than scenes created earlier by Miss Rosa or Mr. Compson.

Quentin's involvement is subtly changed in accordance with Shreve's expanded narrative role. Earlier he had frequently responded "Yes" to Shreve's summation of events and corrected him on minor points, such as the proper address of Rosa Coldfield. Now, however, Quentin has withdrawn to the extent that he barely responds at all except to protest that the relationship Shreve describes between Bon and Judith is not love, and to answer "I dont know" when Shreve requests confirmation of his theories (405). Early in the chapter, Quentin provides the distance from Jefferson to Oxford, but by the end, Shreve must coerce him into agreeing with his assessment of why Bon was carrying the picture of the octoroon and child on the day he was murdered. Otherwise Quentin is silent throughout the long chapter, allowing Shreve his chance to play. We must read into his silence and withdrawal the same anguish and despair which the narrator had voiced as occupying Quentin's mind in the preceding section.

Perhaps in anticipation of the greater role of the narrative persona in the last section of the novel, the narrator's importance is magnified at this point, though with carefully described limits. For the first time, the narrative voice evaluates interpretations of the characters/narrators, pointing out that the creations of Shreve and Quentin are "probably true enough" (419). The word *probably* defines precisely the extent of the narrator's knowledge: he understands more than the characters, but he is denied total omniscience. At times, however, the narrator voices attitudes which suggest a more fully realized personality, such as in his extended analysis of the reasons for the South's defeat (431–32). Most of the interruptions of Shreve's discussion describe the setting, stressing Quentin's sullen bemusement and Shreve's animation in telling the story. Moreover, the narrator frequently asserts that Quentin and Shreve share a similarity of vision:

> They stared—glared—at one another, their voices (it was Shreve speaking, though save for the slight difference which the intervening degrees of latitude had inculcated in them (differences not in tone or pitch but of turns of phrase and usage of words), it might have been either of them and was in a sense both: both thinking as one, the voice which happened to be speaking the thought only the thinking become audible, vocal; the two of them creating between them, out of the rag-tag and bob-ends of old tales and talking, people who perhaps had never existed at all anywhere, who, shadows, were shadows not of flesh and blood which had lived and died but shadows in turn of what were (to one of them at least, to Shreve) shades too) quiet as the visible murmur of their vaporising breath. (378–79)

A later narrative passage goes even further in defining the level of identification between the young men at Harvard and the characters they envision; Bon is "this shade whom they discussed (rather, existed in)" (395). The parenthetical insertion provides one of the novel's most direct intimations of the influence of the past on the present. At this point the people who inhabit Quentin and Shreve's shared visions of the past are more real than their own identities. For Quentin at least the level of identification is dangerously complete.

The communication between the roommates, almost telepathic at times, gives rise to the only real narrative difficulties of the chapter. At two points the narrative voice enters to describe a shared image, first of the Southern army's retreat across Carolina[5] and Bon's decision to return to Judith (433–37). The passage ends with Henry's being summoned to his camp meeting with Sutpen, and appropriately it resumes to describe the meeting itself as well as the later confrontation between Henry and Bon in which Bon offers his pistol (444–47). These passages provide the climax of the chapter, presenting the scenes of greatest emotional turmoil between Henry and Bon (the murder itself is never directly projected, not even reconstructed by any of the character/narrators). We might guess that the details owe a great deal to Shreve's active imagination, but the emotional intensity reveals the presence of the obsessed and depressive Quentin.

The relationship between the roommates in chapter 8 implies, however, that Quentin has not been so gloomy throughout his stay in Cambridge, an idea also supported by the relationship between the youths in *The Sound and the Fury*. In the earlier novel, Mrs. Bland twice arranges to provide a new roommate for Quentin, since she considers Shreve an inappropriate companion for a Southern gentleman. But the Canadian proves his fitness as roommate and friend in several ways: his concern that Quentin attend chapel and class; his defense of Quentin against the accusations of their classmates; his support of Quentin when he is arrested and when he attempts to fight Gerald Bland. Had Shreve considered Quentin in a negative light, he would surely have taken the occasion provided by Mrs. Bland to move out. His staying shows his loyalty to his friend; perhaps he sensed that such a young man as Quentin could profit from the concern of a more well-adjusted youth like Shreve, one ostensibly so different in background and interests.

More extensive descriptions of Shreve by the narrator, delayed until late in the novel, underline his youth and apparent chubby health. Forsaking his deep breathing exercises, Shreve has put on his overcoat, buttoned awry over his bathrobe, in which "he looked huge and shapeless like a disheveled bear . . . " (367). He is nineteen and looks exactly that age. His bearing contrasts dramatically with Quentin, who is described as "hunched in his chair, his hands thrust into his pockets as if he were trying to hug himself warm between his arms, looking somehow fragile and even wan in the lamplight . . . " (367). Set against this contrast is Shreve's attempt to obtain Quentin's assent to his view of Bon and Judith's relationship. He relies on his own meager knowledge of women's behavior and of men's reactions. When Quentin responds that he does not know very much about such matters, he is being more honest than Shreve can really recognize. But Shreve admits that he perhaps does not either, that at his age and in his culture his experience has been similarly limited, though his curiosity is healthy, as his very speculation about Bon and Judith attests. His is no voyeuristic interest, such as the fascination of the Reporter with the lives of the fliers in *Pylon*. Unlike Quentin, Shreve approaches the story of Bon, Judith, and Henry for what he can learn about human nature and how men and women relate to one another. He has no obsessive need to make sense of the tragedy, so he measures it against his own experience and develops from it a credible explanation. When he has completed his reconstruction, when for him it is dramatically complete, he leaves it to retire. Thus is set up the contrast between Shreve's youthful optimism and Quentin's despairing observation, in chapter 9, that he is older at twenty than many people who have died.

Anticipating their shared perception later in the chapter, the narrative persona describes the two as "something both more and less than twins" (367). The Mississippi River has already been seen linking together their native regions and further parallels of language and approach are established as chapter 8 progresses. Their identification with one another grows in intensity as their imaginative linking with Henry and Bon matures. In words that recall the homoerotic overtones of Mr. Compson's theorizing in chapter 4, the narrator describes how Quentin and Shreve stare at each other: "There was something curious in the way they looked at one another, curious and quiet and profoundly intent, not at all as two young men might look at each other but almost as a youth and a very young girl might out of virginity itself—a sort of hushed and naked searching . . . " (373–74). Such an observation, recalling the taunts in *The Sound and the Fury* in which Shreve is called Quentin's husband, does not necessarily suggest a homosexual attraction between the youths. It does predispose the reader to an understanding of Shreve's version of the Bon/Henry relationship. More than anything else, the passage is a clear indication of the closeness of the two young men, their mutual understanding. Each is sensitive, Quentin excruciatingly so; each is captured by the story they recreate together. So close is their identification with each other and with the characters they describe that the fluidity of time relates them not only to the adolescents they recently were, but to the tragic young men whose fortunes they follow through the Civil War.

Shreve begins his reconstruction of the story *in medias res*. He uses the information which Quentin has learned at Sutpen's Hundred in order to revise Mr. Compson's version of the Bon/Henry/Judith relationship, and he takes as his starting point the confrontation between Sutpen and Henry at Christmas 1860. Mr. Compson had advanced the marriage to the octoroon mistress as Sutpen's (and Henry's) objection, but Shreve's more extensive understanding provides a much more satisfactory explanation: "'So the old man sent the nigger for Henry. . . . And Henry came in and the old man said "They cannot marry because he is your brother"'" (366). Shreve's view of Sutpen is more sympathetic than Mr. Compson's had been, despite his easy incorporation of Miss Rosa's term demon; in Shreve's account, the father grieves for Henry, realizing the closeness between his son and Bon, knowing the suffering inflicted upon Henry by the full import of his revelation: not only is Bon your brother, but he has known all along of his identity.

Shreve accepts Mr. Compson's conjecture that Henry's response had been that his father had lied. But this new interpretation adds considerable weight to that reply; Henry had believed his father, knowing his father would not lie about Bon's parentage, but he could not accept that Bon had acted in such a cold and malicious fashion. Thus Shreve begins to voice his and Quentin's theory of Bon's actions, a theory at least partially supported by the narrative persona. The young men accept much of what they have heard, frequently alluding to something said by Mr. Compson or—Shreve is generally doing the talking—"Aunt" Rosa.[6] But they invent a great deal as well to explain the gaps in their knowledge.

From the beginning of the chapter, the narrator insists that though Shreve is speaking, both young men share in the reconstruction of events. There are more frequent reminders of the setting here than in the preceding two sections; these underline an atmosphere alien to Quentin, "the Southerner, whose blood ran quick to cool, more supple to compensate for violent changes of temperature perhaps, perhaps merely nearer the surface" (367). The time is around midnight, and the cold is great enough for Shreve, the native, to wrap himself in both his robe and his overcoat. The room grows progressively colder; Faulkner compares it to a tomb as the chapter progresses. The image suggests the remoteness of the characters the young men create—all are now dead—but it also hints at the numbing effect the repetition of the story has upon Quentin, the excruciating agony and despair which will cause him to join the other figures of the drama in death before the end of the term.

Twice in the chapter's second paragraph, the narrator attributes the story Shreve tells to both young men (367, 368) and suggests that the essential truth of their account is satisfying, though the details are perhaps inaccurate. The two are projected from their sitting room to the scene of the confrontation between father and son, the library at Sutpen's Hundred in December of 1860. They imagine the heads of the lovers passing the window as they walk in the garden where Shreve visualizes various spring and summer flowers in bloom. We are told that "it would not matter here [in Cambridge]" (368) that those blossoms would not be open in December and that the time would have been night, so an observer in the house could not have seen them. What does matter is the identification between the youths, Quentin and Shreve, who tell the story and those, Henry and Bon, who had actually participated in it. Thus begins the gradual merging of perception, the two speakers becoming four as the story progresses and the identification becomes more complete.

Shreve acknowledges that Bon had not known what had transpired between father and son, and he appears to assume that Bon had been unaware of his parentage, at least initially. (Likewise, Shreve makes no mention of Bon's presumed fraction of Negro blood.)[7] In order to explain the circumstances leading up to Henry's repudiation of heritage and home and the eventual murder, however, Shreve is obliged to assume that Bon *did* know that Sutpen was his father. He fashions a lengthy account which, though completely without substantiating evidence, is quite plausible and complete. Simply, he must explain Bon's presence in north Mississippi, at the university, where one would not expect a young man of his age and background to be. Shreve also seems unconvinced by Mr. Compson's analysis of Henry's initial attraction to Bon, and he postulates a sort of intuitive understanding of the fraternal relationship which the information Sutpen later provides Henry merely confirms.

In order to explain Bon's peculiar presence at the university and his subsequent friendship with Henry, Shreve weaves a portrait of Bon's mother which probably owes its inception to General Compson's imagination. The general had been amazed at Sutpen's naive belief that his first wife could have been placated by money, inviting the perception of her as a woman riveted by her hatred and desire for revenge. Added to General Compson's possible constructions, Shreve seems to bring to bear something of what he knows about Rosa in creating the image, as well as something of the fierce dedication of Rosa's aunt. Even Clytie is recalled in Shreve's picture of the relationship between mother and son when Bon is a small boy, a relationship arising from an almost complete lack of comprehension on the child's part, as Charles Etienne had failed to understand Clytie's vigilant protection of him.

Creating the character as a composite of other women in the story, Shreve invests Bon's mother with considerable vehemence and a design for revenge arising from a naiveté and simplicity of understanding which would rival Sutpen's own. She figures that the best way to mold Bon to her ends is to deny that he had ever had a father until the time came for him to accomplish her vengeance:

> "Maybe she was grooming him for that hour and moment which she couldn't foresee but that she knew would arrive some day because it would have to arrive or else she would have to do like the Aunt Rosa and deny that she had ever breathed—the moment when he would stand side by side (not face to face) with his father where fate or luck or justice or whatever she called it could do the rest (and it did, better than she could have invented or hoped or even dreamed, and your father said how being a woman she probably wasn't even surprised). . . . " (370–71)

The influence of the story's earlier interpreters is clear in this passage, which combines allusions to Rosa's monologue with quite typical references to Mr. Compson's misogyny, though nowhere does the novel record the conversation in which he tells Quentin his view of Bon's mother's character. (The conversation would have to have taken place after Quentin's visit to Sutpen's Hundred, since it presents Mr. Compson in possession of information he had not known until Quentin tells him what he had learned there. Neither does the novel detail Quentin's apprising Shreve of his father's comment.)

Shreve expands the idea of Bon's early upbringing at some length, fashioning a typically irreverent analogy to their relationship in the millionaire who owns a race horse and trains and cares for it himself. He pictures the mother swooping down upon the child at play and almost physically attempting to transfer to him her sense of betrayal, her passionate hatred, though the boy understands nothing of what she is trying to communicate, assuming that her behavior is merely a typical manifestation of the love which also provides his biological and material needs. So Bon grows up with his own conception of his Caribbean background, knowing it as a place which had been the fountain of his mother's " 'incomprehensible fury and fierce yearning and vindictiveness and jealous rage' " (373) which he does not understand, just as he does not understand the importance she attaches to his lacking a father, leading him to the conclusion that he shares his condition with all children. Shreve evokes language reminiscent of Rosa's monologue to make the point: " 'all boy flesh that walked and breathed stemming from that one ambiguous eluded dark fatherhead and so brothered perennial and ubiquitous everywhere under the sun——' " (373).

A narrative depiction of the setting at Harvard with Quentin and Shreve staring at each other provides a transition to Shreve's conjectures about Bon's adolescence. He guesses that as Bon had grown older, he had merely accepted his mother's vituperation without questioning the reason for it, assuming that he would discover her purpose soon enough. In preparing his typescript, Faulkner added a passage which explains Bon's lack of concern: " 'because probably by that time he had learned that there were three things and no more: breathing, pleasure, darkness; and without money there could be no pleasure, and without pleasure it would not even be breathing but mere protoplasmic inhale and collapse of blind unorganism in a darkness where light never began' " (374).[8] The addition owes a good deal to Mr. Compson's analysis of Bon's character as the jaded fatalist, but it also emphasizes the cynical posture which Shreve appropriates in conveying the story, a posture which an earlier narrative interpolation had identified as hiding the extent of his emotional commitment.

The idea that Bon would use his mother's obsession to extort money from her provides the initial rationale for the presence of the lawyer, whom Shreve invents as the trustee of the mother's estate. He alone would check Bon's desire for the money. Eventually, however, pleased by his creation, Shreve expands the lawyer's role dramatically, to the extent that the lawyer supplants Bon's mother as the manipulator of events which bring him within reach of Henry and Sutpen's Hundred. His motivation is money, and his approach is much more cool and restrained than his client's. Thus Shreve is able to explain how Bon is brought to the University of Mississippi without being made aware of the identity of his father or of Henry, a fellow student. Shreve supposes that the mother's anger would eventually have forced a revelation, perhaps before Bon could be persuaded to go to school in Oxford. The lawyer cleverly orchestrates the affair to prevent such a disclosure in order to fulfill his own desire for gain, sure that when the time comes he can manipulate Bon as easily as Bon's mother could force him to her will.

Shreve resorts to the introduction of the lawyer for reasons similar to those which had led Mr. Comspon to ascribe so much of the development of the tragedy to fate: a need to reconcile order out of chaos, to explain what otherwise appears to be only blind chance operating with devastating effect upon human lives. Certainly Shreve's creation provides a more satisfactory explanation than Mr. Compson's, but like Compson's own reasoning, Shreve's version tells us a good deal more about its narrator than about what actually happened. In his youthful optimism, Shreve is convinced that the tragic series of circumstances will yield itself to a rational explanation that will preserve the essential purity of motives in the participants which Shreve so much desires; the presence of the lawyer provides such an explanation. Shreve is a romantic, and he declines to consider other apparent possibilities which could account for Bon's presence at the newly founded college and his involvement with the Sutpen family. An obvious one would be Bon's early awareness of his identity coupled with a desire to work his revenge. Admittedly, none of the narrators seems to want to consider this possibility seriously, though it appears to be perfectly logical that Bon's mother would have been in a position to keep track of Sutpen's whereabouts and that, informed at an early age of the reasons for Sutpen's abandoning them, Bon would have shared his mother's outrage. Only later would his motives perhaps change as his love for Judith had begun to complicate his original plan. That Shreve refuses to consider such a conjecture at all illustrates the extent to which he too is caught up in the attractiveness of a romantic past, though his interest obviously arises from sources vastly different from Quentin's.

The lawyer of Shreve's imagining follows the accumulation of Sutpen's wealth closely, postulating at various points how he could use his knowledge of the first wife to translate Sutpen's possessions into his own. He knows that the presence of children makes the possible threat to Sutpen's respectability much greater, though he decides that the the bigamy threat is useless because he is not in a position to make his move until Bon's own maturity. Further he wants to milk Bon's mother of as much cash as possible in a bogus effort to locate the very man whose wealth he has designs upon. (Shreve does not comment on the fact, but the lawyer would almost certainly be aware of the woman's mixed racial heritage—a heritage which Shreve takes for granted whether his assumption is valid or not—and this factor would also nullify the bigamy threat.) He notes the births of Sutpen's son and of his daughter, though he seems immediately to have hatched the diabolical plan of using the daughter and Bon to threaten Sutpen with incest and thereby blackmail him into relinquishing his wealth.

Shreve becomes carried away by the ease with which events can be attributed to such a rational and coldly persistent manipulator as the attorney. He even goes so far as to suggest that the lawyer had arranged the marriage with Bon's octoroon in order to prevent his establishing a romance which would render him useless to the lawyer's incest plot. He would use the octoroon as " '*a block. Not a tether: just a light block of some sort, so he cant get inside of anything that might have a fence around it*' " (377). So he plays Bon's possible discovery of his father against his mother's impatience; the anticipation of acquiring Sutpen's fortune against what he could steal from his client at any time. The incest threat remains valid, however, since he imagines that the result of it would bring the greatest calamity, create the most complete disaster from which he could scavenge his profits.

The narrative voice interrupts again to picture Quentin and Shreve staring at one another, and to underline their shared consciousness, the increasing cold, and the progression of time: the chimes sound for midnight. The "snow-sealed" window (379) stresses the tomblike aspect of the setting as Shreve continues his story. He shifts his attention briefly back to Bon's mother, " 'the old Sabine' " (379), who does not know what she wants, only that she will require Bon's maturity before she can achieve it. She would visit the lawyer's office to inquire about Sutpen, sure that he is dead and outraged that he could be allowed to die before being forced to admit his crime and to suffer for it. (Shreve here again seems to be recalling Miss Rosa's comments about women's desire for men to admit their mistakes [212].) Her monomania rivals Sutpen's own in attempting to track him down and to punish him for his repudiation of her. Shreve imagines that she does not care for anything else, letting herself go, paying no attention to her clothes, taking no pleasure in her possessions, no pride in her growing son. Though Bon would not yet be old enough to make sense of her behavior, he could certainly recognize the extent of her obsession. He imagines the hatred she manifests when reading the faked letter from the lawyer informing her that he is growing close to locating Sutpen. Though to the young Bon the obsession is comparable to nakedness, in Mr. Compson's eyes her hatred itself could clothe her like modesty.

All Bon knows is that he has been created by mother and lawyer for a mission he does not understand. He thinks, as he goes to college at Oxford at the age of twenty-eight, that he will find that revelation which will make sense of his entire life. Shreve's interpretation here stretches the limits of credulity. Indeed, throughout, as Hugh Ruppersburg has recognized, Shreve's narration "depends on the cooperation of a much more submissive and passive Bon than other narrators have portrayed, than Bon's letter to Judith suggests."[9] Shreve is uncertain about the ostensible reason for Bon's schooling at that age; he merely posits that Bon would by now be aware that both his mother and the lawyer are up to something, though he understands the goals of neither.

The suggestion that the mother had Bon sent away because of the octoroon betrays Shreve's belief that her taint in Sutpen's eyes had been black blood. Shreve guesses she may have discovered that Bon had actually married his mistress, thereby potentially repeating the sin of his father. The confrontation between the two on this issue is nicely imagined, since for Bon's mother to demonstrate her true feelings about the situation, she would have to reveal Bon's own family background which she has kept hidden from him all these years: " 'her eyes blazing at him, her voice trying to blaze at him out of the urgency of alarm and fear, but she managing to keep it down since she could not talk about betrayal because she had not told him [about his father] yet, and now, at this moment, she would not dare risk it' " (384).

Ironically, Bon's mother contributes to his repeating Sutpen's crime. Shreve conjectures that after her frustrating interview with Bon she would have gone to the lawyer to get him to extricate Bon from the marriage in order to fit him for her purpose. Bon is aware of this, though not of her motivation. Nonetheless it plays right into the lawyer's hands. By sending his ward to the University of Mississippi, he can both distance Bon from his morganatic wife and put him within reach of the Sutpens in order to bring into play the incest threat. He finds the only problem in his scheme solved: " 'how to get Bon where he would either have to find it out himself, or where somebody—the father or the mother—would have to tell him' " (386). When Bon's mother wants to get him out of town, the lawyer makes the most of the situation. He places him in an environment conducive to his discovery of his parentage, confident that once Bon knows who Sutpen is, he will act on the knowledge. In the lawyer's mind, the incest threat grows from "possible" to "credible" to "certain" (387).

Once more we are reminded of the shared understanding between Quentin and Shreve, who never has to identify a vague pronoun since Quentin always knows to whom it refers. Shreve's lack of concern with factual details is also evident; when Quentin offers more information about the distance from Jefferson to Oxford, Shreve does not even pause. He envisions how the lawyer justifies his choice of the University of Mississippi to Bon. When Bon offers to study law, the lawyer begins to say his mother will agree, threatening a revelation that she is using the lawyer to manipulate her son. But he changes his line almost without hesitation to say she will " " "be pleased" ' " (389).

Shreve postulates that the lawyer would not leave to chance a meeting between Henry and Bon and so would have written a letter of introduction. He also assumes that Henry would have shown it to Bon, at which point Bon would certainly have deduced the reason for the letter, for his being sent to the University of Mississippi, for his whole past life. He would have looked at Henry and sensed the kinship in " 'a glare . . . in which he stood looking at the innocent face of the youth almost ten years his junior, while one part of him said *My brow my skull my jaw my hands* and the other said *Wait. Wait. You cant know yet. You cannot know yet whether what you see is what you are looking at or what you are believing. Wait. Wait* ' " (391–92). Shreve by and large accepts Mr. Compson's suppositions about Bon and Henry's friendship at school, grafting on only knowledge of the kinship which Mr. Compson had not possessed. Henry imitates Bon's dress and gait, his mannerisms and attitudes. Once more, however, Shreve's imagined scene becomes a bit strained when he creates Henry's stumbling confession of affection for Bon: " ' "If I had a brother, I wouldn't want him to be a younger brother. . . . I would want him to be older than me" ' " (394). Bon responds coolly, reflecting Shreve's view that he is interested only in his own discovery and his need to confirm what he believes is true. In Shreve's account, though, Bon follows the pattern of several other Faulkner characters, such as Joe Christmas and Isaac McCaslin, in accepting his supposition without proof. Though Bon never is given any hard evidence—Quentin had asserted baldly that no one knew if he had ever been aware of his parentage (335)—in Shreve and Quentin's reconstruction of events he begins immediately to act as though he has that proof and is merely attempting to force an acknowledgment from his father.

In their account, Bon falls in love with Judith by accident, only later sensing in the situation another avenue of coercing recognition. Shreve's transition to the courtship between Bon and Judith must have stung Quentin: " 'And now . . . we're going to talk about love' " (395). The narrator comments that this is the subject both young men are most interested in, that all the rest of the story had been merely a prelude to this subject. Before passing to Judith, though, Shreve reviews a good many of Mr. Compson's theories concerning Henry and Bon but with the perspective transformed by his greater understanding. He imagines Bon recognizing the power he held over Henry, feeling bitterly that Henry had been reared and nurtured by the father denied him. Though at times he would question his assumption about his parentage and at times even wish to cast Henry aside (" '*That young clodhopper bastard*' " [397]), he basically remains passive, listening to Henry's talk, considering his private questions. He agrees to accompany Henry home for Christmas, not to meet Judith, who could not be a part of his thinking at this point, but in order to get a glimpse of Sutpen, perhaps even a clandestine and private acknowledgment. Shreve phrases Bon's desire for such recognition in terms again recalling Rosa's monologue, in which she had explained the significance of Clytie's touch, joining flesh with flesh: " 'the physical touch even though in secret, hidden—the living touch of that flesh warmed before he was born by the same blood which it had bequeathed him to warm his own flesh with' " (399). The language also echos Sutpen's concern with his own progeny.

Sutpen offers no sign. His lack of acknowledgment fascinates Shreve, who uses it to create some of the novel's most vivid and emotionally wrenching scenes. He imagines Bon's thinking when he meets Sutpen, aware that he is indeed young despite his world-weariness and satiation. He is young because the acknowledgment means so much to him, because he had not even been aware of the lengths he would go to in order to obtain it. Confronted with the lack of evidence, Bon merely creates the proof in Sutpen's face. Assured that his assumption is valid, he is now possessed by the need to understand his father's reason for not recognizing him, if only to tell him to leave and not return. To Bon, the denial is a sort of cowardice, and he rationalizes that he should have been the one to fail because of that quality in his mother's blood which had been the cause of Sutpen's rejection of them.

Quentin, perhaps moved by the suggestion of weakness in a father which he could not fail to associate with his own father's limitations, begins to gather himself to break in, as if at this point in his listening such an interruption requires a supreme effort. But Shreve anticipates him and quickly advances the story to include Judith. Bon must have seen Sutpen's failure to raise an objection to the courtship as proof that he had not been Bon's father, though Shreve also hints that such an approach might have been Bon's rationalizing his attraction to Judith. Regardless of his knowledge, real or supposed, Bon recognizes at Sutpen's Hundred that he could easily have her; Shreve uses the typically careless analogy of a man who chooses between the after-dinner cocktail and the cleansing dessert of lemon sherbet, which Judith must have represented to the jaded Bon.

Quentin interrupts Shreve, pointing out that the analogy does not define love, implying that he cannot understand how love between Bon and Judith could have existed under the conditions Shreve describes. Quentin here indicates that his view of this courtship has been more deeply influenced by Miss Rosa than by his father. Largely for her own reasons, Rosa had maintained that Bon had been merely a ghost figure, that Judith, not bereaved at his death, could not have loved him. Mr. Compson had accepted the love and offered Bon's letter (seemingly forgotten by Quentin though Shreve alludes to it later) as proof. Quentin's view allies him with Rosa; his personal obsessions are closer to hers, and he stubbornly refuses (or, as Elisabeth Muhlenfeld suggests, is unable)[10] to recognize love.

Shreve is faced with no such obstructions, and he can easily imagine how love had grown between the couple. Bon knows that he would come to love her, like the man leaving the dinner table who would realize that he wants only the sherbet, had wanted nothing else for a long time. For Bon, Judith represents a renewal (Shreve even interrupts his narrative to describe the springtime during which Bon would recognize his love). Shreve's view recalls Mr. Compson's theory that Judith and Sutpen's Hundred had represented a welcome respite and release for Bon. But Shreve goes even further to suggest an idea that *The Sound and the Fury* records Quentin as broaching in his August 1909 talk with his father about Caddy: incest between brother and sister. Again, Shreve is perhaps drawing on hints provided by Mr. Compson (recorded in chapter 4), who had pictured the relationship between Henry and Judith as exceptionally close, even resorting to a homoerotic image to convey it. Homosexual overtones had also been used by Mr. Compson to describe the feelings between Henry and Bon. With his knowledge of their kinship, Shreve would view even this relationship as bordering on incest.

His real justification, however, seems to be a logical imaginative extension of Mr. Compson's view of Bon. Satiated with women and made too completely aware at this point in his life of " 'the vain evanescence of the fleshly encounter' " (323), Bon may have seen in incest a way of making the union of man and woman more permanent, more meaningful. An addition made in the preparation of the typescript explains Shreve's theory in language echoing Quentin's section of *The Sound and the Fury*:

> "Who has not had to realise that when the brief all is done you must retreat from both love and pleasure, gather up your own rubbish and refuse . . . and retreat since the gods condone and practise these and the dreamy immeasurable coupling which floats oblivious above the trammelling and harried instant, the: *was-not: is: was:* is a perquisite only of balloony and weightless elephants and whales: but maybe if there were sin too maybe you would not be permitted to escape, uncouple, return.—Aint that right?" (404)[11]

Shreve prefaces this notion with the comment that those men without sisters may have believed this; he says he does not know about the others. Once more the allusion to *The Sound and the Fury* is obvious. Before attacking Gerald Bland, Quentin demands if he has a sister (*TSTF,* 206). Though the scene with Bland occurs chronologically after *Absalom* and Quentin's conversation with Shreve, the parallels are unmistakable. They are made even more clear in that Quentin, who had earlier prepared to interrupt Shreve, answers only " 'I dont know' " (405). The narrator points out that Shreve had paused to listen to Quentin's protest, though he makes none. Shreve's comment about what men without sisters think is an open invitation for Quentin to counter with the viewpoint of men who have sisters—either to corroborate or to attack his theory. Quentin fails to respond because he has apparently told his roommate nothing of his obsessions with Caddy, or perhaps he has related merely enough to arouse Shreve's curiosity. To elaborate would reveal too many of his own neuroses. Unknowingly, Shreve has broached a topic of particular relevance to Quentin, one which is at the heart of his interest in the Sutpen history. Forced to rehearse once more the story that has so closely reflected his own experience and to hear his roommate bring it pointedly to bear upon his personal obsessions, Quentin is now virtually in a state of shock.

Shreve does not let up. He wants confirmation of his theory, and because of his fascination with the characters' motivations, he seems not to notice Quentin's withdrawal. He admits that he may not know about the incest notion either, but that at some point " 'you are bound to fall in love' " (405). Quentin again maintains ignorance, and Shreve scoffs at him, thinking Quentin is suggesting that love does not matter to him, has not touched his experience. He resumes his analysis of Bon, postulating that the love between him and Judith would take care of itself, would be part of their fate, that they, Sutpen's children, would have to pay out the debt which Sutpen, like Abraham of old, had incurred and escaped through age and weariness.

Bon does not concern himself with his love for the woman he suspects may be his sister; he begins to think of that love as a lever, a sort of catalyst to spur Sutpen into an acknowledgment of kinship. He expects a letter from Sutpen containing a single line of recognition, the name Charles, even a lock of hair. Grasping at straws, Bon assumes that if a letter of his to Judith should return unopened, it would be a sign. When the June visit is planned,[12] he supposes that Henry might get a letter instructing him not to bring Bon, some note which would be a tacit acknowledgment, but that letter does not come either. So the two make the visit, Bon aware that Henry has offered both his own life and that of his sister to his friend. Once more the language Shreve uses to phrase Henry's offer has particular relevance for Quentin: " ' "I used to think that I would hate the man that I would have to look at every day and whose every move and action and speech would say to me, I have seen and touched parts of your sister's body that you will never see and touch: and now I know that I shall hate him and that's why I want that man to be you. . . ." ' " Rather pitifully, Quentin again protests: " 'That's still not love' " (410).

Shreve ignores Quentin, wrapped up in the image of Bon he has created, picturing Bon as he arrives for the visit in June 1860 to find Sutpen gone. Bon jumps immediately to the conclusion that he has gone to New Orleans to make sure of Bon's identity. Even with the pledge of both Henry and Judith's devotion, Bon resolves to abandon them with Sutpen's acknowledgment, though he cannot understand why Sutpen had chosen such a roundabout method of revealing himself. Bon returns to New Orleans expecting to meet his father, but he does not. Nor does he find evidence of Sutpen's visit. His mother is the same, and the lawyer offers only implicit confirmation of what Bon had suspected as his motives in sending him to the University of Mississippi in the first place—so he could meet Henry Sutpen.

According to Shreve's account, Bon's hope gradually acquires a tinge of bitterness. When he returns to the university, Henry reproaches him for not writing, and he does so, with his name prominently written on the outside of the envelope. He remains convinced that Sutpen has proven to himself in New Orleans that Bon is his son, and Bon thinks once more that the letter may return unopened. But now he is not sure what he will do. The acknowledgment would have come too late, and Bon perhaps would have proceeded with the courtship. At the last Christmas visit, Bon seems to share something of Rosa's clairvoyance; he knows when Sutpen enters the house, though he is walking with Judith in the garden. He senses when Sutpen sends for Henry, sees Henry entering the library. Anticipating the catastrophe, he sends Judith, disappointed in her own understanding of what love is, away while he waits for Henry to emerge.

The narrative persona takes over to reiterate that the story is a shared reconstruction, Shreve speaking for both of them, and to show the two men become four as Charles-Shreve and Henry-Quentin ride over the countryside toward the river. Henry thinks that Sutpen has destroyed them all, and he takes Bon's failure to write to Judith over the summer or to propose to her as confirmation of his father's assertions. Reflecting the tenor of Shreve's narration, the persona recounts the New Orleans visit, drawing, like Shreve, from Mr. Compson's version but with the new information that the two men had been brothers. The narrator gives partial authority to Shreve and Quentin's visualizations of the Haitian wife's drawing room and to their description of her. Support is also given to Shreve's analysis of her character as revealed in her reaction to meeting Henry: " 'So she has fallen in love with him [Charles]' " (419), she says, laughing at Henry's obvious discomfort. The two had visited the octoroon mistress as well, though the narrator makes clear the differences in the interview as imagined by Mr. Compson and as conjectured by the two young men:

> And Bon may have, probably did, take Henry to call on the octoroon mistress and the child, as Mr Compson said, though neither Shreve nor Quentin believed that the visit affected Henry as Mr Compson seemed to think. In fact, Quentin did not even tell Shreve what his father had said about the visit. Perhaps Quentin himself had not been listening when Mr Compson related it that evening at home; . . . (419–20)

This comment both confirms and undercuts. It adds credence to Quentin and Shreve's account, since it tends to support their interpretation based upon greater understanding than Mr. Compson had had in chapter 4. Though Quentin has obviously given Shreve the "facts" of the New Orleans visit as his father had outlined them, he has omitted Compson's interpretation, since what Quentin had learned at Sutpen's Hundred rendered that interpretation obsolete. The fact that Quentin had perhaps not been listening, and apparently did not need to be, joins with the conditional modifiers and verbs to undercut the authority of his and Shreve's account. The narrator will go only so far as he had earlier in supporting their theory: it is "probably true enough" (419).

Once more Shreve resumes the telling, picking up where the narrator had left off—the interview with Bon's mother. Bon now fully understands what her plan had been, along with the lawyer's schemes. He goes to see the lawyer, who may even have written a letter, after he could be sure Bon had discovered his father's identity demanding " '*I know you are a fool, but just what kind of a fool are you going to be?*' " (420). Since the lawyer's thinking and needs embrace only money, he cannot understand Bon's love of Judith and so offends him by suggesting that he blackmail his father and seduce Judith into the bargain. Bon reacts violently in Shreve's account, assaulting the lawyer and even debating killing him. Shreve is apparently thinking of the young Sutpen's debate concerning Pettibone, for Bon comes to the same conclusion his father had reached years before: " '*I could shoot him. I would shoot him with no more compunction than I would a snake or a man who cuckolded me. But he would still beat me.*' " (423). The lawyer has beaten Bon by leading him into a situation from which he cannot escape, driven by his need of recognition and by his love of Judith. Shreve imagines that he may have beaten him further by absconding with Bon's mother's money, leaving the octoroon without means.

The attention shifts to Henry, who has to reconcile himself to the idea of incest, since Bon seems determined to marry Judith, though Shreve assumes that he had not known what he would do. Shreve accepts Mr. Compson's theory of the durance, the waiting period during the war, though he suggests that the reason had been to allow Henry time to accept the idea of incest. Bon explains that he must pursue the courtship to punish Sutpen for not recognizing him as his son. Henry pleads with him to think of Judith, but both seem aware that Judith is in love, that the taboo of incest will not prohibit her at all. (This notion is perhaps the strongest indication yet of Shreve's romanticism and lack of understanding of women, factors which had earlier contributed to his need to create the lawyer.) The durance represents an impasse: " ' Bon who didn't know what he was going to do and had to say, pretend, he did; and Henry who knew what he was going to do and had to say he didn't' " (426).

The picture of the two men, stalemated as they await the beginning of the war, prepares for the conflicts which provide the climax of the chapter. Henry struggles to accept the incest which his heritage has forbidden out of love for Bon; he cites precedents of incestuous relationships, especially that of John, Duke of Lorraine, who had loved his sister and been excommunicated by the pope. Bon tries to reconcile himself to his father's indifference. Henry permits him to write Judith a letter informing her of the durance, to which she responds by sending him the picture of herself in the metal case. Henry becomes fixated on the Duke while Bon withdraws into a numb nihilism, hurt to the point where nothing matters. Shreve imagines him inviting suicide after he becomes an officer, tormenting Henry by suggesting that Henry might shoot him while Bon leads a charge.

Henry's reaction, his feverish panting and pleading for Bon to stop, anticipates Quentin's reaction to meeting Henry in the following chapter.

The dramatic success of Shreve's account leads to his most egregious alteration of the facts as he has received them. Extending his conception of divisions in Henry's mind regarding Bon and Judith, Shreve postulates that Henry, not Bon, had been wounded at Shiloh. This alteration makes little difference to the climactic event—the murder—but it allows Shreve to present Henry begging Bon to allow him to die and thus escape his dilemma.[13] Shreve pictures Henry fighting to die: " "Let be! Let me die! I wont have to know it then" " (430).

As if Shreve's fancy has twisted the story as much as it can bear, the narrator again interrupts to describe the two young men in their room, which is now "indeed tomblike" (431). Quentin declines even to put on his overcoat; both accept the cold "as though in deliberate flagellant exaltation of physical misery transmogrified into the spirits' travail of the two young men during that time fifty years ago . . . " (431). The interruption justifies the South's ultimate defeat and once more underlines the identification of the roommates with the brothers in the war—"the two the four the two facing one another in the tomblike room" (432).

The shared vision is now voiced by the narrative persona, who brings the chapter closer to its climax in an italicized interpolation picturing the conflict between Henry and Bon against the progressive decline of the South. Bon realizes suddenly that he has not made a decision about his course because he is still waiting for Sutpen to change his mind, to avail himself of the possibility of acknowledgment. He sees the retreat of Johnston's corps across Georgia and into Carolina as bringing him closer to his father, giving his father one more chance. He even hopes against hope that the war will have changed Sutpen, will have given him cause to be straightforward and direct with his first son. When Sutpen's regiment is detached by Lee, Bon even sees his father, places himself in his way, but still he gets no nod, not the barest hint of recognition. So Bon decides as a final act of desperation to return to Judith.

Henry's reaction is one of relief that a decision has been made at last. He allows Bon to write the letter, anticipating almost with joy the damnation he sees in store for the family: " '*And we will all be together in torment and so we will not need to remember love and fornication, and maybe in torment you cannot even remember why you are there. And if we cannot remember all this, it cant be much torment*' " (434). The narrative voice, translating Shreve and Quentin's joined reconstruction, recalls Shreve's earlier comments about how sin transforms experience, gives it greater meaning. The reader familiar with *The Sound and the Fury* is again reminded of Quentin's assertion to his father that he and Caddy had committed incest and of his visions of them in torment where the pain of their experience would be constantly renewed.

Bon's conversation with Henry as Shreve and Quentin relate it, reflects the fatalism of the last line of his letter to Judith, but otherwise his comments on what is left after food and clothes and honor and God are abandoned sound little like the author of the letter. He does maintain the need to continue to live: " *'Only there is something in you that doesn't care about honor and pride yet that lives . . . that probably even when this is over and there is not even defeat left, will still decline to sit still in the sun and die . . . ' "* (436). But he again becomes passive in Shreve's view, again withdrawn and content to be manipulated by events rather than to influence them. This certainly is not the Bon who leads the charge which captures the stove polish and can laugh at the absurdity of the result. Once more, having made his decision, Bon slips into the background, allowing Shreve and Quentin to focus on Henry's predicament. The italicized interruption breaks off at the point when the orderly summons Henry to the colonel's tent.

Shreve's resumption of the story jumps ahead to the subject of the final chapter—Quentin's visit to Sutpen's Hundred with Miss Rosa. The placement of the material delays briefly the climactic scene between Henry and Sutpen and anticipates the supposition which ends chapter 8—Shreve's explanation for why Bon replaced Judith's picture with the octoroon's. Shreve recounts how Quentin had come by the knowledge of what the metal case had contained from Clytie, though he is ambiguous about how the information had actually been transferred; Clytie " 'didn't tell you in so many words anymore than she told you in so many words how she had been in the room that day when they brought Bon's body in and Judith took from his pocket the metal case she had given him with her picture in it; she didn't tell you, it just came out of the terror and the fear . . . ' " (437–38).[14] Shreve goes on in summary fashion, as he had in chapter 6. (Indeed the paragraph here picks up where chapter 6 had ended, with Quentin and Miss Rosa's arrival at Sutpen's Hundred.) He recounts how Rosa had struck Clytie down in order to ascend the stairs, as she had done on the day of Bon's death.

When Shreve breaks off—the interruption is a single paragraph—the narrative voice takes over, pointing out, as it had in earlier chapters, that Quentin is not listening to the speaker. Instead, both he and Shreve have compounded their identification with Henry and Bon, and they follow Bon into the tent. Italics again signal the shared vision, as the chapter builds toward its climax. The present tense adds a greater sense of immediacy, of shared participation between the living men and the shades whose story they reconstruct. Chronology is again wrenched. The narrator backs up to describe the bivouac fires, the opposed troops, as the orderly seeks Henry, described as gaunt and ragged (as Quentin had envisioned him at the end of chapter 5 and the beginning of chapter 6).

Like much of the narration in chapter 8, the scene of Henry's camp meeting with his father reflects earlier narrators. That such a meeting had taken place had been confirmed by General Compson, in command of the division in which Bon and Henry had served. Shreve's supposition about Henry instead of Bon being wounded at Shiloh is incorporated, as is Rosa's notion about an almost superhuman sentience possessed by Sutpen. Henry does not wonder how Sutpen knows of

Bon's decision, does not even suspect that Judith has written him or that Clytie has communicated the fact: *"To him it is logical and natural that their father should know of his and Bon's decision . . . "* (441).

Henry does not suspect, however, what his father has called him to reveal. Sutpen senses that Henry will allow the marriage, and in confirming the fact, Henry repeats almost verbatim Bon's earlier despairing statements about what little would be left after the war. His use of Bon's language confirms that the bond between them remains strong, that the deprivation of the four years has intensified the love, not destoyed it: *"Yes. I have decided. Brother or not, I have decided. I will. I will"* (443). He has not counted on something else besides breathing which will still matter—the racial integrity on which the old social and cultural standards had been built. In Quentin and Shreve's explanation, Sutpen conjures the single taboo which Henry cannot accept: miscegenation. They visualize the youth as calmer after seeing his father, certain of what his response would have to be, dependent only on Bon now to show him what action he must take.

That Bon is part Negro is purely the supposition of Shreve and Quentin, though it is a perfectly plausible explanation of the taint which Sutpen had discovered in his first wife. Sutpen does not reveal the nature of her problem to General Compson, and at a couple of points earlier in the chapter, Shreve presents Bon as unaware of his father's objection to his mother. The narrator presents the idea, which originated with the young men, as though it is authoritative, though certainly such a presentation does not constitute proof of any kind. Cleanth Brooks has suggested that an "organic disability or chronic disease or some neurosis" would be stumbling blocks just as potent to threaten Sutpen's design.[15]

That there is no proof of this assertion should remind the reader that the scene so cogently presented by the narrative persona for Shreve and Quentin is by no means definitive; other possibilities exist. We might question, for instance, whether the threat even of miscegenation would be more damning to Henry than incest. After all, he had grown up with a half-black sister, and no narrator presents him as being bothered by the mixed blood of Bon's mistress; indeed, Mr. Compson envisions him as being practically indifferent to it. Immediately, then, we are invited to question the interpretation provided by the two character/narrators. Would it not be as likely that the objection of Christmas 1860 was much more mundane—simple disapproval of the suitor, fatherly jealousy, the desire to protect Judith? Perhaps Sutpen had discovered that Bon was not as wealthy as he has been assumed to be and had feared that he was merely seeking to establish a fortune through marriage. Any such possibility would explain Sutpen's early objection, and Henry's loyalty to his friend could have easily led him temporarily to abandon home and inheritance until the events of the war intervened and prevented him from repairing the rupture.

More substantial evidence would point to a crucial meeting between Henry and his father, since General Compson had been aware of it; that a serious objection did exist is evident in the murder.[16] Perhaps Sutpen had revealed not Bon's black blood but his parentage to Henry at the camp meeting. Henry's loyalty to Bon would be explained along with his extreme final action to prevent the marriage. We must acknowledge that interest in incest is one of Quentin's obsessions, one he may have transferred to Shreve in telling him the story. That in Quentin's mind Henry could be made to accept incest probably tells us a great deal more about Quentin than about Henry.

A two-line space serves as a transition to another italicized passage, which dramatizes the confrontation between Bon and Henry. Though the murder itself is not described, the pain of this imagined scene is as intense as any which the murder scene could occasion. Bon is solicitous of Henry, offering him his own cloak, as Shreve will offer Quentin means of added warmth in chapter 9. Ironically the time is dawn as Bon learns of his mother's taint in a conversation the narrator does not record. Bon begins with the bald statement, "*—So it's the miscegenation, not the incest, which you cant bear*" (445). Bon is outraged that he has been sent no word; he informs Henry that he will now marry Judith despite Henry's objections.[17] When Henry intimates he will stop the wedding regardless of the cost, Bon offers him a pistol and tells him to "*do it now*" (446). Henry responds by calling Bon his brother, and Bon taunts him unmercifully, as if attempting to commit suicide by forcing Henry to kill him at that moment. Henry seizes the gun, but finally casts it aside in what approaches a state of hysteria.[18] The scene ends with Bon's ominous threat that Henry will have to kill him to prevent the marriage.

Readers of *The Sound and the Fury* are again reminded of the similarity of this confrontation between Bon and Henry to that between Dalton Ames and Quentin. Dalton also offers Quentin a pistol which he is unable to use (though certainly Henry is brought to use his pistol eventually). Faulkner perhaps expects his best readers to make the connection, since the scene is labelled a shared creation of Quentin and Shreve, and Quentin's identification has been with Henry throughout the chapter, while Shreve has been associated more directly with Bon, the outsider. Quentin's identification with Henry at this point explains much of his violent reaction to the story described at the beginning of chapter 9; it also intensifies the drama of his meeting with Henry himself in the novel's climax.

In the chapter's closing paragraphs, Shreve returns to his summarizing style to telescope the return of the two anguished young men to the gate of Sutpen's Hundred, where the murder had occurred. Shreve's final view of Bon is a rather romantic one, predictably so, since Shreve has been extremely sympathetic to Bon throughout. He suggests that Bon had substituted the picture of the octoroon for Judith's in order to say to her, "'*I was no good; do not grieve for me*'" (448), in case Henry made good on his threat. He practically forces Quentin to accede to this interpretation before repeating the line which had closed chapter 7, "'Let's get out of this refrigerator and go to bed'" (448). Having satisfied himself by making sense of the murder, having explained the characters' motivations to his own satisfaction, Shreve is ready to retire. As the following chapter will demonstrate, Quentin does not find it so easy to leave the story alone.

Elisabeth Muhlenfeld questions whether the substitution of the photographs had not perhaps been intended to inform Judith of the existence of the mistress and child: "Judith seems to have accepted it as a message, a commission to care for Bon's quasi wife and son."[19] In order to make such a request, Bon would had to have understood the nature of his beloved much better than any of the narrators gives him credit for. But the suggestion is hardly outlandish.[20] (Judith's behavior might seem more understandable if we posit, as I have earlier, that she had been aware that Bon was her half-brother.) On this point, as on practically all the others in this gripping but largely conjectural chapter, we are free to draw our own conclusions, to create independent ways of interpreting characters and events. Faulkner himself stated at the University of Virginia that the composite drawn by the reader is the one "which I would like to think is the truth" (*FIU*, 274).

"Nevermore of peace": Quentin's Encounter with Henry

The final chapter of *Absalom, Absalom!* is the shortest but also the most intense in its impact. The reader is at last allowed to accompany Quentin on his trip with Miss Rosa to Sutpen's Hundred, an expedition which had been hinted at in the novel's first movement and which had its initial stages described at the opening of the second movement in chapter 6. There, Quentin's impressions of the dust rising from the buggy as he and Rosa had traveled in the September night had been evoked by the letter from Mr. Compson announcing Miss Rosa's death. The letter and Quentin's remembrance unite once more in the final chapter, making it a capstone for the entire book.

The reader eagerly anticipates what he will learn about the visit, for he has been tantalized by hints in preceding sections. Quentin tells Shreve in chapter 7 that his father had understood the story of Bon and Henry only after he had explained it following this journey (332, 342), and in chapter 8, Shreve comments that Quentin himself had understood only when he had been to the rotting mansion and seen Clytie (437–38). Hence, we eagerly expect to learn exactly what Quentin had discovered, but of equal importance, how he had discovered what he knows. Such hopeful greed for certainty, however, is defeated by Faulkner's method, which denies authoritative confirmation of *any* of the "facts" Quentin and Shreve have used to explain the Sutpen tragedy. Such confirmation would destroy much of the novel's carefully considered effect, arising from the extensive ambiguities involved in interpreting the past. Far from lessening the uncertainties, Quentin finds that encountering a living relic of that past merely multiplies them.

Quentin's experience at Sutpen's Hundred confirms his observation in chapter 6 that if he had been present to observe Sutpen's bringing home the gravestones he could *"not have seen it this plain"* (238). Quentin sees clearly Miss Rosa's visit to rescue Henry in December 1909, though he had not been present. But the descriptions of his own visit in September are shrouded in darkness, as Gary J. Williams has pointed out.[1] Again and again, Quentin must rely on senses other than sight to provide information. (The darkness in the room at Harvard now that

Quentin and Shreve have retired offers a parallel to his memory.) He recalls tasting the dust, noticing Miss Rosa's scent of camphor, which he associates with old women, smelling the horse, feeling the sweat crawl on his flesh, hearing the buggy wheels in the road (451–52). He hears Rosa's whimpering, and he identifies the hatchet she gives him "not [by] sight but touch" (455). Miss Rosa shares his blindness, and he must help her up the steps; he feels his way to the window and through it as he moves toward the front door. When Clytie strikes a match, in Quentin's heightened state of awareness it is "like an explosion, a pistol" (459). The entire scene acquires a nightmarish, surreal quality, an atmosphere of unreality, as contrasted with those episodes which Quentin imagines. Quentin remains more comfortable in the realm of imagination, though the terrors he confronts there are as genuine to him as those of his actual experience.

Significantly, everything he "sees" on his trip relates in some way to that portion of the Sutpen story which he finds most moving: the conflict between the Sutpen children. He looks at the gate posts of the plantation and wonders from what direction Henry and Bon had approached them, speculating about "what had cast the shadow which Bon was not to pass alive" (454). He sees Clytie, and she hints about the identity of the person she is hiding upstairs; without that hint he would not have felt the compelling need to be a witness himself. Finally, he confronts Henry, and the impact is so intense that even four months later he pants uncontrollably just remembering it. His vision in the present catalyzes his imagination, his reconstruction of the past forcing him into a greater sense of participation and identification.

Much of chapter 9 is delivered by the narrative persona, who reports the conversation between the roommates and presents Quentin's memories. The section comprises the longest involvement of the narrator since the passage describing the community's response to Sutpen's arrival in Jefferson in chapter 2. But the voice of the narrator becomes more objective than in the preceding section, in which it had evaluated Quentin and Shreve's reconstructions and commented independently upon aspects of the story, such as the reasons for the South's defeat. The narrator voices Quentin's thoughts but does not comment upon them, nor does he provide supplementary information. The greater objectivity functions in a manner similar to the use of the third-person narrator in the fourth section of *The Sound and the Fury.*

The narrative persona begins by reiterating the setting of Quentin and Shreve's dormitory room, as most of the chapters in the second movement open. But now a new element is added—the darkness intensifies the cold: "At first, in bed in the dark, it seemed colder than ever, as if there had been some puny quality of faint heat in the single light bulb before Shreve turned it off . . . " (449). Shreve has opened a window, an action which again underlines his being an alien to Quentin after the linking of the two as almost close as twins in the preceding section. Though concerned about Quentin's welfare, Shreve does not understand the reasons for his roommate's convulsive shaking. He attributes it to the cold, as though unaware of the pain the recitation of the Sutpen story has caused his friend. He offers to cover him with the coats, but Quentin maintains that he feels fine.

That Shreve seems unaware of the extent of Quentin's involvement is curious, since he has been withdrawn and brooding during Shreve's long narration. The Canadian's lack of insight signals a return to the irreverent badgering which he had exhibited at the beginning of chapter 6, in which he had ridiculed Southern culture to incite Quentin into explanation and defense.[2] To a degree, of course, he has never abandoned his tone of careless flippancy, which at one point the narrator identifies as a mask. But he now becomes less solicitous in questioning Quentin, almost abusive. He doubts if even Quentin understands the region he comes from, and again makes seemingly intentional mistakes—surely even a Canadian freshman at Harvard in 1910 would know that Pickett's charge took place at Gettysburg, and Quentin has often corrected his referring to Rosa as Aunt instead of Miss. At the novel's close, he facetiously predicts the racial future of the South and of the entire country despite Quentin's statement that he does not want to hear what Shreve thinks. Thus, Shreve moves further and further away from Quentin as the chapter progresses, indicating that he misunderstands not only the South but his friend as well.

We assume that Quentin has related the tale of his plantation visit to Shreve already, since Shreve refers to what his roommate had learned there, and at the end of the preceding chapter he had reconstructed it in his summary fashion. The emphasis in chapter 9 is thus considerably different from that of the other sections of the second movement. Information is not being transferred, as in chapters 6 and 7, or interpreted, as in chapter 8. Instead, the section focuses almost exclusively upon Quentin's reactions to the story that Shreve already knows. Quentin says little; most of the talking is done by Shreve, but Quentin's compulsive memories cover a great deal of which his roommate is unaware, precipitating an almost violent reaction which Shreve attributes merely to the cold.

Despite his flippancy and his ignorance, Shreve does exhibit what is apparently an honest desire to understand southern culture. What he finds most baffling is the southern preoccupation with the past, with its pervasive influence on the present. To him, the Sutpen tragedy is a paradigm of that influence, particularly in the person of Jim Bond, a character who fascinates Shreve at the end of the chapter for this reason. In correcting Shreve's mistake about Gettysburg, Quentin disappoints his expectation: "'You cant understand it. You would have to be born there'" (451).

Shreve suspects an evasion and questions if Quentin himself understands it. At first, Quentin is hesitant, employing the "'I dont know'" he had used earlier, but he quickly adds, "'Yes, of course I understand it'" (451). Eventually though, he repeats honestly that he does not know. Shreve's accusation that Quentin did not even understand "the Aunt Rosa"—Quentin corrects him for the final time—leads to his long remembrance of that September night. As if to express his reluctance to reconsider his memory, the passage begins with the single word he actually speaks to Shreve, "'No'" (451), acknowledging his own lack of understanding.

Specifically, Quentin fails to understand Miss Rosa's feelings as they journey toward the old house, what he thought "derived from terror, alarm, until he found that he was quite wrong" (452). Miss Rosa continues to view Sutpen in the same way she has always, as though he were a supernatural demon who still existed, still owned the land and dominated it, though he had been dead nearly a half century. But as always, Quentin is affected by Rosa's passion, and though he seems generally little concerned with Sutpen himself in the final chapter, he conjures a vision of Sutpen riding his black stallion, very much as he had created an image of him from Rosa's words in chapter 1. Now, however, Quentin views Sutpen more sympathetically, imagining his position at the end of his life after his return from the war, when Milly Jones had been "all remaining to look at him with unchanged regard" (453). The image provides quite a contrast from the "man-horse-demon" who had erupted onto the peaceful scene earlier (4).

Occasional reminders bring the reader back to the bedroom in New England, but Quentin's thoughts remain focused on the events of that previous September night. When Rosa hesitates, Quentin thinks she is afraid, and indeed she seems to be. She is concerned that Clytie might prevent the discovery; as her monologue had demonstrated, Rosa invests Clytie with superhuman powers derived from the demon's own. Quentin half-heartedly attempts to persuade her to return to town, while his imagination is seized by the site of Bon's murder. Its influence on his thinking is symbolized by the imagery of continuing life: he wonders if "some living tree which still lived and bore leaves and shed or if some tree gone, vanished" (454) had witnessed the crime, cast the fateful shadow. Ironically, Quentin even wishes Henry were present to turn Rosa back, as indeed he will when she sees him.

Rosa soon makes clear that what she fears is more real than a ghost. She bemoans the fact that Quentin had not brought a pistol, and she makes him take the hatchet. They make their slow way up the "rutted tree-arched drive" in which the darkness is "intense" (455). Like Quentin after the visit and as he remembers it later at Harvard, Rosa trembles badly. The approach to the house seems excruciatingly long,[3] and when they reach it, it towers over them:

> It loomed, bulked, square and enormous, with jagged half-toppled chimneys, its roofline sagging a little; for an instant as they moved, hurried, toward it Quentin saw completely through it a ragged segment of sky with three hot stars in it as if the house were one of one dimension, painted on a canvas curtain in which there was a tear; now, almost beneath it, the dead furnace-breath of air in which they moved seemed to reek in slow and protracted violence with a smell of desolation and decay as if the wood of which it was built were flesh. (456–57)

This description is the culmination of several in the book which approach the house as a gothic setting, investing it with an almost human quality. For Miss Rosa it is the personification of Sutpen himself, but for Quentin it acquires a more dreamlike, less real association, perhaps due in large measure to his stated reluctance to discover what lies hidden inside it.

Rosa feels no such reluctance, however, and Quentin realizes that she is not afraid after all; as he admits to Shreve, he does not understand what emotions motivate her. He barely restrains her long enough to enter through a window before she seizes the hatchet to assault the front door. Inside he must feel his way while fighting terror from an unknown source. His eyes strain in the darkness until Clytie startles him by lighting her match. Quentin must already fight for control: "He could not even move for a moment even though something of sanity roared silently inside his skull: 'It's all right! If it were danger, he would not have struck the match!'" (459). As his memories become more intense, their effect upon Quentin in the present becomes more pronounced; his breathing quickens, "now that peace and quiet had fled again" (459).

When Clytie opens the door, she and Rosa repeat the scene which had occurred on the day of Bon's death. Clytie attempts to prevent Rosa's ascension of the stairs, even using the same words: "'Dont you go up there, Rosie'" (460). But unlike the earlier occurrence, in which Judith had intervened, Rosa strikes Clytie down and runs up the stairs, leaving Quentin to help her up and talk briefly with her. Nothing passes between the two which is remarked either by Quentin himself or by the narrator, suggesting that if Quentin did learn something significant from her on this occasion, the novel does not record it. Such a possibility is hardly remote, since Quentin attempts to control his impressions of the night very carefully, refusing to dwell on any information which elicits the greatest terror or grief from him. Obviously he did learn something, but he never reveals exactly how.

After identifying him by relating him to General Compson, Clytie seems willing to talk both honestly and openly with Quentin. She begs him to take Rosa away, though it seems somewhat unusual that she would think Rosa had come to bring Henry to justice: "'Make her go away from here. Whatever he done, me and Judith and him have paid it out'" (461). A slightly different interpretation of her meaning arises because of the ambiguity of Clytie's reference. Most obviously, she refers to Henry himself, but her statement contains just as much truth if by her "Whatever he done" she had meant Sutpen. If she had intended Sutpen—such an interpretation would certainly be applauded by both Mr. Compson and Miss Rosa—it would be only natural to assume that she might explain in greater detail exactly what he had done within the limits of the time Rosa spends upstairs. And indeed, it had been Clytie and Henry and Judith who had borne much of the burden for the crimes against human sensibility which Sutpen had committed.

The length of time Quentin talks to Clytie is uncertain, but he soon ascends the stairs himself and encounters Rosa returning in a state of shock: she "looked full at him as if she had never seen him before—the eyes wide and unseeing like a sleepwalker's . . . '" (461). Again, Quentin is unable to identify the emotion, suspecting that it might even be triumph. J. R. Raper draws an interesting correlation between Rosa's visit to the mansion with Quentin and her entry on the day of Bon's death in terms of the obsessions which had been the subject of her monologue:

> There is no Judith to stop Rosa this time. She simply completes the running stride, in the middle of which her movement stopped in 1865, runs to the closed door, and throws it open, thereby giving renewed animation to the picture which was stopped in 1865. That Henry, who waits beyond the door, is old, wasted, unfit to be her lover, is no matter, for Rosa has substituted the symbol for the reality; in opening that door she symbolically fuses 1865 and 1910 [sic], and restores forward movement to her stunted life. Three months later she dies.[4]

Though he hears Clytie instruct Jim Bond to take Rosa to the buggy, Quentin realizes that he too must see. But he avoids rehearsing *what* he sees, jumping in his memory immediately to his return to the buggy, catching up with Rosa and Jim Bond on the drive. Rosa falls and asks Bond his name; she does not recognize his kinship to the family: "'You aint any Sutpen! You dont have to leave me lying in the dirt'" (462). Though she seems to be referring to Thomas, her comment could indicate that she has been in some way repulsed by Henry. If so, it would in part explain why Miss Rosa postpones for three months her attempts to rescue Henry by securing treatment for him. Her comment also indicates that she is unaware of Charles Bon's kinship to Sutpen; she is wrong, since Jim Bond *is* a Sutpen, the last descendent of the demon of her imagination. Apparently, Rosa is not privy to whatever sources of information Quentin discovers inside the mansion.

Rosa remains stunned by finding her wasted nephew and apparently says nothing more to Quentin except to tell him goodnight. Quentin's reaction to Henry's presence, however, is more than he can control, and he returns home, whipping the horses even into the stable lot:

> He sprang out and took the mare from the buggy, stripping the harness from her and tumbling it into the harness room without stopping to hang it up, sweating, breathing fast and hard; when he turned at last toward the house he did begin to run. He could not help it. He was twenty years old; he was not afraid, because what he had seen out there could not harm him, yet he ran; even inside the dark familiar house, his shoes in his hand, he still ran, up the stairs and into his room and began to undress, fast, sweating, breathing fast. "I ought to bathe," he thought: then he was lying on the bed, naked, swabbing his body steadily with the discarded shirt, sweating still, panting. . . . (463–64)

It is Quentin's memory of his reaction, with its significant overtones of sexual exhaustion, which leads him eventually to recall the crucial interview with Henry that he longs to forget. His anguish is so intense that he can remember, can focus his mind on nothing else: "waking or sleeping it was the same and would be the same forever as long as he lived" (464). His pain is numbed somewhat in the intervening months, and he has managed to avoid in his memory the most excruciating parts of the interview by weaving a cyclical pattern of the less painful questions and responses—Henry's identity, his reason for returning, the length of time he had been there.

What Quentin learns from Henry has occasioned considerable critical controversy, since the novel does not record the transmission of any particularly relevant information. Cleanth Brooks believes that Quentin learned the secret of Bon's parentage from Henry in a passage not recorded in the novel; he states that the conversation provided is a "fragment" which "does not pretend to give more than the awesome confrontation. There is no warrant for concluding that it represents all that was said."[5] Hugh Ruppersburg agrees, stating that the italics of the exchange "indicate, as elsewhere, imagined or reconstructed speech. The dialogue's puzzling elliptical form reflects how it runs endlessly through Quentin's mind, how he cannot free himself of it"; Ruppersburg further suggests that Faulkner purposely obscured what Quentin learned as a means of extending his theme of the unknowability of the past.[6] Gerald Langford's transcription of the manuscript of *Absalom, Absalom!* indicates that in that version the interview between Henry and Quentin is punctuated conventionally, using quotation marks, while other conversations of that night recalled by Quentin are recorded in italics. In the preparation of the typescript, Faulkner reversed the procedure.[7] The critical debate continues to rage, promoting various possibilities to explain how Quentin had uncovered Bon's true identity, including intuition from looking at Clytie,[8] associating Jim Bond with the Sutpen features,[9] and pure imaginative clairvoyance.[10]

That the mystery is intentional is without doubt, since had Faulkner wanted us to discover exactly what Quentin had learned and how he had learned it, he could have included the specific episode of revelation. By this point in the novel, however, the reader should be used to accepting conversations which he does not witness directly. An obvious example is the scene of the confrontation between Judith and Henry which Quentin had been unable to "pass" at the end of chapter 5. Though Rosa alludes to the scene (167), she does not present it the way Quentin remembers it. Obviously, he may have imagined the details of this episode for himself, but other examples exist as well. We never see a conversation between General Compson and his son, though this is the conduit for much of Quentin's information about Sutpen and his children. Similarly, Shreve refers on several occasions to specific points raised by either Mr. Compson or Miss Rosa. At times these points are traceable to narration in the first five chapters, but a couple seem to refer to things which Quentin has related but which the novel does not present, including a comment that Mr. Compson had been right about how Clytie had kept

Bond on the lookout for Rosa's return to arrest Henry (465). Such is also the case with the story of Quentin's trip with Miss Rosa: Shreve summarizes it at the end of chapter 8, but nowhere do we see Quentin relating it to Shreve. Given the numerous earlier examples, it should require little faith to accept that Quentin has learned something at Sutpen's Hundred which the novel does not record, and that it is quite likely not recorded for a thematic reason—Quentin's own reluctance to remember it.

Shreve spurs Quentin's visualization of how the house burns as Rosa returns for Henry, though Shreve cannot manage to get Quentin to respond to any of his comments for quite a while. The narrator points out on four separate occasions that "Quentin did not answer" (465, 466, 468). Instead he labors hard to control his breathing and practically wallows in his despair: "He lay still and rigid on his back with the cold New England night on his face and the blood running warm in his rigid body and limbs, breathing hard but slow, his eyes wide open upon the window, thinking 'Nevermore of peace. Nevermore of peace. Nevermore. Nevermore. Nevermore'" (465). The pattern of his thinking parallels his memory of his conversation with Henry, which he has forced into a similar repetitive structure. Quentin cannot be brought to speak until after he "sees" Rosa's return to the mansion.

Shreve postulates that Rosa delays in going back for Henry because she fears cutting off the source of the hatred which had sustained her all these years—a typically far-fetched idea, since the object of her fanatic bitterness is not Henry but his father. Also characteristically, the narrative voice informs us that Quentin is not listening, having been caught up in the scene as he conjectures it, since he has no recorded source for his details. He pictures her leaning forward as she had in his buggy, shouting for the ambulance to go faster when they see that the house is on fire. Miss Rosa would be in hysterics, as would Jim Bond, whose howling provides a weird obbligato to the scene. Quentin pictures Rosa as doll-like, struggling against the men who would have held her (he remembers her as being doll-like at the return of their earlier visit as well). His final vision of Clytie would have been worthy of Rosa herself: "And then for a moment maybe Clytie appeared in that window from which she must have been watching the gates constantly day and night for three months—the tragic gnome's face beneath the clean headrag, against a red background of fire . . . " (468). After the collapse of the house, all that remains is "the sound of the idiot negro" (468). Bond's cries provide an appropriate commentary on the ultimate results of Sutpen's design, perhaps on the futility of all human endeavor, as James Guetti has suggested: "Bond represents the entire story: he is potential meaning, always out of reach, but asserting in his idiot howling the negation of meaning."[11]

Shreve makes a joke of the fact that Rosa herself had to return to town in the ambulance she had brought for her nephew, but again Quentin does not respond. The narrator even points out his failure to correct Shreve's "Aunt Rosa" (468). His reference to her death reminds Quentin of his father's letter once more, and he strains to make it out in the darkness, while he seems compulsively to remember reading it earlier in the evening. For the final time, the images of Mississippi, wisteria, his father's cigar, and fireflies, combine with the cold and darkness of New England, as the words begin to emerge so that Quentin can almost read them. He tries to visualize them as an antidote to his despair: "It was becoming quite distinct; he would be able to decipher the words soon, in a moment; even almost now, now, now" (469).

His attempt is unsuccessful, and when Shreve comments, " 'The South. Jesus. No wonder you folks all outlive yourselves by years and years and years,' " Quentin responds, " 'I am older at twenty than a lot of people who have died' " (469). Shreve's rejoinder is both ominous and heavily ironic: " 'And more people have died than have been twenty-one.' " Even readers unfamiliar with *The Sound and the Fury* can appreciate Shreve's unintended irony, since the Chronology of *Absalom, Absalom!* (which many in frustration will have frequently referred to by this point) lists Quentin's date of birth as 1891 and his death as 1910. He will be among those who die before reaching legal maturity.

Quentin completes the reading of the letter which he had begun at the opening of chapter 6. His father rather characteristically supposes that instead of escaping the hatred and outrage which had marked the last forty-three years of her life, Rosa had repaired to a beyond in which Sutpen would be the direct object of those feelings, where he would have to suffer her vituperation as his punishment. The idea is related to Shreve's account (obviously borrowed from Quentin or his father) of Sutpen and Wash in the afterlife not being able to remember their conflict of so long ago. Mr. Compson's mention of the weather, the cold which made difficult the digging of Miss Rosa's grave, provides a potent analogue to the cold in the dormitory room. The image of the worm which is turned up living and is soon again frozen, like Jim Bond's howling, provides a reminder of the eventual results of human striving and vanity.

Shreve's final goading concerns Jim Bond, as if the Canadian is trying to draw a moral from the tale.[12] He provides a facetious interpretation of the entire story, concluding with the notion that " 'it takes two niggers to get rid of one Sutpen' " (470). Once more Quentin does not answer. But even Shreve's sarcastic attempt to make sense of the story is ultimately futile, since " 'You've got one nigger left. One nigger Sutpen left' " (471). He uses Jim Bond to forecast interracial breeding to the extent that racial distinctions will no longer be of any consequence at all. At that point, the regional differences and the cultural taboos which precipitated the downfall of the house of Sutpen would no longer matter either. Thus, Shreve is able to sublimate his involvement with the tragedy into a farcical theory of social Darwinism. John V. Hagopian elaborates on Shreve's ideas: "Jim Bond is what inevitably will come of the white's refusal to accept the black man as both black and a man. Since Shreve believes that the South is hopelessly mired in provincial ignorance and obsessive racism, it can create only a gothic distortion of life—rotting plantation houses and the idiot progeny of hatred and despair."[13]

Shreve's final taunting question provokes an outburst which Quentin has seemingly been trying to avoid since the two youths had gone to bed:

> "Now I want you to tell me just one thing more. Why do you hate the South?"
>
> "I dont hate it," Quentin said, quickly, at once, immediately; "I dont hate it," he said. *I dont hate it* he thought, panting in the cold air, the iron New England dark; *I dont. I dont! I dont hate it! I dont hate it!* (471)

We immediately sense that Quentin protests too much, too quickly.[14] The repetition of the phrases recalls the memory of his talk with Henry and his earlier anguish over the loss of his mental balance.

On the surface, Shreve's question seems irrelevant, having practically nothing to do with the line of conversation he has been pursuing.[15] When examined more carefully, though, it explains a good deal about his misunderstanding of Quentin's obsessive concern with the Sutpens. Though he continues to badger his friend, Shreve cannot be insensitive to Quentin's reactions. He is aware of Quentin's uncontrollable shaking after he goes to bed, has watched him brood over his father's letter all evening long, has heard his despairing statement that he is older at twenty than many people who have died. That Shreve does not seem more concerned with Quentin's mental balance is a reflection of his lack of comprehension of both the nature and the extent of Quentin's involvement.

Indeed, the reader himself must question the violence of Quentin's reaction to his meeting Henry Sutpen. Frequent references, increasing in intensity in the second half of the novel, have pointed to Quentin's reluctance to hear the story again and his need to make sense of it. But why is he so upset by his meeting with Henry? An obvious answer would be that actually seeing a central character in the tragedy brings home to him more than ever the nature of the suffering Sutpen's design has created. But we have seen that on other occasions Quentin has found his imaginative reconstructions more satisfying than actual experience, closer to the reality he creates. Perhaps he sees in Henry a symbol of the futility of existence, but he has supported Shreve's contention that both Henry and Bon had found value in life even after their defeat in the war, and that interpretation has been assembled well after his meeting. We might conclude that Quentin is a young man of unusually sensitive perceptions, that he is moved by the same types of emotions the reader himself experiences in reading the novel, only that his closer contact with the story obliges him to react to it with greater emotional violence. But we have seen that Shreve too is a sensitive individual, capable of great compassion, and that he too is moved by what he hears, but he exhibits no signs of emotional scars because of his interest.

In short, none of these explanations is entirely satisfactory, and they invite us to look elsewhere. The most obvious alternative is that Quentin is distraught by what Henry has told him, that his new knowledge of Bon's identity darkens the story almost unbearably in his mind, bringing to the forefront the issues of incest, paternal rejection, and fratricide. The first two of these are important concerns in *The Sound and the Fury*. If we bring a knowledge of Quentin's problems there to our reading of *Absalom, Absalom!*, we arrive at perhaps an even more convincing explanation. We have seen that one of the reasons for Quentin's obsession with the Sutpen tragedy is its bearing on his own experience. Thus, he is particularly interested in the relationship between Bon and Sutpen's later children, Judith and Henry, because of the reflection of his own relationship with his sister Caddy. He becomes fixated on the confrontation between Henry and Judith after the murder, and his imagined reconstruction of the episode in which Bon offers Henry a pistol is reminiscent of his own attempt to banish Dalton Ames. In each case, Quentin's fascination results from Henry's ultimate ability to act in a decisive manner, to sublimate his love both for his sister and for his friend to his abstract definition of honor. Quentin is incapable of such a decisive action, though he admires Henry at the same time that he is horrified by him.

In *The Sound and the Fury*, Mr. Compson defines Quentin's desire as "to sublimate a piece of natural human folly into a horror and then exorcise it with truth" (*TSTF*, 220). Toward that end Quentin had woven his lie about incest. But his father had not taken very seriously either his lie or his veiled threats of suicide. Mr. Compson's own withdrawal from the active forces of life leads him to the position that *no* human action can have significance, that everything is futile—in his own words, "nothing is even worth the changing of it" (*TSTF*, 96). Much of Quentin's desire to understand the Sutpen history arises in general from his need to refute his father's nihilistic position. He sees Sutpen as a man of action, an idealist who is capable of setting a goal and striving to obtain that goal regardless of the consequences. To an extent, Henry inherits the same qualities, though his circumstances require of him no similar mission to fulfill an abstract design. In the end, though, Henry acts, and Quentin must view that action as an affirmation of meaning. For reasons of his own, he has to see in the murder a significant accomplishment.

Though Shreve views Henry's dilemma sympathetically (as does Quentin in their shared visions), the image of him awaiting death in the decaying mansion once again forces the reader to reconsider what he knows about Sutpen's second son. Largely through Quentin's identification with him, we are led to admire Henry's courage in taking action to prevent the marriage and to pity the suffering that action had caused him. But Quentin's memory of the dying Henry invites a closer examination of his reasons for the murder—the episode in Henry's life which has eventually brought him to this pitiable state. Viewed in this new context, Henry becomes more closely identified with his father's adherence to a rigid, inhumane code of behavior. In the final analysis, Henry kills to preserve Sutpen's design—a reluctant tool in his father's futile attempt to preserve what he had built. But a difference between father and son exists, as Robert Dale Parker explains: "Coldness gives Sutpen an excuse for cruelty, whereas Henry has no excuse. . . . Judith is strong willed and loving, Sutpen strong willed and unloving. Henry is loving, but his will is petty. He acts not from love but despite love."[16]

His meeting with Henry Sutpen denies the affirmation Quentin has associated with his act, suggesting that the family honor for which he had killed (and which to Quentin is all important) had been as hollow and empty as the honor of the defeated South. The action affirms nothing but a sterile principle and effectively wastes the lives of all the Sutpen children. Quentin, then, is not paralyzed by his confrontation with a relic of the past in the present, but by a living symbol of the futility of one example of the abstractions which he has exalted. Deborah Robbins has recognized this point: "As Faulkner's depiction insists, Henry Sutpen is an appalling spectacle of human waste; he is not the champion of human value asserted and preserved, but a figure of terrible deprivation. . . . [I]t is clear from Quentin's suffering as he relives the moment in memory that he received no satisfying answer that night to his search for value and meaning in the Sutpen history."[17] Henry's wasted form and pitiful aspect confirm to Quentin one of his father's most memorable expressions of futility in *The Sound and the Fury*: "Because no battle is ever won he said. They are not even fought. The field only reveals to man his own folly and despair, and victory is an illusion of philosophers and fools" (*TSTF*, 93).

Quentin's psychological impotence makes it impossible for him to profit from the negative example of Henry Sutpen's life. As *The Sound and the Fury* demonstrates, much of that impotence derives from Quentin's incorporation of Mr. Compson's nihilistic philosophy, but whatever the source, by the end of *Absalom, Absalom!*, Quentin has lost all hope of rescuing himself from despair. Quentin and his father both fail to discover meaning because they are unable to "make the failures of their past yield a new and revitalizing image of their humanity," as Richard Forrer asserts.[18] John W. Hunt summarizes the nature of Quentin's tragedy thus: "By an act of imagination, Quentin . . . solves the mystery of why Sutpen's design fails. The character of his solution is important because it embodies a view of the past which leaves him in despair over the possibility of meaning in the present."[19]

Shreve is unaware of the parallels between Quentin's family problems and the story of the Sutpens; in fact, the absence of any mention of Caddy in *Absalom, Absalom!* underlines Shreve's ignorance of how Quentin's personal obsessions might affect his response to the tale. It is natural, then, that he ascribes his friend's unusual and intense reaction to hatred of the South, since this is an explanation he can understand and since Shreve has always seen the Sutpen story as emblematic of southern culture in general. Readers of *Absalom, Absalom!* who bring no knowledge of Quentin's character from *The Sound and the Fury* are obliged to come to similar conclusions and interpret Quentin's reaction as arising from his ambivalence to the moral dilemma of racism and economic exploitation, from his confusion about the problem of man's understanding of his past, and from his peculiar identification with the extreme sufferings of the members of a unique southern family. Those aware of the clues to Quentin's psychological paralysis in *The Sound and the Fury* understand more fully the impact of the Sutpens upon this sad and sensitive young man; in that family's tragedy he finds reflected his own.

Conclusion

Absalom, Absalom! marks a milestone in Faulkner's career as a novelist. One of his most ambitious works, only *A Fable* would offer more problems in composition; one of his most demanding, none would require more careful and dedicated attention from his readers. It begins Faulkner's life-long relationship with Random House, with what was to be perhaps the most handsomely manufactured of all of Faulkner's books. And the map at the end, drawn by Faulkner himself and produced in two colors of ink, seems to cement the author's hold on his mythical county and underline the connections between *Absalom, Absalom!* and the earlier novels of the Yoknapatawpha series.

To an extent, *Absalom, Absalom!* departs from the other novels set in Yoknapatawpha County. While the books which preceded it are richly endowed with a sense of locale, *Absalom* is the first which could with justification be called "southern"—the first in which the regional setting contributes significantly to thematic development. Various characters see Sutpen as representative of traits endemic in southern society. Rosa goes so far as to advance him as God's excuse for the South's defeat. Mr. Compson seems to discover in his story justification for his own sense of futility, since Compson's own life has been attenuated by the era of southern humiliation. Sutpen's career parallels the rise and fall of the entire region as a powerful economic and political entity, and the issue of the white man's exploitation of the blacks—the theme of southern racism—brings about the destruction of both Sutpen's design and the social system which gave it birth. Little wonder, then, that Quentin apparently offers Sutpen's story in response to the demand to *"Tell about the South"* (218).

Faulkner, however, was in no sense a narrowly defined "regional" writer, and the concerns of *Absalom, Absalom!* far transcend the subject of southern consciousness. The novel's power lies in its presentation of conflicts which achieve the magnitude of genuine tragedy. At the book's end, Quentin gives voice to a despair similar to that encountered by many of the novel's characters: "'Nevermore of peace'" (465). With his myopic view of the world, Quentin focuses on his own reaction to the violent history of the Sutpen family, but the phrase is equally applicable at one time or another to practically all the participants themselves. Sutpen embarks on the pursuit of his design with ruthless monomania at the age of only fourteen. Ellen's stunned incomprehension at the end of her life surely encompasses her entire involvement with her husband from the time of their engagement. Their children find themselves caught up in a set of circumstances they can neither understand nor control, circumstances which banish the son and condemn the daughter to a spartan existence largely devoid of purpose. Charles Bon, regardless of which interpretation of his motives we accept, is a figure torn between conflicting loyalties and visions of himself; in Shreve's account, he becomes one of Faulkner's most memorable examples of what his Nobel Prize address calls "the human heart in conflict with itself." From her own account, Rosa is destined for a barren existence practically from birth; her outrage at age twenty merely intensifies and confirms her childhood tendencies to withdrawal and isolation. All the book's important characters, then, arrive at a moment of recognition similar to Quentin's at the end when they realize that the perilous encounter between personalities and events has rendered their lives largely devoid of contentment and the possibility of human fulfillment. Peace is lost to them all.

The final outlook in *Absalom, Absalom!*, as in any great tragedy, is not entirely bleak, though; some assertion of individual dignity is occasionally possible. Sutpen's captive architect, for instance, manages to endure with his spirit largely intact, as does Charles Etienne St. Valery Bon, who eventually makes an effort to accept his lot before he contracts his fatal illness. Even Clytie finds a purpose in rearing Jim Bond and caring for the wasted form of Henry Sutpen, and the episode where she completes payment for Charles Etienne's tombstone twelve years after his death is one of the book's most haunting combinations of dedication and endurance. An even more important portrait of these qualities is found in Judith, whose strength in facing her changed circumstances is indeed heroic. Her selfless devotion to Charles Etienne, her acceptance of Milly Jones, her acts of kindness to Rosa after the outrage all testify to a woman of remarkable character and perseverance. Her comments to Mrs. Compson when delivering Bon's letter into her keeping underline Judith's firmly held belief in the principle of life, in the possibility of change and growth. Her example provides the novel's most potent contrast to the sterility and negation of her father's adherence to an abstract design.

The tragic elements and the emphasis upon human endurance link *Absalom* with much of Faulkner's earlier fiction, but artistically the novel represents a new direction. It extends the author's career-long trait of innovation and experimentation, exploring more effective methods of fictional expression. The techniques which establish the outlines of the Sutpen story and deliver that story to the reader are uniquely challenging. The multiple narrators, constant uncertainties, and conflicting testimonies guarantee that the experience of reading the novel becomes an exercise in interpretation on the most fundamental level.

Toward that end, Faulkner uses the device of positing a unique relationship between *Absalom* and *The Sound and the Fury*. While his earlier fiction has occasionally made use of characters who survive with their personalities essentially unchanged from one work to another—a practice he would continue throughout his career—never before had Faulkner relied so heavily upon the reader's knowledge of a character's earlier life and personality in order to grasp the full implications of the story he is telling. The incorporation of Quentin Compson, a central narrator from the earlier novel, to assimilate the various versions of the Sutpen saga and magnify their impact for the reader signals one of Faulkner's boldest and ultimately most successful fictional experiments.

At the highest level, Faulkner designed *Absalom, Absalom!* for the most dedicated and discriminating reader, perhaps more so than any other of his books. Certainly he has provided adequate explanations of Quentin's obsessive interest in the Sutpen story for those who approach *Absalom* purely on its own terms, and the rewards for such a reader rival those of the highest achievements in American fiction. Those readers familiar with *The Sound and the Fury*, however, perceive even more ripples expanding from the pebble dropped into the pond and gather an even higher appreciation for the greatest of William Faulkner's novels.

Appendix

The Chronology of *Absalom, Absalom!*

As with many of Faulkner's novels, the chronology of *Absalom, Absalom!* is complicated and contains certain inconsistencies which cannot be resolved. Many of these inconsistencies are probably the result of the author's changing conceptions of characters and events during the process of composition, but others almost certainly derive from the sheer length and complexity of the work. The novel is unique in the Faulkner canon in that both a Chronology of selected events and a Genealogy of seventeen characters are appended to the text, though the two are not consistent with each other or with the text itself; indeed, inconsistencies occur within the Chronology alone, which lists the date of Sutpen's birth as 1807, yet proclaims that he had been fourteen years old in 1820, when he ran away from home (473).

In all probability, as Elisabeth Muhlenfeld has suggested, Faulkner prepared the Chronology and Genealogy after completion of the typescript setting copy.[1] Whether he sensed that the reader might have difficulty keeping the events of the Sutpen family history straight, or whether Faulkner was reacting to a suggestion made by one of his editors at Random House is impossible to ascertain. Two versions of the chronology were apparently used by Faulkner as he wrote the novel. The earlier is a manuscript listing of the years between 1807 and 1910, with annotations differing in several important respects from the published Chronology and from the novel (see *TS*, 485–86). The most important of these differences, as Noel Polk has pointed out, is the manuscript version's assertion that in 1831 Sutpen discovers that his wife has Negro blood and repudiates her for this reason (*TS*, x). The specific reason for Sutpen's abandoning his first wife is deliberately withheld in the final typescript of *Absalom*. The working chronology also erroneously lists the date of Rosa and Quentin's visit to Sutpen's Hundred as 1910, an inconsistency perpetuated in the first edition. The novel suggests the year of Sutpen's birth is 1808, though all the versions of the chronology offer 1807 as the date.

A two-page typescript version of the chronology was evidently prepared at a later point in composition.[2] Though it covers the same years as the manuscript version, it emphasizes dates of birth and death and the ages of characters at various points, rather than broadly outlining the entire Sutpen saga, as the manuscript listing does. Sutpen's repudiation of his first wife is not mentioned, and the date of Rosa's discovery of Henry and the burning of the Sutpen house has been changed to 1909. A manuscript insertion on the second page of the typescript notes "60 days without rain./42 no dew," a description which finds its way into the published novel (109).

The Genealogy offers some information not contained in either the text or the Chronology. While some of this new information is incidental—such as the name of Sutpen's first wife, Eulalia—some is more significant, such as the updates about Quentin Compson and Shreve McCannon. Quentin's death is recorded, and Shreve's history is advanced to include his war service and his present practice of medicine. These additions tend to support Polk's assertion that "The genealogy is a more formal piece of work which seems to have been conceived especially for inclusion in *Absalom's* appendix" (*TS*, x). The preparation of such materials was particularly interesting to Faulkner, as his writing of the Compson Appendix for the *Portable Faulkner* later indicated.

Evidence in the typescript setting copy of *Absalom* indicates that Faulkner made an effort at internal consistency at a late stage, perhaps even as a result of his work on the Chronology and Genealogy he prepared. Manuscript corrections in Faulkner's hand accurately establish the differences in age between Rosa and Judith and Henry in chapter 1. Occasionally editorial hands can be recognized performing the same duty. Not all the inconsistencies were caught in preparation of the first edition, however. For instance, the period of Rosa Coldfield's outrage is properly forty-three years (from her insult in 1866 to 1909); in the typescript, however, Faulkner had originally set the period at forty-five years, and this number was preserved in passages where the error was not caught, as on page 6 of the typescript setting copy (*TS*, 23). Thus, many of the discrepancies most likely represent the failure of Faulkner and his editors to locate and correct errors resulting from the author's changing conceptions.

A different motive, however, may have been at work as well: Faulkner's reluctance to attempt total consistency. Some of the discrepancies may very well be intentional. Several of the characters, for example, have a tendency to round off numbers when discussing the passage of time, and some of the dates offered by such narrators as Mr. Compson and Miss Rosa, ultimately the sources for all of Quentin and Shreve's knowledge, are based upon conjecture and hearsay. Given Sutpen's admitted confusion about his age, for instance, no one could have been certain that Sutpen had been twenty-five when he arrived in Jefferson in 1833, yet that age is advanced at three points in the novel (16, 35, 275).

Many of the internal discrepancies must thus remain unresolved, but their very presence helps underline some of the novel's main themes, as several critics have maintained.[3] The discrepancies highlight differences in the narrators' perceptions as well as in their interests and obsessions. The mere placement of references to specific dates or periods of time is instructive. The early chapters, as one would expect, are most densely punctuated with such references, though other important ones congregate around the recapitulation of the story by Shreve in chapter 6, which includes the Compsons' visit to the cemetery.[4] Several lengthy passages contain relatively infrequent references to chronology, and these sections usually suggest an imaginative reconstruction of events based upon scanty evidence, such as Mr. Compson's version of Henry's trip to New Orleans with Bon at Christmas 1860 or Shreve's fanciful construction of the relations between the lawyer and Bon and his mother in chapter 8. Similarly, Rosa's monologue contains few pieces of concrete information about chronology which do not relate specifically to her own obsessions. To a degree, then, each narrator's use of chronology provides a clue to his relative accuracy and reliability.

Such clues cannot be pressed too far, though, since no single character is noticeably more reliable than any other. Certain inconsistencies remain unquestioned by all the narrators, and virtually all accept conflicting bits of information. Thus, the final repository of the Sutpen legacy lies not within the realm of fact, but of imagination, as Carl E. Rollyson suggests: "The remarkable coherence of the Sutpen story . . . is the product of a long historical process which relates past and present, not through an agreement of all the facts which are the ephemeral surface of a particular moment in time, but through the human imagination (historical and artistic) which constantly turns over the facts to see what significance they now possess, whenever 'now' happens to be."[5] Faulkner himself made a similar point in a 1946 letter to Malcolm Cowley: " . . . I dont care much for facts, am not much interested in them, you cant stand a fact up, you've got to prop it up, and when you move to one side a little and look at it from that angle, it's not thick enough to cast a shadow in that direction."[6]

No one would argue that factual inconsistencies interfere with fictional truth. A careful cataloguing and examination of the discrepancies in this important novel, though, may reveal a great deal about Faulkner's method of presenting Thomas Sutpen's story. More importantly, they may help us to understand more completely Faulkner's method of creating the world of which he proclaimed himself "Sole Owner & Proprietor" ([487]).

The following listing attempts to incorporate all references to periods or events mentioned in the novel and its appended Chronology and Genealogy. It ignores references of a purely conjectural nature, especially those made by Shreve in chapter 8 and those for which dates are nowhere suggested. Where the testimony of one character contradicts another's, the episode is dated by the source which seems more reliable. For example, Rosa's dating of events in her own life is generally preferred over Mr. Compson's versions, though the inconsistencies between the two accounts are pointed out.

Dates established in the Chronology and Genealogy are listed by the abbreviations C and G. Other page references are to the corrected edition of *Absalom, Absalom!*. The editor of that edition, Noel Polk, explains that "the chronology and genealogy have been corrected in several instances to agree with dates and facts in the novel" (473). However, many contradictions and inconsistencies "with dates and facts" have been allowed to stand. Since the alterations are questionable, based upon the editor's judgment rather than reference to extant documents, they have been pointed out in notes. Valid arguments can be advanced for allowing the errors and discrepancies in the Chronology and Genealogy to remain as they appeared in the first edition, even when they obviously contradict testimony provided in the text of the novel itself.

Chronology

1807	Birth of Thomas Sutpen (C, G). Rosa lists Sutpen's age in 1833 as twenty-five, an assumption attributed to the townspeople's perception as well, which would establish his birth date as 1808, as Shreve maintains (16, 35, 275).
1817	Sutpen family moves to Tidewater, Virginia when Thomas is ten (C); according to Quentin, Sutpen was ten when his father acquired the cart used in the move (279). On the trip, Sutpen became confused about his age, so "he did not know within a year on either side just how old he was" (283). This confusion is echoed several times by Quentin (284, 286, 288, 292).
	Ellen Coldfield born October 9 (C, G, 236).[7] Mr. Compson gives her age as her late thirties in the 1850s (82).
1820	Sutpen leaves home (C). According to the Chronology, Sutpen is fourteen when he leaves, which would contradict the stated date of his birth. Both Mr. Compson and Shreve affirm this age at the point of his departure (62, 275).
1821 or 1822 (?)	Sutpen goes to school for three months one winter as "an adolescent boy of thirteen or fourteen" (300, 301, 303).
1823 (?)	Sutpen goes to sea, according to Quentin's account, which suggests that his age then had been fourteen or fifteen (299). Quentin later asserts that Sutpen had been fourteen (305).

1827   Sutpen marries Haitian wife (C, G), whose name in the Genealogy is Eulalia Bon. Quentin asserts that Sutpen had been "at least twenty years old" during the siege which resulted in his engagement (307). The siege itself develops over a matter of some eight days (315, 316, 317). Quentin establishes the period of six or seven years between Sutpen's decision at age fourteen to go to the West Indies and the siege, during which time he had learned to speak the language (307–8, 309). This period introduces a contradiction unless we assume that Sutpen spent three years between leaving home (1820) and going to sea (1823), an unlikely possibility considering the easy availability of ships in the Tidewater area.

1828   Goodhue Coldfield and family move to Jefferson (C, G); Coldfield had arrived ten years before Sutpen's engagement to Ellen (49, 58).

1831   Birth of Charles Bon in Haiti (C);[8] Bon's tombstone lists his age at death as thirty-three years and five months (239), suggesting that he had been born in early January, 1832. Shreve asserts, though, that he had been twenty-eight when he arrived at the University of Mississippi in the fall of 1859 (383, 390).

Sutpen's repudiation of his wife when he discovers her Negro blood (C, G). Sutpen tells General Compson that the crisis over Bon had occurred over thirty years after he had repudiated his first wife (330; see also 340, 345), which would suggest an earlier date. However, Shreve says that the period was twenty-eight years at the Christmas of 1859 (331), indicating the year 1831. Later, however, Shreve also apparently rounds the period off to thirty years (369, 411).

1833   Sutpen's appearance in Yoknapatawpha County on a Sunday morning in June (C, G, 9, 34, 98, 223). Three days later he gives his pistol demonstration (37). After acquiring his land he leaves for two months and returns with the architect and his slaves (39).

1833–35   Period during which the Sutpen house is built (39, 42, 43, 46, 48, 73).

1833–38   According to Rosa, the time her sister Ellen had had to watch Sutpen before their marriage (17); according to the narrator, the period during which Sutpen is "driven." General Compson computes it as until about "nine months before his son was born" (38). The townspeople in Mr. Compson's account several times remark the passage of five years between Sutpen's arrival and marriage (55, 56, 60, 61, 73).

1834   Birth of Clytie (C, G). Rosa mentions her age in September 1909 as seventy-four (169). Shreve incorrectly gives her age in 1909 as "more than eighty years" (438), which would have put her birthdate before 1829.

The architect attempts to escape and Sutpen tells Compson about his early life and Haitian experiences; Quentin says it was during the second summer of construction on the house (272).

1835–38   Period Sutpen lived in his uncompleted house (15, 44, 46, 47, 48, 56, 60). During this time he begins to invite parties of men out to witness his fights (45).

1838   Sutpen leaves for three months and returns with furnishings for his house (50).

Sutpen becomes engaged and is arrested in April (51, 58, 60, 68).

Marriage of Sutpen and Ellen Coldfield in June (C, G, 56). At the rehearsal the night before the wedding, Ellen and her aunt realize the disapproval of the townspeople (63). General Compson and his wife were "just married" at this time (64).

1839   Birth of Henry Sutpen (C, G). Shreve asserts that Henry had been born almost ten years after Charles, who had been born in 1831 (392, 394), but Shreve is probably just rounding off the number.

1841   Birth of Judith Sutpen on October 3 (C, G, 264). Shreve says Bon, born in 1831, is ten years older than Judith (400).

1845   Birth of Rosa Coldfield (C, G). Rosa's mother, "at least forty," dies in childbirth (70). Rosa and Mr. Compson list the difference between her age and Henry's as six years (21); between her age and Judith's as four years (14, 21, 70, 180). She also gives her age at the time of Bon's death in 1865 as nineteen (167, 176, 177), at her engagement to Sutpen in 1866 as twenty (18). Though Mr. Compson asserts that she was twenty when her father died in 1864, he gives the date of her birth as 1845, seven years after her sister's marriage (70) and lists her age as fifteen in the summer of 1860 when she sees Henry ride through town (88). Mr. Compson also refers to her as "a spinster doomed for life at sixteen," apparently in 1860 (91).[9]

1848 (?)	The races to the church when Rosa is three (23, 24).

According to Mr. Compson the time by which Sutpen had his plantation running smoothly (87).

1849 (?)   Rosa's first trip to Sutpen's Hundred when Judith rebels against riding to church in the phaeton. Rosa remembers being four (27); Judith's age is six when she incites the runaway, according to Rosa (26).

1850   Wash Jones moves to abandoned fishing camp at Sutpen's Hundred with his daughter (C). Shreve says that Sutpen had given permission for Jones to squat in the camp fourteen years before his involvement with Milly, dated about 1867–68 (229). He also states that the granddaughter was one year old at the time. The former date is in conflict with that listed in the Chronology, suggesting instead 1853–54 as the year Jones first moves to Sutpen's Hundred. However, the general figure of twenty years is advanced as that of the involvement between Jones and Sutpen (354, 358, 359, 360), suggesting either 1849 or 1850 as the correct year.

1853   Birth of Milly Jones (C, G); Shreve gives her age at the time Sutpen first takes an interest in her (about 1867) as fifteen (229) and as eight in 1861 when Sutpen departed (231); Quentin agrees (351).

1854 or
1855 (?)   Episode of Sutpen's fight with the slave; Rosa refers to the six years since the racing episode during which she has seen little of Sutpen (29, 30). She also says, however, that her aunt was gone by this time (29), which would suggest a later date. Mr. Compson establishes Henry's age at this point as fourteen, which would put this episode around 1853 (62).

1855   Period during which Rosa would see Sutpen on her trips to visit with her father; Mr. Compson gives her age during this period as ten (76); Henry is sixteen and Judith fourteen (78). Despite later evidence to the contrary, Mr. Compson states that Rosa's aunt had already eloped at this point (76, 77).

1858 (?)   General Compson's wife relates the story of Ellen's aunt and the wedding invitations; Mr. Compson recalls her reaction to her memory twenty years after the event (65).[10]

1859   Meeting of Henry and Charles at the University of Mississippi in September (C, 414). Mr. Compson supports the date (84). Shreve gives Bon's age at this point as twenty-eight (383) and suggests that Henry spent the three months between September and Christmas telling Bon about Judith (406–7).

According to Mr. Compson, Mr. Coldfield and Rosa stop making their annual trips to Sutpen's Hundred when Henry goes away to school (80).

Charles visits Sutpen's Hundred at Christmas and meets Judith and presumably Sutpen (C, 125, 331, 398, 399, 407, 409). Mr. Compson says they stayed two weeks (126), a period which Quentin repeats to Shreve later (334). Shreve himself, though, puts the length of Bon's stay at ten days (400, 402, 411).

(?) Rosa's aunt elopes. Rosa dates her "summer of wistaria," the summer of 1860, as in the year following her aunt's departure, which would fix the date as 1859 (181). Mr. Compson refers to the first sixteen years of Rosa's life during which she lived with her father and aunt (71), which would put the aunt's departure around 1861. However, Compson also refers to her having been gone four years when Judith and Ellen visit in the summer of 1860 (85), signalling 1856. Several references seem to suggest this earlier year (29, 76, 77), hinting that Faulkner may have changed his mind about dating this episode.

Birth of Charles Etienne St. Valery Bon (C, G, 239). Mr. Compson gives his age during the summer of 1870 as eleven (241).

1859–60   The period according to Mr. Compson during which Henry had devoted himself completely to Bon (132).

1860   Henry brings Charles to meet Rosa the day after New Year's, but she is not home (86, 181).

Shreve speculates that during this spring Bon would have realized that he loved Judith (403, 407). Shreve supposes that Bon and Judith would have written each other about every two weeks during this spring (408).

The Genealogy states that Judith became engaged to Charles Bon in 1860, though this is not confirmed by the text of the novel.

Charles visits Sutpen's Hundred in June; Mr. Compson records the length of this visit as both "about a week or so" (84) and later as two days (127, 128); Quentin and Shreve support the latter period (335, 408, 409, 410, 411, 412). Ellen begins to spread news of an engagement (95), though according to Rosa, Ellen had been planning the engagement for the six months between New Year's and June (182).

Sutpen leaves Sutpen's Hundred "on business," according to Mr. Compson (85, 127, 410), who lists the period of his absence as two weeks (127). Quentin tells Shreve he went to New Orleans (335). Mr. Compson theorizes that Bon would have learned of the visit as soon as he arrived home (113), and he asserts that probably both General Compson and Clytie knew that he had gone to New Orleans (85). Rosa mentions his absence as coinciding with a trip made by her father; she stays at Sutpen's Hundred while her father is away (181).

Ellen and Judith stop to visit Rosa on the way to Memphis to buy clothes in the summer, according to Mr. Compson (84). Compson mistakenly gives Judith's age at the time as seventeen, though she would have to be either eighteen or nineteen if she had been born in 1841.

Rosa's "summer of wistaria," during which she remembers her age to have been fourteen (178, 179), the summer after Bon's first Christmas visit and his brief stop at the end of the school term (181), the last summer before the war (186).

Shreve speculates that Bon would have waited until September to decide about returning to school (415).

Mr. Compson supposes that during the fall of 1860 Bon would have sent weekly letters to Judith at Sutpen's Hundred (130). He later asserts that there had been other letters sent by Bon "after that first Christmas" (159).

Bon's visit to Sutpen's Hundred at Christmas (130, 335–36, 415). Mr. Compson tabulates the period of Bon's visits as "three times in two years, for a total period of twelve days" (122, 125, 149).

Sutpen forbids marriage between Judith and Bon at Christmas (C).

Henry's repudiation of his birthright on Christmas Eve (C, 95, 96, 111, 130, 154, 336, 369). Mr. Compson presumes that at this point Henry discovered the nature of Sutpen's absence the previous June (129).

Departure of Henry and Bon for New Orleans at Christmas (C, 111, 131, 417, 418, 419). Mr. Compson mentions that Henry is "scarcely twenty" (112). Ellen retires to her room where she remains until her death, "two years later," according to Mr. Compson (95, 130, 156).

1860–61   Shreve speculates that during this period as the war approached, Henry had wrestled with the threat of incest posed by Bon (425, 426, 427).

1861   Bon and Henry leave New Orleans and go north during the spring, according to Mr. Compson (147).

Sutpen, Henry, and Bon depart for war (C, 97, 336, 356). Mr. Compson says that at this point Sutpen's age was nearly fifty-five (97).

Until Sutpen's departure Jones had not been allowed to approach the front of the house and for the duration gets no closer than the kitchen door, according to Shreve (229).

1861–65   The period during which Henry and Bon are not heard from; Mr. Compson calls it the probation, though several characters refer to these four years as both a period of waiting and as those occupied by the war (8, 107, 110, 111, 112, 119, 122, 123, 125, 132, 146, 147, 149, 156, 159, 160, 161, 162, 163, 164, 167, 175, 186, 200, 201, 205, 211, 307, 358, 433, 436, 437, 440, 441, 442, 443, 445, 446).

1862   Bon wounded at Pittsburg Landing, carried to the rear by Henry (154, 337). Shreve asserts that Henry, not Bon, had been wounded on the second day of the battle (430).

Sutpen voted colonel during regimental elections, dated the summer before Ellen's death by Mr. Compson (156, 237).

Rosa's aunt last heard of trying to pass Yankee lines; Mr. Compson fixes the date as two years before Mr. Coldfield's death (103).

1863   Death of Ellen Coldfield on January 23 (C, G, 136, 236).[11] Rosa suggests that Ellen's death occurred in 1862 by listing the period between it and Bon's death as three years (14). Later she fixes the period of two years between Ellen's death and Charles' murder (166, 167). According to Mr. Compson, Rosa is seventeen at the time of her sister's death (104).

1864   Death of Goodhue Coldfield (C, G, 70). Mr. Compson at one point gives four years as the period Rosa had fed Mr. Coldfield in the attic (81); later he puts the time as three years (101). Rosa herself fixes the period as "almost four years" (192). Mr. Compson also mistakes the passage of two years between the deaths of Ellen and her father (103).

Sutpen brings the tombstones to Sutpen's Hundred in the late fall (238, 337).

Sutpen visits General Compson when he brings home the tombstones and talks to him about his design (337); Quentin stresses the period of thirty years after Sutpen's first conversation with Compson (299, 307, 308, 323, 325, 327, 330). Sutpen asserts on this occasion that his design would be delayed by fifty years regardless of his decision (340), and he refers to his humiliation at the plantation door as having occurred "fifty years ago" (342). He seems generally to round off the period occupied by his design at fifty years (343), a practice followed by the other characters (347).

Retreat of Confederate troops, including Henry and Bon, across Georgia into Carolina during the winter (433).

1865   Bon's letter to Judith concluding they have waited long enough (160).

Bon and Henry spend January through March waiting for the war's end in Carolina (434, 435).

Henry's murder of Bon on May 3 (C, G, 239).

Judith's discovery of the photograph of the octoroon and child (110).

Rosa's move to Sutpen's Hundred (C). She tells Quentin that she had been nineteen at the time (167, 176, 177) and remembers the move as occurring five years after her "summer of wistaria" in 1860 (185, 186). At the beginning of chapter 3, Mr. Compson incorrectly asserts that she had moved after her father's death (70, 72), though he contradicts himself at the end of the chapter (106–7) and later (156).

Judith's delivery of Bon's letter to Mrs. Compson, one week after his burial (156).

1866   Sutpen's return from the war in January (73, 74); Rosa fixes the date as seven months after Bon's death (197, 199) and as five years after Sutpen's original departure (209), a figure Shreve echoes (224). The date is nearly two years since he had come home with the tombstones (346). Shreve mentions that Sutpen is almost sixty years old at his return (225). Mr. Compson comments that Rosa had not seen Sutpen in six years when he returns (81).

A deputation of nightriders threatens Sutpen in early March, according to Rosa (201).

Sutpen's engagement to Rosa in April (C, 17, 222) and his insult to her (C). She refers to the three months it took her to arrange for the engagement and mentions her age at the time as twenty (197, 202, 203, 206); the engagement occurs five years after Sutpen's departure for the war (209). Shreve repeats the period of three months between Sutpen's return and the engagement (347). According to Rosa, Sutpen was fifty-nine (200). She also refers to the date of Ellen's marriage as almost thirty years earlier (205). Rosa tells Quentin that she had lived "under the same roof" with Sutpen for two years (18), which would put the engagement and insult in 1868. However, she gives her age at the time as twenty, which would indicate 1865–66 (18), and she often refers to the forty-three years of her outrage in the narrative present of 1909 (3, 7, 12, 13, 17, 109, 210, 212, 218, 221; see also 437). Shreve rounds the number off to fifty years in discussing both Rosa's period of outrage and Clytie's time of despair (437, 451).

Rosa's return to Jefferson after her insult in June (C); she refers to the two months that passed between her engagement and the insult (206) and remarks that it occurred on the day Sutpen had learned how much of his land he would be able to retain (210). Shreve later fixes the period between engagement and insult as three months (226), and Quentin mistakes Sutpen's age at this time as "past sixty" (348). Rosa hints that the town did not discover that she had returned for two months (212).

1867   Sutpen's "courtship" of Milly Jones (C). Mr. Compson says that during this year Sutpen's "fat, the stomach" became prominent (98). Shreve gives Milly's age as fifteen (229). Quentin suggests that the courtship had lasted three years (352), perhaps thinking of the period between Rosa's insult in 1866 and Sutpen's death three years later (355).

Sutpen loans Wash Jones his scythe; Shreve and Quentin mention the loan as occurring two years before Sutpen's death (223, 228, 232, 358).

1868   General Compson overhears the argument in the store between Wash and Sutpen (354); Quentin tells Shreve that the scene occurred a year before Sutpen's death (355). Wash says in the episode that he is "past sixty" and Milly is fifteen (354), an age which agrees with her birthdate in the Chronology, but contradicts evidence elsewhere in the text.

1869   Birth of Milly's child, August 12 (C, 236).

Jones's murder of Sutpen, Milly, and her child on Sunday, August 12 (C, G, 232, 234, 236). Shreve remarks that Judith had worn the same expression on her face for four years, since the death of Bon, as she held the door open for Sutpen's body to be brought in (231) and that she was a woman of thirty (233), contradicting other evidence.

Death of Jones (C, G); Quentin comments that he is past sixty at the time (361).

1870   Week-long visit of Bon's mistress and Charles E. St. V. Bon to Sutpen's Hundred in summer (C, 241, 243). Charles E. St. V. Bon is eleven at the time, according to Mr. Compson (241).

Judith sells Sutpen's store (239, 241).

1871   Clytie brings Charles E. St. V. Bon from New Orleans to Sutpen's Hundred (C, 240). Mr. Compson says the trip took three weeks in December (240, 245). Charles E. St. V. Bon's age is twelve (245,

246, 251). While Clytie is away, Judith brings money for her ward's tombstone to General Compson (240).

1873   Either Clytie or Judith finds Charles E. St. V. Bon's broken mirror, two years after his arrival when he is fourteen (250).

1878 or   Judith involves General Compson when Charles E. St. V. Bon is
1879 (?)   arrested (252). Apparently in 1872, General Compson remembers seeing the boy two years before when he and his mother had visited Bon's grave; the episode of the arrest occurs eight or nine years after that visit (252). This date, however, is contradicted by Compson's assertion that Judith was forty at the time, which would set the year around 1881, when Charles E. St. V. Bon would have been twenty-two years old (252). Later Mr. Compson fixes the episode as occurring eight years after Bon's arrival, putting the date at 1879 (256).

1879   Marriage of Charles E. St. V. Bon (G).

1881   Charles E. St. V. Bon returns to Sutpen's Hundred with Negro wife (C). The return follows a year's absence, according to Mr. Compson (257), which would set the episode of Bon's arrest around 1880. However, Mr. Compson also refers to a period of about four years during which Bon visited Jefferson only three times (262), an impossibility given the date of his death.

1882   Birth of Jim Bond (C, G); listed as a year after Bon's return by Mr. Compson (257).

1884   Death of Judith Sutpen on February 12 (C, G, 239).[12] Judith's death is listed as twenty-five years before 1909 (12).[13]

        Death of Charles E. St. V. Bon (C, G, 239).

1885   General Compson sees the portfolio of Rosa's poetry (101).

1890   Birth of Shreve McCannon (G). The narrator gives Shreve's age in January 1910 as "nineteen, a few months younger than Quentin" (367), an assertion which contradicts the Genealogy.

1891   Birth of Quentin Compson (G). The text establishes that Quentin and Shreve had been born "within the same year" (322), and points out on several occasions that Quentin's age, both in September 1909 and January 1910, is twenty (7, 9, 12, 405, 463, 469).

1896   Clytie finishes paying for the tombstone for Charles E. St. V. Bon; Mr. Compson refers to the twelve years since his and Judith's deaths while she had saved the money (263); he also refers to the period of twenty-four years since Judith had commissioned the tombstone in 1871 (263).

1905   Henry returns to Sutpen's Hundred. Rosa seems certain someone has hidden in the house for four years (216), and Henry himself gives four years as the period of his residence in 1909 (438, 464, 465).

1909[14]   September, Quentin's afternoon talk with Miss Rosa, from "after two oclock" to "almost sundown" (3, 4, 7, 9; see also 452). There have been "sixty days without rain and forty-two without even dew" (109, 219–20).

Quentin's talk with his father after supper on the gallery (10, 34, 218, 227, 259, 420, 469).

Quentin and Rosa's visit to Sutpen's Hundred, where they find Henry, later in the evening following his conversation with his father (C, 218, 219, 221).

Quentin informs his father of revelations concerning the Sutpen story the day after his visit with Rosa to Sutpen's Hundred (227, 332). Shreve comments that Mr. Compson had waited forty-five years—the period since Sutpen's conversation with General Compson—to discover anything new about the family tragedy (332).

Rosa's attempt to fetch Henry to town in December, three months after her visit with Quentin (C, 465, 466, 468).

Clytie sets fire to the Sutpen house in December (C).

Death of Henry Sutpen in December (G).

Death of Clytie in December (G).

1909–10   Quentin Compson attends Harvard (G).

1909–14   Shrevlin McCannon attends Harvard (G).

1910   Death of Rosa Coldfield in January (G).

Mr. Compson's letter to Quentin, dated January 10, 1910, suggests January 8 as the date of Rosa Coldfield's death and January 9 as the date of her burial (217). Compson announces that she had lain in a coma "almost two weeks" (217).

Quentin and Shreve's attempt to reconstruct the Sutpen story in January; described as five months after the September talk with Mr. Compson (34; see also 419). At another point the narrator establishes the date through references to the years of the Civil War (431, 438, 439). Several comments in the final three chapters detail the period of time covered by the conversation: the first, in the middle of chapter 7, suggests that the time is shortly before eleven as Quentin describes the capture of the architect (318), though the roommates have obviously been talking a good while at this point; some time after eleven Quentin describes Sutpen's return to the war in 1864 (343); chapter 8 begins just before midnight (366); the midnight chimes ring during Shreve's analysis of "the old Sabine" (379); during Shreve's attempt to demonstrate love in the Bon-Judith relationship, we are told that the midnight chimes "would have rung some time ago" (405); the one o'clock chimes ring while Quentin reconstructs the fire at the Sutpen mansion (465, 466).

Disappearance of Jim Bond (G).

Death of Quentin Compson (G).

1914–18   Shreve's service in the Royal Army Medical Corps (G).

Notes

Introduction

1. Elisabeth Muhlenfeld, Introduction, *William Faulkner's Absalom, Absalom!: A Critical Casebook* (New York: Garland, 1984), p. xv.

2. James B. Meriwether, *The Literary Career of William Faulkner*, Authorized Reissue (Columbia: University of South Carolina Press, 1971), p. 172.

3. Of these, only "Mistral," included in *These Thirteen* (1931), had been published. The others are included in *Uncollected Stories*. For a discussion of the "Don-and-I stories," see Estella Schoenberg, *Old Tales and Talking* (Jackson: University Press of Mississippi, 1977), pp. 20–23. Schoenberg discusses "Evangeline" on pp. 30–48.

4. Muhlenfeld, p. xxiv.

5. Brenda G. Cornell in an article entitled "Faulkner's 'Evangeline': A Preliminary Stage" (*Southern Quarterly*, 22 [Summer 1984]), examines the relationship between the story and the novel. She recognizes the story's structural sophistication, with "its consistent rhythmic sectional pattern of exposition, climax, and denouement during sectional transitions. Within each of these seven parts, there is a building of tension to climax . . . followed immediately by a tension release, signaled by some spatial movement . . . , light-dark contrast, or natural physical release, such as the shift from the image of the burning house at the end of Section VI to that of the pre-dawn rain at the beginning of Section VII" (p. 25). John Pilkington's *The Heart of Yoknapatawpha* (Jackson: University Press of Mississippi, 1981) also discusses parallels between "Evangeline" and the novel (pp. 162–66).

6. Joseph Blotner, *Faulkner: A Biography*, 2 vols. (New York: Random House, 1974), p. 819. Neil D. Isaacs' "Götterdämmerung in Yoknapatawpha" (*Tennessee Studies in Literature*, 8 [1963]: 47–53) offers a valuable critical examination of "Wash" from the point of view of the archetypes it incorporates.

7. Malcolm Cowley, *The Faulkner-Cowley File: Letters and Memories, 1944–1962* (New York: Viking, 1966), p. 26.

8. Blotner, pp. 822–25.

9. Muhlenfeld, p. xviii.

10. Blotner, p. 828.

11. Louis Daniel Brodsky, "The Textual Development of William Faulkner's 'Wash': An Examination of Manuscripts in the Brodsky Collection," *Studies in Bibliography*, 37 (1984): 250.

12. Ibid., pp. 250–51.

13. I am indebted to Professor James B. Meriwether, who suggested this idea to me. Meriwether theorizes that Faulkner may have planned to use "Evangeline" as the basis for an expanded work as early as the year of its composition. His sending schedule indicates that he submitted the story only to the *Post* and to *Woman's Home Companion*, both of which rejected it in July of 1931 (*Literary Career*, p. 172). He continued to submit his other stories until he placed them or decided to use them in another context, as was the case with "This Kind of Courage." The limited number of submissions of "Evangeline" perhaps indicates that as early as the summer of 1931 Faulkner may have had other plans for it.

14. See "An Introduction for *The Sound and the Fury*," ed. James B. Meriwether, *Southern Review*, 8 (Autumn 1972): 705–10 and "An Introduction to *The Sound and the Fury*," *Mississippi Quarterly*, 26 (Summer 1973): 410–15.

15. Blotner, pp. 810–13.

16. Ibid., pp. 820–21.

17. Quoted by Blotner, p. 960. Professor Meriwether pointed out to me the possible relevance of Faulkner's close acquaintance with the *published* text of the novel.

18. David Minter has suggested the possible connection between Faulkner's work on the introductions for *The Sound and the Fury* and the composition of *Absalom, Absalom!* in *William Faulkner: His Life and Work* (Baltimore: Johns Hopkins University Press, 1980), p. 157.

19. Blotner, pp. 884–85.

20. Ibid., p. 828; see also Muhlenfeld, who quotes liberally from the manuscript drafts, pp. xviii-xx.

21. Quoted by Muhlenfeld, p. xx.

22. Blotner, pp. 828–29; Muhlenfeld also quotes from the description of the room in this fragment.

23. Muhlenfeld, p. xxi.

24. Blotner, p. 829; see also Muhlenfeld, p. xxi.

25. Ibid., p. 841.

26. Ibid., pp. 851–53.

27. Several critics have commented on the relevance of the title. Lennart Björk notes the implied irony in "Ancient Myths and Moral Framework of Faulkner's *Absalom, Absalom!*" (*American Literature*, 35 [May 1963]: 196–204). Lynn Gartrell Levins concludes that none of the Old Testament parallels is "clear cut" in *Faulkner's Heroic Design* (Athens: University of Georgia Press, 1976), pp. 37–38. John T. Irwin's *Doubling and Incest, Repetition and Revenge* (Baltimore: Johns Hopkins University Press, 1975) suggests that Faulkner uses the allusion to question the morality of a society which had both tolerated and justified slavery in terms of the Bible (pp. 148–51). In "What is Gothic about *Absalom, Absalom!*" Max Putzel relates the allusion to David's anguish to the passage in *Macbeth* which gives Faulkner the title of *The Sound and the Fury*: "In each case the hero's soliloquy summarizes the despair that comes over him as his ambitious career passes in review before his eyes and he sees himself diminished by the punishment it has invited" (*Southern Literary Journal*, 4 [Fall 1971]: 5). By far the most comprehensive examinations of the meaning of the title of *Absalom* are John V. Hagopian's "The Biblical Background of Faulkner's *Absalom, Absalom!*" (*The CEA Critic*, 36 [January 1974]: 22–24) and Stephen M. Ross's "Faulkner's *Absalom, Absalom!* and the David Story: A Specula-

tive Contemplation" in *The David Myth in Western Literature*, ed. Raymond-Jean Frontain and Jan Wojcik (West Lafayette, Indiana: Purdue University Press, 1980, pp. 136–53). Ross emphasizes that an easy correspondence cannot be found and that Faulkner intends his title to allude to the entire career of the ancient king, not just to his relationship with his son Absalom.

28. Blotner, pp. 858–60.

29. Ibid., p. 873.

30. Ibid., p. 877.

31. Ibid., pp. 882–84.

32. Ibid., pp. 885–87.

33. See the transcription of the manuscript in Gerald Langford's *Faulkner's Revision of Absalom, Absalom!* (Austin: University of Texas Press, 1971), p. 43.

34. *The Achievement of William Faulkner* (New York: Random House, 1966), p. 150. Noel Polk adds more details, including that "the first half of the manuscript shows that Faulkner shifted many page groupings many times" in his "The Manuscript of *Absalom, Absalom!*" (*Mississippi Quarterly*, 25 [Summer 1972]: 363).

35. Blotner, pp. 896–900.

36. Ibid., pp. 900–904.

37. See Langford, p. 150.

38. Blotner, p. 909.

39. Ibid., p. 917.

40. Ibid., p. 920.

41. Meta Carpenter Wilde reveals in her memoir of their relationship, *A Loving Gentleman*, written with Orin Borsten (New York: Simon and Schuster, 1976), that Faulkner never discussed the novel he was working on at the time. That he was able to make such steady progress on the novel while beginning a serious love affair is testimony to the powers of concentration Faulkner could summon.

42. See Langford, p. 362.

43. Blotner, p. 930.

44. Ibid., p. 934.

45. One of the sheets of typescript is a version of the novel's last page and bears the date April 8, 1935, suggesting that Faulkner had completed the typescript on that date, though further changes required some retyping. I am grateful to Professor Meriwether for allowing me to examine these documents in his collection.

46. The manuscript chronology is reproduced in *William Faulkner's Manuscripts 13: Absalom, Absalom!*, pp. 485–86.

47. See *The Making of William Faulkner's Books, 1929–1937: An Interview with Evelyn Harter Glick* (Columbia, S.C.: Southern Studies Program, University of South Carolina, 1979) for a discussion of the materials appended to *Absalom, Absalom!* (p. 47).

48. Blotner, p. 891.

49. Muhlenfeld suspects that Faulkner "almost certainly worked out [the chronology] after he had finished typing the novel" (p. xxxii). Support for this idea may be found in the typescript setting copy, which has several alterations of dates and periods of time apparently made by Faulkner himself.

50. Ibid., p. xxxi.

51. Ibid., p. xxxi. Both the manuscript and published chronologies specify that Sutpen had repudiated his first wife when he discovered her taint of Negro blood (TS, 485).

52. Millgate, p. 151.

53. Blotner, pp. 928–29.

54. Polk, p. 361. Polk points out that the extent of editorial tampering with *Absalom, Absalom!* was much greater than suggested by Millgate: "it is in fact the most heavily and worst-edited of any of the Faulkner typescripts with which I am familiar, excluding 'Flags in the Dust.' My own collation of the setting copy with the published book reveals some 1400 variants, the vast majority of which are identifiably editorial in origin . . . " (p. 361).

55. Muhlenfeld, p. xxxii.

56. Blotner, pp. 936, 941.

57. Millgate, p. 151.

58. Blotner, pp. 945–46.

59. Muhlenfeld, p. xxxiii.

60. *Count No 'Count* (Jackson: University Press of Mississippi, 1983), p. 131.

61. Blotner, p. 927.

62. Joseph Blotner, *Faulkner: A Biography*, One-Volume Edition (New York: Random House, 1984), p. 411.

63. William Faulkner, "Upon Receiving the Nobel Prize for Literature," *Essays, Speeches and Public Letters*, ed. James B. Meriwether (New York: Random House, 1965), p. 120. In 1938 Faulkner sent a letter to the president of the League of American Writers making his position regarding the Spanish Civil War clear: "I most sincerely wish to go on the record as being unalterably opposed to Franco and fascism, to all violations of the legal government and outrages against the people of Republican Spain" (*Essays, Speeches and Public Letters*, p. 198).

64. Since Walter Sullivan's "The Tragic Design of *Absalom, Absalom!*" (*South Atlantic Quarterly*, 50 [October 1951]: 552–66) and Richard B. Sewall's chapter on the novel in his book *The Vision of Tragedy* (New Haven: Yale University Press, 1959, pp. 133–47), numerous critics have discussed the novel as an outstanding example of modern tragedy and have examined Sutpen as a tragic hero.

65. Richard Poirier, "'Strange Gods' in Jefferson, Mississippi: Analysis of *Absalom, Absalom!*," *William Faulkner: Two Decades of Criticism*, eds. Frederick J. Hoffman and Olga W. Vickery (East Lansing: Michigan State College Press, 1951); rpt. *William Faulkner's Absalom, Absalom!: A Critical Casebook*, ed. Elisabeth Muhlenfeld (New York: Garland, 1984), p. 3.

66. Bernard DeVoto first noted the relationship in his review "Witchcraft in Mississippi" (*Saturday Review of Literature*, 15 [October 31, 1936]: 3), and he has been followed by several others. A. C. Hoffman acknowledged but did not explore the connections in a note ("Faulkner's *Absalom,*

Absalom!," *Explicator*, 10 [November 1951], Item 12). He was followed by Olga Vickery in *The Novels of William Faulkner: A Critical Interpretation* (Baton Rouge: Louisiana State University Press, 1959; rev. ed., 1964, pp. 92, 101). Robert M. Slabey in "Faulkner's 'Waste Land': Vision in *Absalom, Absalom*" (*Mississippi Quarterly*, 14 [Summer 1961]) suggests that the novel "helps to explain why [Quentin] kills himself" (p. 155). The interrelationship between the two novels was also recognized by Duncan Aswell in "The Puzzling Design of *Absalom, Absalom!*" (*Kenyon Review*, 30 [Issue 1, 1968]: 67–84) and by M. E. Bradford in "Brother, Son, and Heir: The Structural Focus of Faulkner's *Absalom, Absalom*" (*Sewanee Review*, 78 [Winter 1970]: 76–98). In "Narration as Creative Act: The Role of Quentin Compson in *Absalom, Absalom!*" (in *Faulkner, Modernism and Film*, eds. Evans Harrington and Ann J. Abadie [Jackson: University Press of Mississippi, 1979], pp. 82–102), Thomas Daniel Young argues that Quentin's experience in *The Sound and the Fury* affects is narration in *Absalom*, a point repeated by John Pilkington (pp. 181–84) and David Minter (p. 158). André Bleikasten uses a slightly different approach in "Fathers in Faulkner" (*The Fictional Father: Lacanian Readings of the Text*, ed. Robert Con Davis [Amherst: University of Massachusetts Press, 1981]). He suggests that the relationship between the two novels is part of a larger pattern: "One may choose to consider Faulkner's novels as discrete, autonomous units; it is no less legitimate to read them as so many fragments of a single text, each novel functioning as a supplement to the previous ones and requiring in turn the supplementarity of its followers—not to be made whole, but to allow the process of completion to continue" (p. 137).

67. Joseph W. Reed, Jr., "*Absalom, Absalom!*," *Faulkner's Narrative* (New Haven: Yale University Press, 1973), p. 168. Reed's position is echoed by several critics, including Melvin Backman in *Faulkner: The Major Years* (Bloomington: Indiana University Press, 1966, p. 88); R. Scott Kellner in "A Reconsideration of Character: Relationships in *Absalom, Absalom!*" (*Notes on Mississippi Writers*, 7 [Fall 1974]: 40); Warren Beck in *Faulkner: Essays* (Madison: University of Wisconsin Press, 1976, pp. 289, 299); John V. Hagopian in "Black Insight in *Absalom, Absalom!*" (*Faulkner Studies*, 1 [1980]: 31–32); John W. Hunt in "The Disappearance of Quentin Compson" (in *Critical Essays on William Faulkner: The Compson Family*, ed. Arthur F. Kinney [Boston: G. K. Hall, 1982], p. 375); and Carl E. Rollyson, Jr. in *Uses of the Past in the Novels of William Faulkner* (Ann Arbor, Michigan: UMI Research Press, 1984), pp. 79–80).

68. Irwin, pp. 25–28.

69. Schoenberg, pp. 7–15. Irwin suggests that Quentin's telling of the Sutpen story is a repetition of the events of August 1909, including his discovery of Caddy's sexual relationship with Dalton Ames and his futile attempt to make Ames leave town (p. 74).

70. In *The Fragile Thread: The Meaning of Form in Faulkner's Novels* (Amherst: University of Massachusetts Press, 1979), Donald M. Kartiganer suggests that Mr. Compson, even more than Quentin, remains the same character from *The Sound and the Fury* to *Absalom, Absalom!*; his cynical pessimism is transferred intact (pp. 78–79).

71. Schoenberg suggests quite plausibly that the title of the novel points to the relationship between Mr. Compson and his son, for whom he will have reason to mourn as David mourns the loss of Absalom (pp. 48–49).

Chapter 1

1. John T. Matthews, "The Marriage of Speaking and Hearing in *Absalom, Absalom!*," *Journal of English Literary History*, 47 (1980): 584–85.

2. Hugh M. Ruppersburg, *Voice and Eye in Faulkner's Fiction* (Athens: University of Georgia Press, 1983), p. 86. Ruppersburg's book contains the most perceptive survey of the shifting

narrative viewpoints in the novel, as well as suggesting useful terms for discussion of narrative difficulties in Faulkner generally. James H. Matlack in "The Voices of Time: Narrative Structure in *Absalom, Absalom*" (*Southern Review*, 15 [June 1979]: 333–54) briefly outlines the shifts in point of view in the novel's first five chapters, though he only hints about the narrative complications of the last four.

3. Virginia V. Hlavsa suggests that hints about the plot in chapter 1 leave one with the feeling that "he knows the story in essence before he knows it in substance" ("The Vision of the Advocate in *Absalom, Absalom!*," *Novel*, 3 [Fall 1974]: 54).

4. John T. Irwin has noticed the similarities between Rosa and Quentin: "They are both virgins and have refused incest, Quentin with his sister, Rosa with her brother-in-law. They are both obsessed by their frustrated desire, and that frustration has turned desire into hatred. In *The Sound and the Fury* Quentin is portrayed as psychologically impotent, while at the very start of *Absalom* Rosa is described sitting in her parlor with an 'air of impotent and static rage' directed against Sutpen, 'the long-dead object of her impotent yet indomitable frustration'" (p. 75).

5. Miss Rosa's comment may carry considerable autobiographical significance for Faulkner. At the time of his writing the novel, the author was frequently in financial need; Joseph Blotner records that often that need was exacerbated by Estelle Faulkner: " . . . there were times when she would buy clothes, spending money they did not have, money her seething husband would have to try to earn with more potboiler stories" (*Faulkner: A Biography*, One-Volume edition, p. 359). Meta Carpenter Wilde recalls a letter which more closely parallels Miss Rosa's prophecy for Quentin: "An earlier letter had hinted of 'uproar' at home. Now [Faulkner] began to confide more about his difficulties with Estelle. He had discovered that in spite of his warnings to local merchants, she had managed to charge up to about a thousand dollars during his absence [in Hollywood]. Among the items were some over-stuffed pieces of furniture and a radio" (*A Loving Gentleman*, p. 103). Wilde quotes Faulkner as having taken " 'a certain amount of sadistic pleasure in ejecting from the house pneumatic divans and Cab Calloways and so forth' " (p. 103).

6. Schoenberg, pp. 8–10.

7. Quentin's difficulty picturing the members of the Sutpen family introduces an important motif in the novel: various characters are pictured as without substance, as mere ghosts. The most obvious example is Rosa's view of Sutpen and of Bon in her monologue, though the same difficulty seems to plague Mr. Compson and the Harvard narrators.

8. Quentin's emphasis on Miss Rosa's voice recalls that Marlow thinks of Kurtz as a voice in *Heart of Darkness*, a novel exhibiting several affinities with *Absalom, Absalom!*.

9. Miss Rosa's interest in the concept of the gentleman would have a particular relevance of which she is unaware to Quentin, whose conversation with his father at the end of section two of *The Sound and the Fury* turns in part upon Mr. Compson's definition of gentlemanly behavior: "no Compson ever disappointed a lady" (*TSTF*, 219–22). Presumably that conversation would have taken place only a matter of weeks before Quentin is summoned by Miss Rosa. Shreve comments on the day of Quentin's suicide that he is glad not to be a gentleman, perhaps alluding to Quentin's concern with the concept and sparking Quentin's memory of another conversation with his father on the subject of gentlemanly standards (*TSTF*, 125–26). At another point Quentin recalls, "*Father said it used to be a gentleman was known by his books; nowadays he is known by the ones he has not returned*" (*TSTF*, 99).

10. John Hagan, "Déjà Vu and the Effect of Timelessness in Faulkner's *Absalom, Absalom!*," *Bucknell Review*, 11 (March 1963): 35–36.

Chapter 2

1. The picture of Quentin listening to his father talk also recalls the opening section of "A Justice," in which the young Quentin chooses not to go fishing in the creek with Caddy and Jason, but instead listens to Sam Fathers "tell me about the old days" (*Collected Stories* [New York: Random House, 1950, p. 344). The story was written in 1931 (Meriwether, *Literary Career*, p. 173).

2. Blotner, *Faulkner: A Biography*, One-Volume Edition, pp. 209, 213.

3. Ruppersburg in *Voice and Eye in Faulkner's Fiction* describes the narrator in some detail: "The external narrator, not a character, ranges freely between past and present, summarizing and describing what the characters themselves cannot; his objectivity counterbalances the subjective perspectives of the characters. Though not part of the story . . . he witnesses all of it. His function is rarely apparent on the surface, primarily because the more personable character narrators overshadow him. He also is not omniscient . . . . But his ability to travel in time and space, his detailed descriptions, and his one sustained external narrative . . . suggest that he occupies a better position to 'know' about events than any of the characters" (pp. 95–96).

4. In "What Happens in *Absalom, Absalom!*" Floyd C. Watkins explains that many of the conflicting details between the versions of the Sutpen story "may be plants by the author to suggest the unreliability of his narrators, who have little real information and who wish to probe the Sutpen family for the smallest facts and the deepest motives" (*Modern Fiction Studies*, 13 [Spring 1967]; rpt. *William Faulkner's Absalom, Absalom!: A Critical Casebook*, ed. Elisabeth Muhlenfeld [New York: Garland, 1984], p. 57).

5. *A Glossary of Faulkner's South* (New Haven: Yale University Press, 1976), p. 40. Professor Meriwether has suggested to me that Sutpen's facility with his pistols provides a clue to the method by which he acquires the capital to get his new start after leaving Haiti. Sutpen's source of funds is also a matter of much speculation among the members of the community.

6. Ruppersburg, p. 89.

7. Donald M. Kartiganer relates Sutpen's fighting with his slaves to his mountain training: he explains to General Compson that in his youth "everybody had just what he was strong enough or energetic enough to take and keep" (221). His physical domination over his slaves demonstrates his strength and energy ("Faulkner's *Absalom, Absalom!*: The Discovery of Values," *American Literature*, 37 [November 1965]: 296).

8. The reference to Sutpen's breeding is one of the early hints of the class conflict which will climax in Sutpen's clash with Wash Jones in chapter 7. It also explains one reason why Sutpen would have chosen General Compson for a friend, since Compson was a representative of the class to which Sutpen aspired.

9. *Faulkner's Narrative*, p. 163.

10. A marginal note by an editor on page 59 of the typescript setting copy reads: "I think you belabor the question of big or little wedding too much. Can't you cut some of it" (*TS*, 76). One of the cancelled passages on the following page contains the explanation: "I don't get this." A later annotation reads: "Same here" (*TS*, 77). Such editorial questions and tampering show an almost complete lack of understanding of Faulkner's purpose and of his methods.

Chapter 3

1. The manuscript punctuates this chapter in a more conventional way, like the preceding one (see Langford, pp. 23, 87).

2. Of course, the chronology makes it impossible that Mr. Compson is thinking of this scene specifically in *Absalom, Absalom!*, since it occurs in the spring of 1910. The resonances between the two passages, however, are unmistakable.

3. In *The Sound and the Fury* Jason at least sees Mr. Compson's drinking as a sort of suicide, comparable in degree if not in efficiency to Mr. Coldfield's denying himself food for the three days before his death.

4. Critics employing a psychoanalytic approach might suggest that Faulkner's declining to mention Caddy directly merely underscores her presence as an example of Quentin's repression of his memory of her; this seems to be too easy an answer.

5. Walter Brylowski in *Faulkner's Olympian Laugh* (Detroit: Wayne State University Press, 1968) explores the novel's classical allusions in some detail. Mr. Compson's fondness of them has led several critics to explain how he forces the Sutpen story into a pattern resembling classical tragedy. See for instance Lynn Gartrell Levins's analysis in *Faulkner's Heroic Design*.

6. On the basis of the unique punctuation of the chapter, John C. Hodgson argues that it occurs after Quentin's trip to Sutpen's Hundred and his explanation of Bon's identity ("'Logical Sequence and Continuity': Some Observations on the Typographical and Structural Consistency of *Absalom, Absalom!*," *American Literature*, 43 [March 1971]: 97–107). Mr. Compson would then know that Bon had been Sutpen's first son. Cleanth Brooks refutes this idea in *William Faulkner: Toward Yoknapatawpha and Beyond* (New Haven: Yale University Press, 1978), p. 326.

7. Brooks, p. 326.

8. Donald M. Kartiganer remarks that Ellen's attitude toward Bon mirrors Sutpen's manipulation of people he uses only to further his design ("Faulkner's *Absalom, Absalom!*: The Discovery of Values," p. 299). This interpretation supports Rosa's view that Sutpen had corrupted Ellen.

9. In the novel the name is incorrectly spelled Sumpter (p. 95).

10. Langford, p. 110.

11. Michael Millgate first called attention to this revision (*The Achievement of William Faulkner*, p. 150).

Chapter 4

1. *The Fragile Thread*, p. 82.

2. "'We Have Waited Long Enough': Judith Sutpen and Charles Bon," *Southern Review*, 14 (January 1978): 72.

3. The hint of a homosexual interest between Henry and Bon (and later between Quentin and Shreve) was first noted by Irwin (p. 72). More recently, the issue has been explored in Don Merrick Liles's "William Faulkner's *Absalom, Absalom!*: An Exegesis of the Homoerotic Configurations in the Novel" (*Journal of Homosexuality*, 8 [1983]: 99–111), which demonstrates that the possibility of a homosexual attraction would explain a great deal of what Compson finds puzzling in Henry and Bon's behavior.

4. Professor Meriwether has suggested to me the possibility that just as Quentin's confused sexual identity may be reflected in his and Shreve's hints of a homosexual interest between Henry and Bon in chapter 8, so perhaps Mr. Compson's initial suggestion of the idea in chapter 4 may reflect Compson's own sexual insecurities. Another explanation is that he senses Quentin's sexual confusion, possibly resulting from latent homosexuality and an incestuous attraction to his sister Caddy. The tragedy of Bon-Henry-Judith then becomes a lesson which Mr. Compson perhaps wishes Quentin to see as vitally related to his own situation.

5. Faulkner inconsistently altered the period Bon could have courted Judith from seventeen to twelve days in the typescript setting copy. Seventeen would seem to be a more defensible number, given Mr. Compson's assertion that that first Christmas (1859) Bon had spent two weeks visiting with Henry and that at the end of the term (June 1860), Bon had visited for two days before returning to New Orleans, where Sutpen had already gone to "investigate" him. The total would be sixteen days, to which could be added the day of Bon and Henry's departure, Chistmas Eve, 1860, for a total of seventeen. His reason for the change may have been that Faulkner wished to make even more remarkable the fact that a lasting commitment had been born between the two in such a short period of time.

6. Lyle Saxon, whom Faulkner knew in New Orleans in the 1920s and with whom he stayed briefly in New York in 1928 (Blotner, *Faulkner*, One-Volume ed., p. 222) described the octoroon mistresses in very similar terms in his book *Fabulous New Orleans* (New York: D. Appleton-Century Co., 1928): "Now it must not be assumed that these women were prostitutes—they were not. They were reared in chastity, and they were as well educated as the times would permit. These were for the greater part the illegitimate daughters of white men and their quadroon mistresses. They were 'free women'—not slaves. Their chastity was their chief stock in trade, in addition to their beauty. Their mothers watched them as hawks watch chickens, accompanied them to the balls where only white men were admitted, and did not relinquish their chaperonage until the daughter found a suitable 'protector.' The protector was usually a young Creole gentleman with enough money to support the quadroon girl in fitting style. The 'little houses along the ramparts' were not houses of ill-fame, but domiciles of these women and the white men who 'protected' them. And the women were proverbially faithful, just as the young white girls of the colony were proverbially innocent. For the quadroon girl's future depended upon pleasing the man with whom she lived. Sometimes the liaisons lasted for years—occasionally for life. But more often than not they were broken off when the young man married" (p. 181).

7. Mr. Compson may again be drawing upon personal experience here. In *The Sound and the Fury* Mrs. Compson maintains that Jason alone has inherited the traits of her family, the Bascombs (pp. 126–27). According to her, the other children are all Compson.

8. The Sutpen code of taking what it is strong enough to hold and keep looks forward to the delineation of the code Sutpen had learned in his mountain childhood in chapter 7. Here Mr. Compson reflects ideas learned from his father, as Quentin will echo both father and grandfather when he becomes the source of narration of Sutpen's early life.

9. Once again, Mr. Compson is perhaps indicating the relative involvement of the women in his own family. Given the personalities of his wife Caroline and of Caddy, it seems only natural he would assume that Judith would not be informed of the nature of the rift between father and son.

10. It is difficult to judge the reliability of Mrs. Compson as a witness, since little about her is known in *Absalom*. She has a slightly more prominent role in *The Unvanquished* (New York: Random House, 1938), especially in the chapter "Skirmish at Sartoris." The original version of that chapter, "Drusilla," was written in the fall of 1934, just before completion of the typescript of

Pylon, after which Faulkner would again turn his attention to *Absalom, Absalom!* (see *USWF*, 683). In this story, Mrs. Compson, though considerably older than the character in *Absalom* (she is of Granny's generation), is clearly aligned with the conservative forces of the community represented by the women outraged by Drusilla's unconventional relationship with John Sartoris.

11. Judith's action looks forward to Cecelia Farmer's attempt to make a lasting mark by scratching her name on a pane of glass in *Requiem for a Nun* (New York: Random House, 1951, p. 229). Faulkner interprets her action as announcing " '*Listen, stranger; this was myself: this was I* ' " (p. 262).

12. "The Evocation of Voice in *Absalom, Absalom!*," *Essays in Literature*, 8 (Fall 1981): 136.

13. " 'We Have Waited Long Enough': Judith Sutpen and Charles Bon," pp. 74–75.

Chapter 5

1. Ruppersburg, p. 86.

2. Schoenberg, p. 145.

3. *Faulkner's Narrative*, p. 160.

4. In "Meaning Called to Life: Alogical Structure in *Absalom, Absalom!*," (*Southern Humanities Review*, 5 [Winter 1971]: 9–23), J. R. Raper links techniques in Rosa's speech to film techniques Faulkner may have learned in Hollywood. Rosa's drawing out over a long period the events of a few minutes is similar to the slow-motion device, and the whole novel's frequent use of juxtaposition of scenes is related to cinematic montage.

5. *William Faulkner: Toward Yoknapatawpha and Beyond*, p. 357.

6. Thadious M. Davis explains Rosa's view of Clytie in this scene: "Begrudgingly, Rosa recognizes her own inadequacies, Clytie's essential harmony with her world and, to a degree, their psychological union. But she does so by making Clytie the personification of all that has prevented her full participation in life. Clytie is . . . the visible proof of Sutpen's sexual activity with someone other than 'wife.' As such, Clytie is the lasting insult to the virgin spinster of Sutpen's denial of her" ("The Yoking of 'Abstract Contradictions': Clytie's Meaning in *Absalom, Absalom!*," *Studies in American Fiction*, 7 [Autumn 1979]: 216).

7. Cleanth Brooks remarks: "The essential metaphor is that which identifies a man with his house. . . . Sutpen's mansion, which he has wrested from the swamp almost as if by supernatural power, has a special relation to him, seems to be an extension of him, and since, in Miss Rosa's eyes, he is a demon, it reveals itself as the fit abode for a demon, a kind of metallic inferno, impervious to fire" (*William Faulkner: Toward Yoknapatawpha and Beyond*, pp. 357–58).

8. Ibid., p. 359.

9. "The Marriage of Speaking and Hearing in *Absalom, Absalom!*," pp. 580–83.

10. Critics of *Absalom, Absalom!* have overlooked the fact that Mr. Coldfield is absent from home on the occasion when Sutpen goes to New Orleans to investigate Bon. Given the structure of Mr. Coldfield's life as described by both Rosa and Mr. Compson, it seems unlikely that he would often have business which calls him away from Jefferson for extended periods. Could Sutpen have again involved him at this point, elicited his aid in attempting to head off disaster? If Mr. Coldfield had learned something about the man courting his granddaughter this summer, it could have at least contributed to his bizarre retreat into his attic during the final years of his life.

11. *The Complete Poems of Emily Dickinson*, ed. Thomas H. Johnson (Boston: Little, Brown and Co., 1951), p. 35.

12. Rosa's concern with Bon's death and burial leads Virginia V. Hlavsa to remark that the "abiding theme of her narration . . . is death, pounded home with murder, slayings, crucifixions, bodies, corpses, coffins, burials, graves, skulls, dust, and immortality" ("The Vision of the Advocate in *Absalom, Absalom!*," p. 62).

13. The cry McCaslin makes, *"Yaaaay, Forrest! Yaaaay, John Sartoris! Yaaaaaay!"* recalls the ending to "Skirmish at Sartoris" (see *USWF*, 73). Though Rosa does not remark Judith's reaction, she must have found this unorthodox cry terribly jarring under the circumstances, perhaps suggesting the opposition of the feminine manifestation of grief and decorum as opposed to the male concern with war and glory, concepts rather foreign and unimportant to Judith, as her comments to Mrs. Compson at the end of chapter 4 indicate.

14. Compare Miss Rosa's earlier comment, ". . . *surely there is something in madness, even the demoniac, which Satan flees, aghast at his own handiwork . . .* " (208).

15. According to Gerald Langford this conversation appears in quotation marks in the manuscript (see Langford, p. 178).

16. Cleanth Brooks has pointed out the dubious attribution of the passage: "This is a scene which Miss Rosa could not have personally witnessed; and though she may, nevertheless, have been capable of giving a detailed account of it, the reader does not hear her do so anywhere in chapter V. . . . Perhaps she had given Quentin an account of the murder and Henry's bursting into Judith's room at some time before her monologue suddenly resumes on page 134; but one should note the consequences of this reasonable deduction. If it was the scene of Henry's confrontation with Judith which so arrested Quentin's attention that he couldn't 'listen' to Miss Rosa, then, if we take the author's statement literally, Quentin didn't listen to *anything* that was said in chapter V" (*William Faulkner: Toward Yoknapatawpha and Beyond*, p. 307).

17. Ibid., pp. 303–4.

Chapter 6

1. Ruppersburg, p. 120.

2. *William Faulkner: The Yoknapatawpha Country*, p. 310.

3. Marvin K. Singleton in an article entitled "Personae at Law and in Equity: The Unity of Faulkner's *Absalom, Absalom!*" (*Papers on English Language and Literature*, 3 [Fall 1967]) explains that the name Shreve evokes *shrieve* or *shire-reeve*, "old terms for sheriff" which are appropriate to his judgmental role in the novel (p. 365). The name is also related to the even more relevant verb *shrive*, meaning to hear one's confession.

4. *William Faulkner: The Yoknapatawpha Country*, p. 313.

5. Another factor contributing to Shreve's lack of understanding of Quentin's involvement is the probability that Quentin has told him nothing about his relationship with Caddy as outlined in *The Sound and the Fury*.

6. See Langford, pp. 179–228.

7. The reference to what Quentin learned on his trip with Rosa to Sutpen's Hundred is also missing from the manuscript version. Faulkner apparently added it as a means of further heightening suspense (see Langford, p. 190).

8. Ruppersburg states, "The participle 'thinking' establishes the italicized narrative's source as Quentin's mind" (p. 119). However, the original source of this material must be Shreve, since Quentin responds "Yes" at the top of page 232. This passage is, then, another example of translated narrative similar to Rosa's in chapter 5.

9. The emphasis on class conflict is in part a carryover from Faulkner's incorporation of "Wash," which had begun as a Snopes story, into *Absalom, Absalom!*.

10. Having Luster present in this scene is a chronological inconsistency with *The Sound and the Fury*, in which Luster, a young black of about fourteen, is Benjy's attendant during the present time of 1928. Clearly, he would have had to have been born after Quentin's death in 1910, and therefore could not have been attending the horses for a hunt which occurred probably in the fall of 1907 or 1908. T.P., Benjy's companion during the scenes of Caddy's wedding, which occurred in April 1910, would be a choice more consistent with the chronology. In the typescript setting copy, the typed name Dan appeared originally; Faulkner then cancelled this name and substituted Luster (*TS*, 248). The name Dan is not used for any of the servants in *The Sound and the Fury*; perhaps Faulkner wanted to draw yet another link to the earlier novel and merely got the names confused.

11. *William Faulkner: Toward Yoknapatawpha and Beyond*, p. 304.

12. Elisabeth Muhlenfeld finds this fact significant: "Judith commits herself *before* he arrives to the life-long care of her dead fiance's son, knowing he is a Negro" ("'We Have Waited Long Enough': Judith Sutpen and Charles Bon," p. 78).

13. Quentin's thought "*Yes, I have had to listen too long*" (p. 243) should not be read as having come to him while listening to his father in the cemetery. Rather, it should remind the reader that he is recalling the conversation at Harvard, probably while listening to Shreve cover the same events, since Shreve's comment introducing the flashback indicates that Quentin has relayed this material to him previously.

14. Yet another possibility is offered by Loren Schmidtberger in "*Absalom, Absalom!*: What Clytie Knew" (*Mississippi Quarterly*, 35 [Summer 1982]), which suggests that Clytie probably was aware of Bon's identity and told Judith "eventually" after his death and after Sutpen's death (p. 259). This interpretation would explain Judith's treatment of Charles Etienne, but not her behavior when her father returns from the war.

15. "'We Have Waited Long Enough': Judith Sutpen and Charles Bon," p. 78.

16. Donald M. Kartiganer in "Faulkner's *Absalom, Absalom!*: The Discovery of Values" reads Charles Etienne's sleeping arrangements as an unwillingness by either Judith or Clytie to grant him full status as either white or Negro (p. 299).

17. The use of the term "demon" seems inconsistent here, recalling Rosa's view of Sutpen rather than that of Mr. Compson or his father. Should it suggest the presence of Shreve, repeating a story heard earlier from Quentin? Given the nature of this part of the narrative, this explanation seems unlikely. Probably the term was a mere oversight on Faulkner's part.

18. *Go Down, Moses* (New York: Random House, 1942), p. 363.

19. Michael Millgate points out the discrepancy in the first edition between the text, in which Judith and Charles Etienne die of noncontagious yellow fever, and the Chronology, which states the cause of death as smallpox, a communicable disease (Millgate, p. 323). (Noel Polk alters the Chronology of the corrected edition to agree with the text.) Faulkner originally typed smallpox in preparing the setting copy, but changed to yellow fever, typed above the cancelled original (*TS*, 275).

20. The attitude of the townspeople toward Rosa is somewhat reminiscent of Jefferson's reaction to Miss Emily when she had become a problem after her father's death in "A Rose for Emily" (*Collected Stories*, pp. 119–30).

Chapter 7

1. James Guetti notices the contrast between Quentin's imaginative verve and the narrative descriptions of him which emphasize his brooding, seemingly withdrawn countenance; the contrast reflects his dual role as passive listener (to Rosa and Mr. Compson) and active creator (for Shreve) of a coherent story ("*Absalom, Absalom!*: The Extended Simile," *The Limits of Metaphor: A Study of Melville, Conrad, and Faulkner* [Ithaca: Cornell University Press, 1967]; rpt. *William Faulkner's Absalom, Absalom!: A Critical Casebook*, ed. Elisabeth Muhlenfeld [New York: Garland, 1984], p. 70.

2. See Langford, pp. 268–69, 281, 335–36.

3. Like the passages underlining Quentin's involvement in the story, these lines were added as Faulkner prepared the typescript, as Cleanth Brooks has pointed out (*William Faulkner: The Yoknapatawpha Country*, p. 438). See also Langford, pp. 272–73.

4. Langford, p. 277.

5. Ibid., p. 281.

6. Ibid., p. 296.

7. Ibid., p. 229.

8. *William Faulkner: The Yoknapatawpha Country*, pp. 296–98.

9. Ibid., p. 308. In a later article which addresses the subject of Sutpen's innocence, Brooks uses an approach based more upon ethical standards and concludes that "Sutpen's innocence is not mere sinlessness, but an inability to comprehend what sin is" ("The American 'Innocence': In James, Fitzgerald, and Faulkner" (*Shenandoah*, 16 [Autumn 1964]: 31).

10. In *Faulkner and the Novelistic Imagination*, Robert Dale Parker stresses Sutpen's lack of imagination, suggesting that he follows patterns established during his childhood for his entire life (Urbana: University of Illinois Press, 1985, pp. 115–19).

11. Essentially the same conclusion may be drawn about Quentin Compson, who looks to his father, the weak and ineffectual Mr. Compson, for guidance in *The Sound and the Fury*. Quentin's interest in the Sutpen story may be traced in part to his searching for a more potent father figure, just as Sutpen himself replaces his father with the design inspired by Pettibone.

12. Irwin, p. 100.

13. Poirier, p. 5.

14. Guetti, pp. 73–82.

15. Ruppersburg, pp. 122–23.

16. Floyd C. Watkins discusses how Wash's view of Sutpen's action is influenced by his lack of understanding of Sutpen's purpose: "Ignorant of the cause of the rejection, [Wash] dies believing that Sutpen arose to see about the birth of a foal rather than of his own child. Inhumane as Sutpen is, poor Wash understandably cannot give him credit for the little humanity he has" ("What Happens in *Absalom, Absalom!*," p. 61).

Chapter 8

1. Carl E. Rollyson, Jr.'s "The Recreation and Reinterpretation of the Past in *Absalom, Absalom!*" offers a useful examination of how the creations of Quentin and Shreve in chapter 8 draw upon information and interpretations provided by earlier narrators.

2. John T. Matthews comments on the discrepancies between differing versions of the Sutpen history: "The apparent conflicts of fact or interpretation between the several accounts do not require resolution. Each teller makes his or her meaning precisely by selecting incidents important enough to dispute . . . " (p. 587).

3. "Conrad's Influence on Faulkner's *Absalom, Absalom!*," *Studies in American Fiction*, 2 (1974): 202–3.

4. *The Fragile Thread*, p. 98.

5. Here again Faulkner's knowledge of history is faulty: he describes a retreat in the front of Sherman's advancing army which did not occur.

6. Stephen M. Ross points out the extent to which Shreve accepts Mr. Compson's interpretation of events. Despite the fact that he is basing his notions on incomplete information in chapter 4, Compson attributes Henry's behavior to his racial and sexual attitudes, the same bases Shreve seizes upon, though he understands a great deal more in chapter 8 ("Conrad's Influence on Faulkner's *Absalom, Absalom*," pp. 202–3).

7. At the University of Virginia, Faulkner commented at length on the extent of Bon's knowledge: "I think that Bon knew all the time that his mother was part Negress, but during Bon's childhood that was not important. He grew up in the Indies or in New Orleans where that wasn't too important. His mother was a wealthy woman. She could have called herself a Creole whether she had Negro blood along with the French or not. It became important only when Bon realized that it was important to his father. I think that Bon got into that business—well, of course, because he formed a friendship with Henry and felt that Henry, the ignorant country boy, had given him a sort of worship, an admiration and a worship which he enjoyed. Then when he saw the sort of stiff-necked man that Henry's father was and knew that that was his father too, he in a way had given his father a chance to say, I will acknowledge you, but if . . . I do openly and you stay here, you will wreck what I have devoted my life to, and so take my love and go, I think Bon would have done it. But this old man was afraid to do that. And Bon tempted him to hold him over the coals in—partly in revenge of his treatment of his—Bon's—mother, until Bon got involved too deeply" (*FIU*, 272–73).

8. See Langford, p. 310.

9. Ruppersburg, p. 124.

10. "'We Have Waited Long Enough': Judith Sutpen and Charles Bon," p. 80.

11. See Langford, pp. 321–22.

12. Shreve describes a Decoration Day ceremony fifty years after the war to characterize Mississippi in June. The image is irrelevant to his present purpose, but it is typical of Shreve, who sees the Sutpen story within the larger pattern of the strange customs of the South. His final question of Quentin at the book's end is similarly irrelevant. In fact the picture of the effete veterans prefigures the appearance of Henry Sutpen himself in the following chapter. Under different circumstances, Henry would have been one of the cheering veterans of the lost cause.

13. Gerald Langford has found evidence that the reversal was a late alteration in the preparation of Faulkner's manuscript. A marginal note by Faulkner states: "Henry saves Bon. H says 'I wish it was me here. That would settle it.' Bon suggests that Henry leave him to die to settle it" (Langford, p. 339). Faulkner added a passage to the typescript in which Shreve attempts to justify his alteration of the facts he has received.

14. Cleanth Brooks finds this passage to be an oversight on Faulkner's part; if it is not, then Brooks thinks it indicates yet another conversation which had occurred at Sutpen's Hundred that chapter 9 does not record and that the novel does not present Quentin relating to Shreve (*William Faulkner: Toward Yoknapatawpha and Beyond*, p. 324).

15. *William Faulkner: Toward Yoknapatawpha and Beyond*, p. 327. Another article by Brooks, "On *Absalom, Absalom!*" (*MOSAIC*, 7 [Fall 1973]), raises the possibility that Sutpen may have discovered that his first wife had not been a virgin or had been pregnant when he had married her (p. 167).

16. In his dissertation, "The Monument and the Plain: The Art of Mythic Consciousness in William Faulkner's *Absalom, Absalom!*" (University of Wisconsin, 1971), Oliver LaFayette Billingslea points out that if miscegenation had been Henry's only motive for the murder he need not have fled, since given Bon's mixed race he would have been pardoned; thus, "the consequences of his action—the forty years of suffering are not motivated" (p. 213).

17. Faulkner added the description of Henry's appearance from Bon's perspective during the preparation of the typescript, apparently to intensify the drama of the scene but also to provide a further link between Henry's behavior and Quentin's as described in the following chapter. See Langford, pp. 348–49.

18. The language describing Henry's face, emphasizing the whites of his inrolled eyes, looks forward to the descriptions of Lucas Beauchamp's face in a similar confrontation in "The Fire and the Hearth" section of *Go Down, Moses* (pp. 55–56).

19. "'We Have Waited Long Enough': Judith Sutpen and Charles Bon," p. 79.

20. Panthea Reid Broughton offers a more negative reason for the substitution of the picture: "if he is killed and the locket opened, Bon wants to be identified with the octoroon mistress, not with Sutpen who rejected him" (*William Faulkner: The Abstract and the Actual* [Baton Rouge: Louisiana State University Press, 1974], pp. 71–72).

Chapter 9

1. "Quentin Finally Sees Miss Rosa," *Criticism*, 21 (Fall 1979): 343.

2. Hugh Ruppersburg attributes a more exalted role to Shreve: "Repeatedly he forces Quentin to recognize his failure of understanding, confronting him with problems more profound than the story he has tried to tell: the nature of the past, the constant flow of time, human mortality, the futility of human endeavor" (p. 128). Michael Millgate credits Shreve with bringing "Quentin to a fuller knowledge of both himself and his region" (p. 157).

3. Compare the difficulty of reaching the house Bayard perceives after he and Ringo have shot the Yankee horse in "Ambuscade," the first chapter of *The Unvanquished* (p. 30).

4. "Meaning Called to Life: Alogical Structure in *Absalom, Absalom!*," p. 22.

5. *William Faulkner: The Yoknapatawpha Country*, p. 441. See also pp. 316–17 and *William Faulkner: Toward Yoknapatawpha and Beyond*, pp. 314, 320–22.

6. Ruppersburg, p. 129.

7. Langford, p. 41.

8. See for instance John V. Hagopian, "Black Insight in *Absalom, Absalom!*," p. 35, and John W. Hunt, "The Theological Center of *Absalom, Absalom!*," *William Faulkner: Art in Theological Tension* (Syracuse: Syracuse University Press, 1965); rpt. *Religious Perspectives in Faulkner's Fiction*, ed. J. Robert Barth (Notre Dame: University of Notre Dame Press, 1972), pp. 156–58.

9. This view is maintained by Duncan Aswell in "The Puzzling Design of *Absalom, Absalom!*," pp. 95–96 and by Hershel Parker in "What Quentin Saw 'Out There,'" *Mississippi Quarterly*, 27 (Summer 1974): 323–26.

10. James Guetti takes this position in "*Absalom, Absalom!*: The Extended Simile," p. 71. Guetti's view is shared by Susan Resneck Parr in "The Fourteenth Image of the Blackbird: Another Look at Truth in *Absalom, Absalom!*," *Arizona Quarterly*, 35 (1979): 153–64. Carl E. Rollyson, Jr. goes even further to suggest that Quentin already knew about Henry's relationship to Bon before their meeting at Sutpen's Hundred, which Rollyson suggests is recorded in its entirety ("The Recreation and Reinterpretation of the Past in *Absalom, Absalom!*," pp. 60–65).

11. Guetti, p. 86.

12. Gerald Langford points out that Shreve's preoccupation with explaining Jim Bond was apparently a late addition by Faulkner, since much of it does not appear in the manuscript (p. 41).

13. "*Absalom, Absalom!* and the Negro Question," *Modern Fiction Studies*, 19 (Summer 1973): 210.

14. Warren Beck suggests that Quentin is Faulkner's "chief representative" in the novel and that his last comment is "perhaps an echo of Faulkner himself" (*Faulkner: Essays*, p. 23). Though the association of Quentin with Faulkner is dangerous, the novel's final lines do look forward to the close of the 1954 fictionalized essay "Mississippi," in which the speaker's ambivalence toward his native region can be more closely identified with the voice of the author: "Loving all of it even while he had to hate some of it because he knows now that you dont love because: you love despite; not for the virtues, but despite the faults" (*Essays, Speeches and Public Letters*, pp. 42–43).

15. M. E. Bradford has recognized the lack of relevance in Shreve's final question and links it to his ignorance of the South's concern with history: "Shreve's last question is . . . imperceptive; it indicates that *no* valid answer Quentin could have offered the Canadian would have given him the understanding he seeks" ("Brother, Son, and Heir: The Structural Focus of Faulkner's *Absalom, Absalom!*," p. 96).

16. *Faulkner and the Novelistic Imagination*, p. 142. Susan Gallagher in "To Love and to Honor: Brothers and Sisters in Faulkner's Yoknapatawpha County" (*Essays in Literature*, 7 [Fall 1980]) makes a similar point: "Henry Sutpen agonizes over placing priorities with individuals or ideals but elects to follow the same inhuman code as his father. His decision is a much more horrible one, for he must eventually kill what he loves for the sake of his conception of honor" (p. 220).

17. "The Desperate Eloquence of *Absalom, Absalom!*," *Mississippi Quarterly*, 34 (Summer 1981): 323.

18. "*Absalom, Absalom!*: Story-Telling as a Mode of Transcendence," *Southern Literary Journal*, 9 (Fall 1976): 44.

19. "The Theological Center of *Absalom, Absalom!*," p. 158.

Appendix

1. Muhlenfeld, Introduction, *William Faulkner's Absalom, Absalom!: A Critical Casebook*, p. xxxii.

2. I am grateful to Professor James B. Meriwether for allowing me to examine these documents from his collection.

3. Many commentators have recognized the novel's chronological inconsistencies and the discrepancies between the novel and its appendices. Among the most important discussions are those of Floyd Watkins, "What Happens in *Absalom, Absalom!*," which focuses on internal inconsistencies, which he attributes to "the tendency of these narrators, like most tellers of stories, to exaggerate or to use round numbers" (p. 61); Duncan Aswell, "The Puzzling Design of *Absalom, Absalom!*," who suggests that the contradictions between the novel and the appended material are intentional, included "in order to develop [Faulkner's] theme still further at the expense of the reader's expectations" (p. 104); Susan Resneck Parr, "The Fourteenth Image of the Blackbird: Another Look at Truth in *Absalom, Absalom!*," who points out the limitations of the knowledge of the narrator in the Chronology and Genealogy (p. 155); and Thomas E. Connolly, "Point of View in Faulkner's *Absalom, Absalom!*," who addresses several of the inconsistencies in the narrative and between the novel and the Genealogy (pp. 259, 262–63).

4. Though the novel nowhere establishes the date of the quail hunt, Cleanth Brooks has postulated the autumn of 1907 or 1908 on the basis of internal evidence, including the season for hunting and the weather during September 1909 as described in the novel (*William Faulkner: Toward Yoknapatawpha and Beyond*, p. 304). The presence of Luster as the Compsons' accompanying servant on this occasion in *Absalom* is probably the result of Faulkner's having forgotten about his relative age, since as an adolescent in *The Sound and the Fury* Luster is charged with tending Benjy on his birthday in 1928.

5. Rollyson, "*Absalom, Absalom!*: The Novel as Historiography," p. 166.

6. *The Faulkner-Cowley File*, p. 89.

7. Both the Chronology and Genealogy of the first edition list the year of Ellen's birth as 1818.

8. The first edition gives 1829 as the date of Bon's birth.

9. Rosa tells Quentin that she had been born twenty-two years too late (22), though her meaning is obscure. That would have put her birth in 1823, the year Sutpen went to sea. A possible explanation is that Rosa had wished to have taken Ellen's place; if this is true, she was born twenty-eight years too late, since Ellen's date of birth was 1817.

10. Mr. Compson's age is not determined in the novel, but his seeing his mother react to her memory of Ellen's aunt twenty years after the wedding (1858) would indicate that he was born sometime in the early 1850s. The narrator comments that Rosa had established herself as the county's poetess laureate in Mr. Compson's youth (8), and she had begun the odes in the early 1860s. These references suggest that Mr. Compson had begun his family relatively late in life, as had his father.

11. The Chronology and Genealogy of the first edition list 1862 as the year of Ellen's death.

12. The Chronology of the first edition attributes the deaths of Judith and Charles E. St. V. Bon to smallpox.

13. Shreve refers to the Sutpen house as having stood "*empty and unthreatening for twenty-six years*" (267, 270) at some point when Quentin and his friends had visited it as children. A logical explanation would be that Shreve dates the time from the death of Ellen and Charles Etienne, but this would put the year of the visit in 1910, an obvious impossibility. Another theory is that he refers to Sutpen's death in 1869, but this would date the visit in 1895, when Quentin would have been only around five years old, probably too young to be allowed to wander so far from home.

14. Both the Chronology and Genealogy of the first edition present these events as occurring in 1910.

Annotated Bibliography

Adamowski, T. H. "Children of an Idea: Heroes and Family Romances in *Absalom, Absalom!*" *MOSAIC: A Journal for the Comparative Study of Literature and Ideas*, 10 (Fall 1976): 115–31; rpt. *William Faulkner's Absalom, Absalom!: A Critical Casebook*. Ed. Elisabeth Muhlenfeld. New York: Garland, 1984, pp. 135–55. A psychoanalysis of Sutpen, who engages in a "quest for autonomy . . . that is analogous to the fantasy of controlling one's own parentage."

––––––. "Dombey and Son and Sutpen and Son." *Studies in the Novel*, 4 (Fall 1972): 378–89. Dickens's novel is comparable to *Absalom, Absalom!* in that both demonstrate the damage of "extreme individualism."

Adams, Richard P. "Work: *Absalom, Absalom!*" *Faulkner: Myth and Motion*. Princeton: Princeton University Press, 1968. Useful general study which emphasizes the mythical patterns operating in the novel: Rosa's Gothic pattern; Mr. Compson's pattern of "classical and Renaissance tragedy"; and "the pattern of romantic narrative" imposed by Quentin and Shreve.

Angell, Leslie E. "The Umbilical Cord Symbol as Unifying Theme and Pattern in *Absalom, Absalom!*" *Massachusetts Studies in English*, 1 (1968): 106–10. The image links Rosa and Clytie, Quentin and Shreve, and finally becomes a metaphor for the relationship between the novel and the reader.

Aswell, Duncan. "The Puzzling Design of *Absalom, Absalom!*" *Kenyon Review*, 30 (Issue I, 1968): 67–84; rpt. *William Faulkner's Absalom, Absalom!: A Critical Casebook*. Ed. Elisabeth Muhlenfeld. New York: Garland, 1984, pp. 93–107. Focuses on the inability of the reader to "know" with certainty the facts in the Sutpen story as Faulkner's theme—the ultimate illusiveness of human experience. Includes a consideration of the Chronology and Genealogy but is largely repetitive of earlier work.

Backman, Melvin. "*Absalom, Absalom!*" *Faulkner: The Major Years*. Bloomington: Indiana University Press, 1966, pp. 88–112; rpt. *Twentieth Century Interpretations of Absalom, Absalom!*. Ed. Arnold Goldman. Englewood Cliffs, New Jersey: Prentice-Hall, 1971, pp. 59–75. Employs an historical approach to examine Sutpen as one of the Old South's "new men," not an aristocrat. Bon's story is "a richly ironic fable of the Old South"; *Absalom, Absalom!* is "Faulkner's most historical novel."

Baldanza, Frank. "Faulkner and Stein: A Study in Stylistic Intransigence." *Georgia Review*, 13 (Fall 1959): 274–86. Both Faulkner and Stein have broadened the boundaries of language by the primitive vigor of their prose. Though the purposes for Faulkner's style are perhaps misinterpreted, the essay analyzes the style of *Absalom* in some detail.

Barth, J. Robert. "Faulkner and the Calvinist Tradition." *Thought*, 39 (Spring 1964): 100–120; rpt. *Religious Perspectives in Faulkner's Fiction: Yoknapatawpha and Beyond*. Ed. J. Robert Barth. Notre Dame: University of Notre Dame Press, 1972. The emphasis on doom and fate in *Absalom* identifies Faulkner with the Calvinistic strain of American Puritanism, an identification traceable throughout Faulkner's career.

Bašić, Sonja. "Faulkner's Narrative Discourse: Mediation and Mimesis." *New Directions in Faulkner Studies: Faulkner and Yoknapatawpha, 1983*. Eds. Doreen Fowler and Ann J. Abadie. Jackson: University Press of Mississippi, 1984, pp. 302–21. Explores narrative strategies in *The Sound and the Fury*, a novel primarily "rendered" (in James's phrase) and *Absalom, Absalom!*, a novel primarily told, that is, delivered by narrators.

Beck, Warren. *Faulkner: Essays*. Madison: University of Wisconsin Press, 1976. Though offering no sustained examination of *Absalom, Absalom!*, Beck's essays refer to it frequently, often citing it as Faulkner's masterpiece. Illuminating comments on Faulkner's use of Quentin as narrator, the style, and the subject of miscegenation in particular. The essays include "William Faulkner's Style." *American Prefaces*, VI (Spring 1941): 195–211, a valuable early consideration of that subject.

Behrens, Ralph. "Collapse of Dynasty: The Thematic Center of *Absalom, Absalom!*" *PMLA*, 89 (January 1974): 24–33. Explores the value of four interpretations of the collapse of Sutpen's design: innocence; hubris; the disintegration of Southern society itself; and failure of the dynastic concept, which parallels the biblical story from which Faulkner takes the title.

Bennett, J. A. W. "Faulkner and A. E. Housman." *Notes and Queries*, New Series, 27 (June 1980): 234. Identifies three allusions not noted by Brooks to *A Shropshire Lad*.

Billingslea, Oliver LaFayette. "The Monument and the Plain: The Art of Mythic Consciousness in William Faulkner's *Absalom, Absalom!*" Diss. University of Wisconsin, 1971. Essentially a study of how the personalities of the narrators affect their view of the Sutpen story. Beginning with Sutpen, the author examines each of the character/narrators in detail, including the voice of the narrative persona, which he identifies with Faulkner.

Björk, Lennart. "Ancient Myths and the Moral Framework of Faulkner's *Absalom, Absalom!*" *American Literature*, 35 (May 1963): 196–204. Discusses allusions which fuse Greek, Hebrew, and Christian cultures to magnify the nature of Sutpen's tragedy.

Blake, Nancy. "Creation and Procreation: The Voice and the Name, or Biblical Intertextuality in *Absalom, Absalom!*" *Intertextuality in Faulkner*. Eds. Michel Gresset and Noel Polk. Jackson: University Press of Mississippi, 1985, pp. 128–43. Unconvincing examination of biblical echoes in the novel.

Bleikasten, André. "Fathers in Faulkner." *The Fictional Father: Lacanian Readings of the Text*. Ed. Robert Con Davis. Amherst: University of Massachusetts Press, 1981, pp. 115–46, 195–202. An examination of the meaning of father figures in Faulkner's major novels from *Sartoris* to *A Fable*. Discussion of *Absalom* draws heavily upon Irwin.

Blotner, Joseph. *Faulkner: A Biography*. 2 Vols. New York: Random House, 1974. Contains a detailed account of Faulkner's life during the composition of the novel, though it must be used with care because of the occasional errors and the sometimes inadequate documentation. The revised one-volume edition (New York: Random House, 1984) is somewhat easier to use because of the condensation of material; however it omits most of the documentation. It adds information about Faulkner's relationship with Meta Carpenter; otherwise the account of Faulkner's life during the composition of *Absalom* remains essentially the same.

Bosha, Francis J. "A Source for the Names Charles and Wash in *Absalom, Absalom!*" *Notes on Modern American Literature*, 4 (Spring 1980), Item 13. Faulkner could have found the names from an advertisement his great-grandfather had placed to sell slaves of those names in 1855.

Bradford, M. E. "Brother, Son, and Heir: The Structural Focus of Faulkner's *Absalom, Absalom!*" *Sewanee Review*, 78 (Winter 1970): 76–98. Basically a consideration of Quentin's role as narrator, with valuable insights into his relationship with Shreve. The essay acknowledges the links between *Absalom, Absalom!* and *The Sound and the Fury* and reads Bon in a strongly negative light.

Breit, Harvey. Introduction. *Absalom, Absalom!* by William Faulkner. New York: The Modern Library, 1951, pp. v-[xii]. An appreciative comment which suggests that "the immediacy of the past and the urgency of the present" fuse to make the novel "a kind of fiery laboratory of its author's triumphs and travails."

Brodsky, Claudia. "The Working of Narrative in *Absalom, Absalom!*: A Textual Analysis." *Amerikastudien*, 23 (1978): 240–59. An examination of the narrators and how the novel's structure encourages reading their comments about the story in light of their own personalities.

Brodsky, Louis Daniel. "The Textual Development of William Faulkner's 'Wash': An Examination of Manuscripts in the Brodsky Collection." *Studies in Bibliography*, 37 (1984): 248–81. Provides a collation of early stages of composition of "Wash" along with the text of a twenty-two-page typescript version. The introduction describes the materials but makes several specious, unsound conclusions about them.

Brooks, Cleanth. "*Absalom, Absalom!*: The Definition of Innocence." *Sewanee Review*, 59 (Autumn 1951): 543–58. Sutpen's innocence is that of modern man; Brooks explores the nature of that innocence by contrasting Sutpen with the novel's other characters and by showing the effect of his story upon Quentin. Appears in revised form in *William Faulkner: The Yoknapatawpha Country*.

_____ . "The American 'Innocence': In James, Fitzgerald, and Faulkner." *Shenandoah*, 16 (Autumn 1964): 21–37; rpt. *A Shaping Joy: Studies in the Writer's Craft*. New York: Harcourt, Brace, Jovanovich, 1971. A perceptive examination of the concept of innocence in *The American*, *The Great Gatsby*, and *Absalom, Absalom!* Innocence is often a destructive quality.

_____ . "Faulkner and History." *Mississippi Quarterly*, 25 Special Supplement (Spring 1972): 3–14. In examining Faulkner's providential view of history, the article examines Sutpen, Shreve, and Quentin for their varying views of the past. Sutpen has no concept of history; Shreve ignores it; Quentin is destroyed by it.

_____ . "Faulkner's Ultimate Values." *Faulkner and the Southern Renaissance: Faulkner and Yoknapatawpha, 1981*. Eds. Doreen Fowler and Ann J. Abadie. Jackson: University Press of Mississippi, 1982, pp. 266–81. Cites Judith as exemplifying love, compassion, and endurance in a general analysis of the virtues of Faulkner's characters.

_____ . "History and the Sense of the Tragic: *Absalom, Absalom!*" *William Faulkner: The Yoknapatawpha Country*. New Haven: Yale University Press, 1963, pp. 295–324; rpt. (in part) *Twentieth Century Views of William Faulkner*. Ed. Robert Penn Warren. Englewood Cliffs, New Jersey: Prentice-Hall, 1966. Perhaps the best single critical article on the novel. Brooks stresses structure and character analysis, dividing his attention between the Sutpens and the narrators. A series of appended notes investigates specific critical points such as the issue of Bon's Negro blood and the chronology of events during Quentin's visit to Sutpen's Hundred.

_____ . "On *Absalom, Absalom!*" *MOSAIC*, 7 (Fall 1973): 159–83. An updating of some issues in Faulkner scholarship which Brooks had instigated in earlier contributions. He takes issue with assertions in Langford's introduction to his collation of the manuscript and the published book, asserts anew that Sutpen is not typical of the Southern aristocracy, and cites other examples of the American quality of Sutpen's innocence. A revision of part of the article appears as an appendix in *William Faulkner: Toward Yoknapatawpha and Beyond*.

_____ . "The Narrative Structure of *Absalom, Absalom!*" *Georgia Review*, 29 (Summer 1975): 366–94; rpt. *William Faulkner: Toward Yoknapatawpha and Beyond*. New Haven: Yale University Press, 1978, pp. 301–28. A useful systematic investigation of how information about the Sutpens is revealed by the narrators.

_____ . "The Poetry of Miss Rosa Canfield [sic]." *Shenandoah*, 21 (Spring 1970): 199–206; rpt. *William Faulkner: Toward Yoknapatawpha and Beyond*, pp. 354–61. An examination of poetic techniques in chapter 5 of *Absalom*.

_____ . "The Sense of Community in Yoknapatawpha Fiction." *University of Mississippi Studies in English*, 15 (1978): 3–18. Cites Jefferson's early view of Sutpen in *Absalom* along with other works to defend Brooks's contention in *William Faulkner: The Yoknapatawpha Country* that the sense of community is vital to understanding much of Faulkner's fiction.

Brooks, Peter. "Incredulous Narration: *Absalom, Absalom!*" *Comparative Literature*, 34 (Summer 1982): 247–68. Influenced by Irwin, a deconstructionist reading of the novel which focuses on narratology. Few new insights offered.

Broughton, Panthea Reid. *William Faulkner: The Abstract and the Actual*. Baton Rouge: Louisiana State University Press, 1974. Refers to *Absalom* frequently (in passages not indexed) for examples of characters who treat others as objects (possessions) or abstractions, as in Rosa's view of Bon.

Brown, Calvin S. *A Glossary of Faulkner's South*. New Haven: Yale University Press, 1976. Contains useful explanations of several terms and references in the novel which may be unfamiliar to the modern urban reader.

Brown, May Cameron and Esta Seaton. "William Faulkner's Unlikely Detective: Quentin Compson in *Absalom, Absalom!*" *Essays in Arts and Sciences*, 8 (May 1979): 27–33. Drawing upon Gidley, asserts that though Quentin has little in common with Chandler's or Hammett's detectives, he possesses qualities in the stories he appears in which make him the ideal detective for *Absalom, Absalom!*.

Brumm, Ursula. "Thoughts on History and the Novel." *Comparative Literature Studies*, 7 (September 1969): 317–29. *Absalom* figures briefly at the end of this consideration of the blending of historical fact and novelistic fiction in the work of Scott, Stowe, Fontane, and Faulkner. Interesting remarks on the nature of the historical novel.

Brylowski, Walter. "Faulkner's 'Mythology.'" *Faulkner's Olympian Laugh: Myth in the Novels*. Detroit: Wayne State University Press, 1968; rpt. *William Faulkner's Absalom, Absalom!: A Critical Casebook*. Ed. Elisabeth Muhlenfeld. New York: Garland, 1984, pp. 109–30. Investigates four levels of myth in *Absalom, Absalom!*: allusions and analogies; myth as plot; mythic mode of thought; Southern myth.

Burns, Stuart L. "Sutpen's 'Incidental' Wives and the Question of Respectability." *Mississippi Quarterly*, 30 (Summer 1977): 445–47. Rosa's idea that Sutpen courted Ellen to gain respectability is not true; instead, it refects Rosa's desire for respectability.

Campbell, Harry Modean. "Faulkner's *Absalom, Absalom!*" *Explicator*, 7 (December 1948), Item 24. Explanation of a passage in chapter 3 which provides a good example of the complexities embodied in the novel's style.

Canine, Karen McFarland. "Faulkner's Theory of Relatively: Non-Restrictives in *Absalom, Absalom!*" *SECOL Bulletin: Southeastern Conference on Linguistics*, 5 (Fall 1981): 118–34. Faulkner's use of non-restrictive clauses challenges traditional grammatical classifications and contributes to the novel's theme of the ambiguous nature of truth.

Carothers, James B. *William Faulkner's Short Stories*. Ann Arbor, Michigan: UMI Research Press, 1985. Includes a brief discussion of the incorporation of "Wash" into *Absalom*; no comments about "Evangeline."

Chabot, C. Barry. "Faulkner's Rescued Patrimony." *Review of Existential Psychology and Psychiatry*, 13 (1974): 274–86. Cites Sutpen as an example of several Faulkner characters who deny their past.

Clark, William Bedford. "The Serpent of Lust in the Southern Garden." *Southern Review*, 10 (Autumn 1974): 805–22. Miscegenation has a long history in Southern literature as symbolic of the South's guilt about slavery. The article surveys the tradition and cites *Absalom* as its culmination. Bon is a "mulatto avenger."

Coanda, Richard. "*Absalom, Absalom!*: The Edge of Infinity." *Renascence*, 11 (Autumn 1958): 3–9. Sensitive appreciation of the novel's style which defends it against early attackers and explores it in terms of baroque painters and the styles of early twentieth-century writers, especially Conrad.

Conley, Timothy K. "Beardsley and Faulkner." *Journal of Modern Literature*, 5 (September 1976): 339–56. Detailed analysis of Beardsley's influence on Faulkner's graphic art and his fiction, including the allusions in *Absalom, Absalom!*. Mr. Compson's descriptions of Bon and his son also seem related to Beardsley types.

Connolly, Thomas E. "Point of View in Faulkner's *Absalom, Absalom!*" *Modern Fiction Studies*, 27 (Summer 1981): 255–72. Despite ascribing too much authority to the narrative persona, a sound recital of the shifts in point of view in the novel, summarizing critical opinions on those episodes which have occasioned most debate.

———— . "A Skeletal Outline of *Absalom, Absalom!*" *College English*, 25 (November 1963): 110–14; rpt. *Twentieth Century Interpretations of Absalom, Absalom!* Ed. Arnold Goldman. Englewood Cliffs, New Jersey: Prentice-Hall, 1971, pp. 101–6. Reconstruction arranged like a genealogy of all events in the novel without distinction between those which are "factual" and those imagined by the narrators.

Cornell, Brenda G. "Faulkner's 'Evangeline': A Preliminary Stage." *The Southern Quarterly*, 22 (Summer 1984): 22–41. A level-headed critical analysis of the similarities between the story and *Absalom, Absalom!*, with emphasis upon narrative strategy, plot line, and characters.

Cowley, Malcolm. Introduction. *The Portable Faulkner*. New York: Viking, 1946, pp. i–xxiv. A highly influential essay which continues to affect criticism of the novel. In a survey of Faulkner's career to 1945 Cowley offers a detailed plot summary of *Absalom* and suggests that it be interpreted allegorically as a part of Faulkner's "legend of the South."

———— . "Magic in Faulkner." *Faulkner, Modernism, and Film: Faulkner and Yoknapatawpha, 1978*. Eds. Evans Harrington and Ann J. Abadie. Jackson: University Press of Mississippi, 1979, pp. 3–19. In a prologue to a discussion of "The Bear" reiterates that *Absalom, Absalom!* and Faulkner's work generally concern the myth of the South. Takes issue with Brooks's view of Sutpen.

———— . "Poe in Mississippi." *The New Republic* (November 4, 1936), p. 22. Though praising *Absalom* as the best and most unified of Faulkner's novels, Cowley's review criticizes the style and finds the book ultimately less successful than it might have been. First appearance of Cowley's influential notion that Sutpen's story represents the rise and fall of the Old South.

Davis, Robert Con. "The Symbolic Father in Yoknapatawpha County." *Journal of Narrative Technique*, 10 (Winter 1980): 39–55. Drawing upon Irwin, a discussion of the fictional father and his effect upon the female persona. Rosa, like Quentin, searches for a father figure, and her view of Sutpen gives the novel its structure. Some interesting comments on Rosa's monologue in particular.

Davis, Thadious M. "'Be Sutpen's Hundred': Imaginative Projection of Landscape in *Absalom, Absalom!*" *Southern Literary Journal*, 13 (Spring 1981): 3–14. *Absalom, Absalom!* is lacking in descriptions of landscape. Instead, the characters—particularly Rosa—project their own personalities into discussions of the past.

———— . "The Yoking of 'Abstract Contradictions': Clytie's Meaning in *Absalom, Absalom!*" *Studies in American Fiction*, 7 (Autumn 1979): 209–19. A perceptive analysis of Clytie's role, particularly in relation to Rosa and Judith. To Rosa she is an indictment; her relationship with Judith "provides a model for sibling cooperation and harmony" suggesting "a different order of social interaction between races in the South."

Davenport, F. Garvin, Jr. "William Faulkner." *The Myth of Southern History: Historical Consciousness in Twentieth-Century Southern Literature*. Nashville: Vanderbilt University Press, 1970, pp. 82–130. A wide-ranging examination of *Absalom, Absalom!* within the context of contemporary Southern intellectual and historical trends. Sutpen's downfall is not Southern, but American and Western. The book's theme is "the necessity of moral responsibility in history."

de Montauzon, Christine. *Faulkner's Absalom, Absalom! and Interpretability: The Inexplicable Unseen*. Berne: Peter Lang, 1985. Uses a variety of critical approaches to examine how the reader must attempt to resolve the meanings of the novel, to "totalize" it, a process which *Absalom* resists.

DeVoto, Bernard. "Witchcraft in Mississippi." *Saturday Review of Literature*, 15 (October 31, 1936): 3–4, 14. An early review which praises Faulkner's technical brilliance while condemning his style and subject matter. The first acknowledgment of how Quentin links *The Sound and the Fury* and *Absalom*.

Dickerson, Lynn. "A Possible Source for the Title *Absalom, Absalom!*" *Mississippi Quarterly*, 31 (Summer 1978): 423–24. The quotation which gives the novel its title appears in Grace Lumpkin's *To Make My Bread* (1932), a book Faulkner owned.

———— . "Thomas Sutpen: Mountaineer Stereotype in *Absalom, Absalom!*" *Appalachian Heritage*, 12 (Spring 1984): 73–78. The character of Sutpen can be traced to traits described by such authors as Horace Kephart and John Fox, Jr.

Donaldson, Laura E. "The Perpetual Conversation: The Process of Traditioning in *Absalom, Absalom!*" *Modernist Studies: Literature and Culture*, 4 (1982): 176–94. Tradition is largely passed on through the spoken word. An examination of the novel in light of several recent theories of oral communication.

Doody, Terrence. "Quentin and Shreve, Sutpen and Bon." *Confession and Community in the Novel*. Baton Rouge: Louisiana State University Press, 1980, pp. 163–83. Sutpen confesses to General Compson for social acceptance; Rosa to Quentin for personal affirmation; Quentin to Shreve for motives approaching Sutpen's. The chapter has some useful insights into Shreve's role, especially regarding his view of Bon.

Doxey, W. S. "Father Time and the Grim Reaper in *Absalom, Absalom!*" *Notes on Contemporary Literature*, 8 (May 1978): 6–7. From the same background as Sutpen, Wash represents time "catching up at last" with Sutpen's design.

Egan, Philip J. "Embedded Story Structures in *Absalom, Absalom!*" *American Literature*, 55 (May 1983): 199–214. The story told by each of the central narrators exhibits its own structural pattern reflecting the personality of the individual speaker.

Flynn, Peggy. "The Sister Figure and 'Little Sister Death' in the Fiction of William Faulkner." *University of Mississippi Studies in English*, 14 (1976): 99–117. Judith, like Caddy in *The Sound and the Fury*, is one of Faulkner's sister figures, seen through the eyes of the males who dominate Faulkner's fictional world.

Forrer, Richard. "*Absalom, Absalom!*: Story-Telling as a Mode of Transcendence." *Southern Literary Journal*, 9 (Fall 1976): 22–46. An interesting and perceptive look at the narrative persona, Mr. Compson, and Quentin as they reveal themselves in the stories they tell. The novel is ultimately bleak because the narrators are unable to translate their brilliantly imaginative reconstructions of the past into a richer understanding of their own humanity.

Gallagher, Susan. "To Love and to Honor: Brothers and Sisters in Faulkner's Yoknapatawpha County." *Essays in Literature*, 7 (Fall 1980): 213–24. A look at the way brother-sister relationships in Faulkner reveal the author's concern with love and honor. Very useful comments about Judith, who chooses love, and Henry, who, like Quentin, prefers an abstract code of honor.

Gidley, Mark [Mick]. "Elements of the Detective Story in William Faulkner's Fiction." *Journal of Popular Culture*, 7 (Summer 1973): 97–123. Although the primary emphasis in this article is upon fiction employing Gavin Stevens—*Intruder in the Dust* and *Knight's Gambit*—Gidley explores Faulkner's familiarity with the detective genre and suggests applications to the role of Quentin and Shreve in *Absalom, Absalom!*.

Glick, Evelyn Harter. *The Making of William Faulkner's Books, 1929–1937: An Interview with Evelyn Harter Glick*. Columbia: Southern Studies Program, University of South Carolina, 1979. Recollections by Mrs. Glick, who worked in production for Cape and Smith, Smith and Haas, and Random House, of manufacturing procedures for Faulkner's novels she worked on, including *Absalom, Absalom!*.

Goldman, Arnold. Introduction. *Twentieth Century Interpretations of Absalom, Absalom!* Ed. Arnold Goldman. Englewood Cliffs, New Jersey: Prentice-Hall, 1971, pp. 1–11. Summary of the plot and of major critical views of the novel's meaning. Irony prevents *Absalom, Absalom!* from being a conventional historical novel.

Gray, Richard. "The Meanings of History: William Faulkner's *Absalom, Absalom!*" *Dutch Quarterly Review of Anglo-American Letters*, 3 (1973): 97–110. History manifests both a personal level and a societal level, both of which are reflected by each of the novel's main narrators: Rosa, whose attitudes toward Sutpen reflect the Northern abolitionists; Compson, whose identification with Sutpen's fall gives him a more Southern outlook; Quentin, whose personal obsessions cause his romantic view of events.

Guerard, Albert J. "*Absalom, Absalom!*: The Novel as Impressionist Art." *The Triumph of the Novel: Dickens, Dostoevsky, Faulkner*. New York: Oxford University Press, 1976, pp. 302–39. An excellent general essay on the novel which focuses on its impressionist technique (derived from Conrad) of giving a sense of reality to imagined or created scenes; hence the novel is concerned with poetic truth, not with the depiction of reality.

———— . "Faulkner the Innovator." *The Maker and the Myth: Faulkner and Yoknapatawpha, 1977.* Eds. Evans Harrington and Ann J. Abadie. Jackson: University Press of Mississippi, 1978, pp. 71–88. Considers *Absalom, Absalom!* in discussing three areas of Faulkner's technical innovations: levels of consciousness (suggested at times by italics); "narration by conjecture" (which Faulkner found in *Chance*); and experiments with the form of the novel. Includes some expansion of the discussion of the characters' language in *The Triumph of the Novel*.

———— . "The Faulknerian Voice." *The Maker and the Myth: Faulkner and Yoknapatawpha, 1977.* Eds. Evans Harrington and Ann J. Abadie. Jackson: University Press of Mississipi, 1978, pp. 25–42. An exploration of the distinctions between the terms "voice" and "style." Includes some observations about the voices of the narrators in *Absalom*, which Guerard sees as individualized, though characteristically Faulknerian.

Guetti, James. "*Absalom, Absalom!*: The Extended Simile." *The Limits of Metaphor: A Study of Melville, Conrad, and Faulkner.* Ithaca: Cornell University Press, 1967, pp. 69–108; rpt. *Twentieth Century Interpretations of Absalom, Absalom!.* Ed. Arnold Goldman. Englewood Cliffs, New Jersey: Prentice-Hall, 1971, pp. 76–100; and *William Faulkner's Absalom, Absalom!: A Critical Casebook.* Ed. Elisabeth Muhlenfeld. New York: Garland, 1984, pp. 65–92. Focuses on how each narrator attempts to order the Sutpen story; Quentin's attempt to tell the story parallels Sutpen's attempt to impose meaning on nothingness. Some valuable insights, though the conclusions weaken the essay in an attempt to relate it to the broader thesis of Guetti's book.

Hagan, John. "Déjà Vu and the Effect of Timelessness in Faulkner's *Absalom, Absalom!*" *Bucknell Review*, 11 (March 1963): 31–52; rpt. *Makers of the Twentieth-Century Novel.* Ed. H. R. Garvin. Lewisburg, Pennsylvania: Bucknell University Press, 1977. Interesting exploration of how the disclosures in chapters 7, 8, and 9 leave the reader with a sort of déjà vu effect because of parallels between characters and events revealed in patterns of imagery, such as that of the closed door.

———— . "Fact and Fancy in *Absalom, Absalom!*" *College English*, 24 (December 1962): 215–18. First detailed examination of the existence of Bon's Negro blood and how Quentin might have learned of it.

Hagopian, John V. "*Absalom, Absalom!* and the Negro Question." *Modern Fiction Studies*, 19 (Summer 1973): 207–11. A perhaps oversimplified account of the issue of racism in the novel which nonetheless makes some valid points: Sutpen is not really a racist; Rosa and Henry (as envisioned by Shreve) are; the novel as a whole "clearly repudiates Southern racism."

———— . "Black Insight in *Absalom, Absalom!*" *Faulkner Studies*, 1 (1980): 29–36. After a long (and somewhat tedious) summary of critical positions concerning what Quentin learns at Sutpen's Hundred, posits that he discovered the fact that Bon was black on that occasion from Clytie.

———— . "The Biblical Background of Faulkner's *Absalom, Absalom!*" *The CEA Critic*, 36 (January 1974): 22–24; rpt. *William Faulkner's Absalom, Absalom!: A Critical Casebook.* Ed. Elisabeth Muhlenfeld. New York: Garland, 1984, pp. 131–33. Examines the application of the biblical story of David and Absalom to the novel.

Hall, Constance Hill. *Incest in Faulkner: A Metaphor for the Fall.* Ann Arbor, Michigan: UMI Research Press, 1986. Contains a chapter on *Absalom* which examines the various instances of incest and explores echoes between the novel and *Paradise Lost*.

Hammond, Donald. "Faulkner's Levels of Awareness." *Florida Quarterly*, 1 (1967): 73–81. A brief justification of Faulkner's use of language atypical of his characters to bridge the gap between their conscious perceptions and their deeper levels of awareness. Methods include verbal indicators, parenthesis, and italics. Some examples are drawn from *Absalom*.

Haury, Beth B. "The Influence of Robinson Jeffers' 'Tamar' on *Absalom, Absalom!*" *Mississippi Quarterly*, 25 (Summer 1972): 356–58. Points out several parallels between the poem and the novel, suggesting a clear pattern of influence.

Hawkins, E. O. "Faulkner's 'Duke John of Lorraine.'" *American Notes and Queries*, IV (October 1965): 22. The allusion is probably to John V, Count of Armagnac.

Henderson, Harry B., III. *Versions of the Past: The Historical Imagination in American Fiction*. New York: Oxford University Press, 1974, pp. 253–69. Quentin and Shreve's attempt to understand the Sutpen story mirrors their need to understand the culture of the South. Their difficulty results from their attempt to reduce the explanation to a single motive.

Herndon, Jerry A. "Faulkner: Meteor, Earthquake, and Sword." *Faulkner: The Unappeased Imagination, A Collection of Critical Essays*. Ed. Glenn O. Carey. Troy, New York: Whitstone Publishing Co., 1980, pp. 175–93. Despite the assertion that Sutpen's story (along with the McCaslin and Compson family histories) represents the rise and fall of the Old South, the article makes some interesting comments about Rosa's view of herself and of Sutpen.

Hlavsa, Virginia V. "The Vision of the Advocate in *Absalom, Absalom!*" *Novel*, 8 (Fall 1974): 51–70. Despite the gimmicky approach of the essay, which examines the novel as a nine-part trial, there are some valuable insights into the narrators' views of their stories and into the structure of the novel itself.

Hodgson, John A. " 'Logical Sequence and Continuity': Some Observations on the Typographical and Structural Consistency of *Absalom, Absalom!*" *American Literature*, 43 (March 1971): 97–107. An interesting but ultimately futile attempt to categorize Faulkner's use of italics, quotation marks, and parenthetical insertions to indicate varying levels of consciousness or periods of time. Unaware that in the manuscript Faulkner punctuates chapter 3 conventionally, Hodgson concludes that it occurs *after* Quentin's visit to Sutpen's Hundred because of its unique punctuation.

Hoffman, A. C. "Faulkner's *Absalom, Absalom!*" *Explicator*, 10 (November 1951), Item 12. Recognizes but does not really explore the relationship between *Absalom, Absalom!* and *The Sound and the Fury*.

_____ . "Point of View in *Absalom, Absalom!*" *University of Kansas City Review*, 19 (Summer 1953): 233–39. A level-headed early look at the novel's narrative structure which attacks Cowley's contention that Sutpen's fall reflects the decline of the Old South.

Holder, Alan. "The Doomed Design: William Faulkner's *Absalom, Absalom!*" *The Imagined Past: Portrayals of Our History in Modern American Literature*. Lewisburg, Pennsylvania: Bucknell University Press, 1980, pp. 53–72. General essay which examines the vantage points of the major narrators. The attempt to understand history in the book is a moral act.

Holman, C. Hugh. "*Absalom, Absalom!*: The Historian as Detective." *Sewanee Review*, 79 (October-December 1971): 542–53; rpt. *The Roots of Southern Writing: Essays on the Literature of the American South*. Athens: University of Georgia Press, 1972. One of the first examinations of Faulkner's use of the conventions of detective fiction in *Absalom, Absalom!*. Holman's comments on history and the novel's historical concerns are of little value.

Hopper, Vincent F. "Faulkner's Paradise Lost." *Virginia Quarterly Review*, 23 (Summer 1947): 405–20. A wide-ranging consideration of Faulkner's romantic theme of man's loss of paradise. Sutpen is a Miltonic hero whose essential conflict is with nature.

Howe, Irving. "*Absalom, Absalom!*" *William Faulkner: A Critical Study*. New York: Vintage Books, 1962, pp. 53–59. Originally published in 1952, Howe's study proved influential despite its essentially condescending attitude. It examines the character of Sutpen, the structure, and the style, which Howe attacks. Sutpen does not fully achieve tragic dignity because he never acquires recognition of his downfall.

Hunt, John W. "The Disappearance of Quentin Compson." *Critical Essays on William Faulkner: The Compson Family*. Ed. Arthur F. Kinney. Boston: G. K. Hall, 1982, pp. 366–80. Interesting speculations on why Faulkner found Quentin a useful narrator, both in his short fiction and in *The Sound and the Fury* and *Absalom, Absalom!*.

_____ . "Keeping the Hoop Skirts Out: Historiography in Faulkner's *Absalom, Absalom!*" *Faulkner Studies*, I (1980): 38–47. An intriguing investigation of Faulkner's use of Quentin and Shreve as narrators who search for historical truth. "Faulkner employs a modified historiographical method in reconstruction by controlling the effects of knowledge of the end upon reader, listener, and narrator." At the end of chapter 8, he must introduce the third-person narrator to take over Quentin and Shreve's role.

———. "The Theological Center of *Absalom, Absalom!*" *William Faulkner: Art in Theological Tension.* Syracuse, New York: Syracuse University Press, 1965, pp. 101–36; rpt. *Religious Perspectives in Faulkner's Fiction: Yoknapatawpha and Beyond.* Ed. J. Robert Barth. Notre Dame: University of Notre Dame Press, 1972, pp. 141–69. An excellent study of the moral positions in the novel which suggests that the final moral vision is Faulkner's, revealed in the way *Absalom* is designed as a work of art. Hunt relates the destruction of Sutpen's design to an imitation of the worst aspects of the traditional society in which he found himself, a society which elevated materialism over love. The design is destroyed because of the love exhibited by Bon, Judith, and Henry, and its failure is crucial to Quentin "because it is the characteristic failure of modern man."

Ilacqua, Alma A. "Faulkner's *Absalom, Absalom!*: An Aesthetic Projection of the Religious Sense of Beauty." *Ball State University Forum*, 21 (Spring 1980): 34–41. Examination of the moral positions in the novel from the standpoint of Jonathan Edwards' vision of the beauty of the world's total order of good and evil. Sutpen fails because he cannot share that vision. Some interesting insights despite the rather odd assertion that Jim Bond at the end represents Faulkner's essential optimism.

Irwin, John T. *Doubling and Incest. Repetition and Revenge: A Speculative Reading of Faulkner.* Baltimore: Johns Hopkins University Press, 1975; rpt. (in part) *Faulkner: New Perspectives.* Ed. Richard H. Brodhead. Englewood Cliffs, New Jersey: Prentice-Hall, 1983. Basically a Freudian reading of Quentin's role in *Absalom, Absalom!* and *The Sound and the Fury,* Irwin makes some useful points, almost in spite of his method. Particularly good regarding Mr. Compson.

Isaacs, Neil D. "Götterdämmerung in Yoknapatawpha." *Tennessee Studies in Literature*, 8 (1963): 47–53. A sound archetypal exegesis of "Wash." Jones views Sutpen as the horse-god and destroys him ritualistically when he becomes old and useless. Brief comments on the incorporation of the story into the novel.

Jackson, Blyden. "Faulkner's Depiction of the Negro." *University of Mississippi Studies in English*, 15 (1978): 33–47. In a general survey of black characters in Faulkner's fiction, Jackson points out that Jim Bond does not represent Faulkner's repugnance at miscegenation. Faulkner's attitude toward blacks was enlightened, cosmopolitan, both in his life and in his fiction.

Jacobs, Robert D. "Faulkner's Tragedy of Isolation." *Southern Renascence: The Literature of the Modern South.* Eds. Louis D. Rubin, Jr. and Robert D. Jacobs. Baltimore: Johns Hopkins University Press, 1953, pp. 170–91. Faulkner's great tragic novels concern the "failure of human responsibility in time." *The Sound and the Fury, Light in August,* and *Absalom, Absalom!*—each exhibits characters whose solipsism leads to their downfalls. Sutpen's tragedy has affinities to Renaissance as well as classical tragedy.

Jehlen, Myra. "The Death of the Prodigal." *Class and Character in Faulkner's South.* New York: Columbia University Press, 1976, pp. 47–73. Error-filled examination of *The Unvanquished* and *Absalom, Absalom!* from the point of view of the agrarian class conflict: *The Unvanquished* defends the cavalier tradition, whereas *Absalom* attacks it through Quentin's view of history.

Jenkins, Lee. "*Absalom, Absalom!*" *Faulkner and Black-White Relations: A Psychoanalytic Approach.* New York: Columbia University Press, 1981, pp. 177–219. The first half of the chapter is essentially a character study of Sutpen, refreshingly free of Freudian jargon. The second half explores Bon as Sutpen's dark double and examines the psycho-sexual relationships among members of Sutpen's family; it is less useful than the former section, which contains some interesting insights into Sutpen's personality.

Jones, Suzanne W. "*Absalom, Absalom!* and the Southern Custom of Storytelling: A Reflection of Southern Social and Literary History." *Southern Studies*, 24 (Spring 1985): 82–112. An examination of how the social and cultural background of the major narrators affects the way they tell the story. Particularly valuable comments about Rosa.

Justus, James H. "The Epic Design of *Absalom, Absalom!*" *Texas Studies in Literature and Language*, 4 (Summer 1962): 157–76; rpt. *William Faulkner's Absalom, Absalom!: A Critical Casebook*. Ed. Elisabeth Muhlenfeld. New York: Garland, 1984, pp. 35–54. Urges reading *Absalom, Absalom!* as epic rather than imposing upon it more limiting categories such as "social allegory" or "gothic myth."

Kartiganer, Donald M. "Faulkner's *Absalom, Absalom!*: The Discovery of Values." *American Literature*, 37 (November 1965): 291–306. Initially a look at how Sutpen represents the values of the traditional Southern community, the essay expands into a consideration of the human values exhibited by the major characters. Bon's values provide the novel's most potent antithesis to those of Sutpen.

———— . "Process and Product: A Study of Modern Literary Form (Part II)." *Massachusetts Review* (Autumn 1971): 789–816. A lengthy examination of Conrad's *Nostromo* and *Absalom, Absalom!* as examples of process literature, in which acts of the imagination are of supreme importance. The climax of *Absalom* is the communal imaginings of Shreve and Quentin in the final four chapters, and the disintegration of this sharing at the end mirrors the conflict between Bon and Henry, the central subject of the reconstruction.

———— . "Quentin Compson and Faulkner's Drama of the Generations." *Critical Essays on William Faulkner: The Compson Family*. Ed. Arthur F. Kinney. Boston: G. K. Hall, 1982, pp. 381–401. Some insights into Quentin's personality in *The Sound and the Fury* and *Absalom, Absalom!* within a larger consideration of generational conflict among Yoknapatawpha families, particularly the Sartorises and Compsons.

———— . "The Role of Myth in *Absalom, Absalom!*" *Modern Fiction Studies*, 9 (Winter 1964): 357–69. An interesting examination of the novel from the viewpoint of Frazer's tribal myth of the fertility god who must recognize and be challenged by his son. Sutpen's failure to recognize Bon deprives the son of the right of challenge.

———— . "*The Sound and the Fury* and Faulkner's Quest for Form." *Journal of English Literary History*, 37 (December 1970): 613–39. Looks at how theories such as Bergson's on the processes of the mind influenced Faulkner's attempt to find unity in disordered experience. Although the primary focus is on *The Sound and the Fury*, Kartiganer makes several points about *Absalom*, which he views as the climax toward which Faulkner's fictional experiments evolved.

———— . "Toward a Supreme Fiction: *Absalom, Absalom!*" *The Fragile Thread: The Meaning of Form in Faulkner's Novels*. Amherst: University of Massachusetts Press, 1979, pp. 69–106; rpt. *Faulkner: New Perspectives*. Ed. Richard H. Brodhead. Englewood Cliffs, New Jersey: Prentice-Hall, 1983. Despite its reliance upon the worn formula that the narrators' stories reveal as much about themselves as about their subjects, this chapter offers some useful insights, particularly into Rosa and the relationship between Quentin and Shreve. It is not so good about Sutpen, whom Kartiganer considers a reliable witness in chapter 7.

Kawin, Bruce. "Faulkner's Film Career: The Years with Hawks." *Faulkner, Modernism, and Film: Faulkner and Yoknapatawpha, 1978*. Eds. Evans Harrington and Ann J. Abadie. Jackson: University Press of Mississippi, 1979, pp. 163–81. In a survey of Faulkner's work with Hawks, Kawin suggests that *Sutter's Gold* may have altered Faulkner's approach to *Absalom, Absalom!*. Though the idea is intriguing, it is not explored here in any detail.

———— . "The Montage Element in Faulkner's Fiction." *Faulkner, Modernism, and Film: Faulkner and Yoknapatawpha, 1978*. Eds. Evans Harrington and Ann J. Abadie. Jackson: University Press of Mississippi, 1979, pp. 103–26. A general consideration of film techniques in Faulkner's work. Suggests that the style and structure of *Absalom, Absalom!* may be explained in terms of montage, the imposition of contrasting images.

Kauffman, Linda. "Devious Channels of Decorous Ordering: A Lover's Discourse in *Absalom, Absalom!*" *Modern Fiction Studies*, 29 (Summer 1983): 183–200. Rosa's language and her obsessive concerns draw upon the tradition of the lover's discourse, in which language is artistically fashioned to fill the lack of the beloved.

Kellner, R. Scott. "A Reconsideration of Character: Relationships in *Absalom, Absalom!*" *Notes on Mississippi Writers*, 7 (Fall 1974): 39–43. Though the Quentin of *The Sound and the Fury* has much in common with Henry Sutpen, the Quentin of *Absalom, Absalom!* should be more directly linked with Bon.

Kerr, Elizabeth M. "*Absalom, Absalom!*: Faust in Mississippi, or, The Fall of the House of Sutpen." *University of Mississippi Studies in English*, 15 (1978): 61–82. Draws upon Leslie Fiedler to examine gothic conventions in *Absalom, Absalom!* but makes no mention of earlier work done on this aspect of the novel. A revised form appears in the author's *William Faulkner's Gothic Domain* (Port Washington, New York: Kennikat, 1979).

Kinney, Arthur. "*Absalom, Absalom!*" *Faulkner's Narrative Poetics: Style as Vision.* Amherst: University of Massachusetts Press, 1978, pp. 194–215. Though it demonstrates the inadequacies of language, *Absalom, Absalom!* is about the potency of words. Despite misreadings of the novel's closing scenes, the chapter contains some interesting insights into Shreve's involvement with the story Quentin tells.

———. "Family Structure in Faulkner." *New Directions in Faulkner Studies: Faulkner and Yoknapatawpha, 1983.* Eds. Doreen Fowler and Ann J. Abadie. Jackson: University Press of Mississippi, 1984, pp. 143–71. A general essay on families in Faulkner, emphasizing the Sartorises, Compsons, Sutpens, and McCaslins. *Absalom, Absalom!* "is the story about the failure of the South seen as the failure to produce a viable family." Despite a superficial approach, the essay suggests a useful metaphor for considering the novel.

———. "Form and Function in *Absalom, Absalom!*" *Southern Review*, 14 (August 1978): 677–91. Essentially a source study, suggesting how Faulkner may have been influenced by William Clark Falkner's *The White Rose of Memphis* and works by Thomas Dixon as well as *The Brothers Karamazov* and his work in Hollywood. The parallels are only superficially recognized, not explored in detail.

Korenman, Joan S. "Faulkner and 'That Undying Mark.'" *Studies in American Fiction*, 4 (Spring 1976): 81–91. Sutpen, Judith, and Rosa all try to achieve immortality: Sutpen through his desire for a son; Judith by giving Bon's letter to Mrs. Compson; Rosa by passing the story on. The subject of immortality in *Absalom, Absalom!* is a new concern in Faulkner's work, one which grows more prominent in the latter half of his career.

Kort, Wesley A. "Social Time in Faulkner's Fiction." *Arizona Quarterly*, 37 (Summer 1981): 101–15. The issue of time in Faulkner is more complex than some critics have recognized. Cites examples from *Absalom* and several other novels to illustrate the premise that "social time" is more inclusive than personal or natural time.

Krause, David. "Reading Bon's Letter and Faulkner's *Absalom, Absalom!*" *PMLA*, 99 (March 1984): 225–41. Examines the "documents" which convey meaning in the novel, focusing especially on how both Bon and Henry interpret the letter Bon writes to Judith near the end of the war.

———. "Reading Shreve's Letters and Faulkner's *Absalom, Absalom!*" *Studies in American Fiction*, 11 (Autumn 1983): 153–69. Argues that the letters Shreve invents are clues to the nature of interpretation and ultimately to how the novel itself is to be read.

Langford, Gerald. *Faulkner's Revision of Absalom, Absalom!: A Collation of the Manuscript and the Published Book.* Austin: University of Texas Press, 1971. Although presenting transcriptions of large portions of the manuscript, the book is flawed by mistranscriptions and errors of fact. The Introduction fails to take into consideration changes made to the typescript by Faulkner's editors and so is practically valueless. As a whole the book must be used with extreme caution.

LaRocque, Geraldine E. "*A Tale of Two Cities* and *Absalom, Absalom!*" *Mississippi Quarterly*, 35 (Summer 1982): 301–4. Compares passages to suggest possible influences of the Dickens novel upon *Absalom, Absalom!*.

Larsen, Eric. "The Barrier of Language: The Irony of Language in Faulkner." *Modern Fiction Studies*, 13 (Spring 1967): 19–31. Language is both the medium of communication and a barrier to complete understanding. Quentin's inability to discover the truth of Sutpen demands the reader's involvement with language as experience.

Lensing, George S. "The Metaphor of Family in *Absalom, Absalom!*" *Southern Review*, 11 (Winter 1975): 99–117. The metaphor of the family symbolizes "all human relations." The concept of Judith/Henry/Bon comprising the ideal family is a damaging oversimplification.

Lenson, David. "Classical Analogy: Giraudoux Versus Faulkner." *Achilles' Choice: Examples of Modern Tragedy*. Princeton: Princeton University Press, 1975, pp. 105–16. *Absalom, Absalom!* is a tragedy in the Nietzschean definition, with the role of the chorus shared by the townspeople, Sutpen's slaves, and the narrators.

Levin, David. "*Absalom, Absalom!*: The Problem of Re-creating History." *In Defense of Historical Literature: Essays on American History, Autobiography, Drama, and Fiction*. New York: Hill and Wang, 1967, pp. 118–39. Interesting essay which suggests that many of the "facts" in the book depend upon "reasonable historical inference," and that though a narrator may be either prejudiced or uninformed, the value of his contribution cannot be totally discounted.

Levins, Lynn Gartrell. "The Heroic Design." *Faulkner's Heroic Design: The Yoknapatawpha Novels*. Athens: University of Georgia Press, 1976, pp. 7–54. General essay which examines the varying viewpoints of the four narrators: Rosa's gothicism; Mr. Compson's Aristotelian tragedy; Quentin's chivalric romance; Shreve's tall tale. Levins then explores the novel's sources in Greek tragedy. The chapter incorporates the author's "The Four Narrative Perspectives in *Absalom, Absalom!*" *PMLA*, 85 (January 1970): 35–47.

Liles, Don Merrick. "William Faulkner's *Absalom, Absalom!*: An Exegesis of the Homoerotic Configurations in the Novel." *Journal of Homosexuality*, 8 (1983): 99–111. Reasoned and intelligent examination of the possibility of a homosexual attraction between Bon and Henry and between Quentin and Shreve.

Lind, Ilse Dusoir. "The Design and Meaning of *Absalom, Absalom!*" *PMLA*, 70 (December 1955): 887–912; rpt. *William Faulkner: Four Decades of Criticism*. Ed. Linda Wagner. East Lansing: Michigan State University Press, 1973. Influential essay which is still a usable overview, despite several errors. Lind links the novel to classical tragedy, analyzes the narrators, the style, and the moral and social implications of Sutpen's tragedy, which she relates to the tragedy of the South.

Longley, John Lewis, Jr. "Thomas Sutpen: The Tragedy of Aspiration." *The Tragic Mask: A Study of Faulkner's Heroes*. Chapel Hill: University of North Carolina Press, 1963, pp. 206–18. A general, largely outdated consideration of Sutpen as a tragic figure representative of the American dream of success.

MacKethan, Lucinda Hardwick. "Faulkner's Sins of the Fathers: How to Inherit the Past." *The Dream of Arcady: Place and Time in Southern Literature*. Baton Rouge: Louisiana State University Press, 1980, pp. 153–80. A study of how several Faulkner characters view the past. Sutpen and Quentin (like young Bayard in *Sartoris*) establish goals derived from "an inaccessible past." Interesting comments about Quentin's view of the Sutpen story.

McClennen, Joshua. "*Absalom, Absalom!* and the Meaning of History." *Papers of the Michigan Academy of Science, Arts, and Letters*, 42 (1957): 357–69. Takes issue with Poirier's analysis of the novel's structural division and the importance of Quentin. Sutpen (representative of the Old South) is the main character, and the narrators' views of him reflect their attitude toward history.

McDonald, Walter R. "Coincidence in the Novel: A Necessary Technique." *College English*, 29 (February 1968): 373–88. *Absalom, Absalom!* is a novel in which coincidence, though justified, is so pervasive as to be viewed as related to fate (as Mr. Compson does).

Marshall, Sarah Latimer. "Fathers and Sons in *Absalom, Absalom!*" *University of Mississippi Studies in English*, 8 (1967): 19–29. Contrasts Sutpen's view of his sons with David's view of Absalom, citing various critical opinions of Sutpen.

Martin, Reginald. "The Quest for Recognition over Reason: Charles Bon's Death-Journey into Mississippi." *South Central Bulletin*, 43 (Winter 1983): 117–20. Poorly reasoned examination of Charles's motives for seeking out Sutpen. Ultimately his reasons cannot be explained logically.

Mathews, James W. "The Civil War of 1936: *Gone with the Wind* and *Absalom, Absalom!*" *Georgia Review*, 21 (Winter 1967): 462–69. Comparative notes on the critical reception of the novels both in the South and in national publications.

Matlack, James H. "The Voices of Time: Narrative Structure in *Absalom, Absalom!*" *Southern Review*, 15 (June 1979): 333–54. A wide-ranging consideration of how the structure and progression of the novel reveal its themes. Matlack argues that the "speaking voice and the fluidity of time" are the primary narrative strategies and that ultimately the novel is about the creation of art itself.

Matthews John T. "The Marriage of Speaking and Hearing in *Absalom, Absalom!*" *Journal of English Literary History*, 47 (1980): 575–94. A thoughtful examination of how the characters use language to "recover the past" or to act as a substitute for it. Rosa uses language to fill her sexual void; she creates Bon and Sutpen alike. Although primary focus is on Rosa and Sutpen, the essay makes valuable observations about several characters. An expanded version appears in the author's *The Play of Faulkner's Language* (Ithaca, New York: Cornell University Press, 1982).

Meriwether, James B. *The Literary Career of William Faulkner: A Bibliographical Study*. Authorized Reissue. Columbia: University of South Carolina Press, 1971. Provides useful bibliographical information about *Absalom, Absalom!* and the stories which precede it.

Millgate, Michael. "*Absalom, Absalom!*" *The Achievement of William Faulkner*. New York: Random House, 1966, pp. 150–64; rpt. *Twentieth Century Interpretations of Absalom, Absalom!* Ed. Arnold Goldman. Englewood Cliffs, New Jersey: Prentice-Hall, 1971, pp. 42–58. Valuable examination of the composition and structure of the novel suggesting European influences (particularly *Jane Eyre*) as well as American ones.

_____ . "'A Cosmos of My Own': The Evolution of Yoknapatawpha." *Fifty Years of Yoknapatawpha: Faulkner and Yoknapatawpha, 1979*. Eds. Doreen Fowler and Ann J. Abadie. Jackson: University Press of Mississippi, 1980, pp. 23–43. An examination of how Faulkner's conception of a group of related works developed, emphasizing the role of Quentin Compson in that conception.

_____ . "Faulkner and History." *The South and Faulkner's Yoknapatawpha: The Abstract and the Apocryphal*. Eds. Evans Harrington and Ann J. Abadie. Jackson: University Press of Mississippi, 1977, pp. 22–39. A revision, with less direct consideration of *Absalom, Absalom!*, of "The Firmament of Man's History" (see below).

_____ . "'The Firmament of Man's History': Faulkner's Treatment of the Past." *Mississippi Quarterly*, 25 Special Supplement (Spring 1972): 25–35. A brief look at *Absalom, Absalom!* along with *Go Down, Moses* as illustrative of Faulkner's concern not with historical fact but with the truths his characters perceive from the past. The South is not Faulkner's essential subject.

Minter, David. "Apotheosis of the Form: Faulkner's *Absalom, Absalom!*" *The Interpreted Design as a Structural Principle in American Prose*. New Haven: Yale University Press, 1969, pp. 191–219. The creative reconstructions provided by the characters reflect the artistry of the author. A general essay which prefigures some of the remarks in Minter's *William Faulkner: His Life and Work* (see below).

_____ . *William Faulkner: His Life and Work*. Baltimore: Johns Hopkins University Press, 1980, pp. 143–60 *et passim*. A skeletal and superficial account of *Absalom's* composition, based upon Blotner, gives way to a critical evaluation. The novel is Faulkner's greatest because of its inclusiveness, and it resists "reduction" by virtue of its narrative strategy and language.

_____ . "Family, Region, and Myth in Faulkner's Fiction." *Faulkner and the Southern Renaissance: Faulkner and Yoknapatawpha, 1981*. Eds. Doreen Fowler and Ann J. Abadie. Jackson: University Press of Mississippi, 1982, pp. 182–203. Faulkner's use of his family in fiction reflects interests in his region and its past, interests which motivate Quentin in *Absalom, Absalom!* as well. Ultimately, though, interests in region or family reflect interest in the self, both for Quentin and his creator.

_____ . "'Truths More Intense than Knowledge': Notes on Faulkner and Creativity." *Faulkner and the Southern Renaissance: Faulkner and Yoknapatawpha, 1981*. Eds. Doreen Fowler and Ann J.

Abadie. Jackson: University Press of Mississippi, 1982, pp. 245–65. *Absalom* is used as an example of the patterns of repetition (dependence on traditional forms) and of play (experimentation) which mark Faulkner's creativity.

Mortimer, Gail L. "Significant Absences: Faulkner's Rhetoric of Loss." *Novel*, 14 (Spring 1981): 232–50. Very interesting article which suggests how concern with structural and thematic absences, defined in terms of shapes, boundaries, and other metaphors, reveals Faulkner's "preoccupation with loss." Several examples are drawn from *Absalom*, and many of Mortimer's conclusions are relevant to the novel.

Muhlenfeld, Elisabeth. Introduction. *William Faulkner's Absalom, Absalom!: A Critical Casebook.* Ed. Elisabeth Muhlenfeld. New York: Garland, 1984, pp. xi-xxxix. By far the most comprehensive account of the evolution of the novel and its early reception. Based upon biographical information provided by Blotner, the essay also outlines the composition of *Absalom* based upon examination of manuscript and typescript materials.

―――― . "Shadows with Substance and Ghosts Exhumed: The Women in *Absalom, Absalom!*" *Mississippi Quarterly*, 25 (Summer 1972): 289–304. The women in the novel are forced into being ghostlike because they are used by men and not allowed to assert and develop their own humanity. Particularly useful comments about Rosa.

―――― . " 'We Have Waited Long Enough': Judith Sutpen and Charles Bon." *Southern Review*, 14 (January 1978): 66–80; rpt. *William Faulkner's Absalom, Absalom!: A Critical Casebook.* Ed. Elisabeth Muhlenfeld. New York: Garland, 1984. A perceptive reading of Bon's letter to Judith which concludes that their love was genuine and that Judith is one of Faulkner's most memorable portraits of long-suffering women.

O'Connor, William Van. "Consequences of the Old Order." *The Tangled Fire of William Faulkner.* Minneapolis: University of Minnesota Press, 1954. Plot summary designed to illustrate the Southern character of the novel. A revision of the author's "Faulkner's Legend of the Old South" in *Western Humanities Review*, 7 (Fall 1953): 293–301.

Owens, Clarke. "Faulkner's *Absalom, Absalom!*" *The Explicator*, 42 (Spring 1984): 45–46. Examines the reasons for Rosa's summons of Quentin offered in the novel's first chapter as examples of movement from "dead history" to moral commitment.

Paddock, Lisa. " 'Trifles with a Tragic Profundity': The Importance of 'Mistral.' " *Mississippi Quarterly*, 32 (Summer 1979): 413–22. Don and the narrator of "Mistral" prefigure Quentin and Shreve in *Absalom*, which, like the story, concerns "the multifariousness of truth."

Page, Sally R. *Faulkner's Women: Characterization and Meaning.* Deland, Florida: Everett/Edwards, 1972, pp. 102–9. A few brief comments about Judith—"one of Faulkner's most admirable women"—and a somewhat longer character analysis of Rosa, linking her with such figures as Miss Emily and Minnie Cooper.

Parker, Hershel. "What Quentin Saw 'Out There.' " *Mississippi Quarterly*, 27 (Summer 1974): 323–26. Quentin learns of Bon's parentage by connecting the Supten features of Jim Bond's and Clytie's faces. The conversation between Henry and Quentin recorded in the novel is apparently complete. Though interesting, the ideas are not completely convincing.

Parker, Robert Dale. *Faulkner and the Novelistic Imagination.* Urbana: University of Illinois Press, 1985. Introduction uses *Absalom* as a primary example of Faulkner's method of maintaining suspense by delaying information. The chapter "Something Happening: *Absalom, Absalom!* and Imagination" offers a general analysis of the book, stressing Sutpen's lack of imagination and the hatred which motivated Henry to kill Bon.

Parr, Susan Resneck. "The Fourteenth Image of the Blackbird: Another Look at Truth in *Absalom, Absalom!*" *Arizona Quarterly*, 35 (1979): 153–64. Takes issue with the critical position that the novel contains reliable evidence of Bon's black blood. On his visit to Sutpen's Hundred, Quentin merely intuits what he and Shreve think they know about Bon.

Paterson, John. "Hardy, Faulkner, and the Prosaics of Tragedy." *Centennial Review*, 5 (Spring 1961): 156–75; rpt. (in part) *Twentieth Century Interpretations of Absalom, Absalom!* Ed. Arnold Goldman. Englewood Cliffs, New Jersey: Prentice-Hall, 1971, pp. 32–41. A comparison of *The Mayor of Casterbridge* and *Absalom, Absalom!*. The richness of language which makes *Absalom* a greater work of art makes it also a lesser tragedy than Hardy's novel.

Pearce, Richard. "Reeling Through Faulkner: Pictures of Motion, Pictures in Motion." *Modern Fiction Studies*, 24 (Winter 1978–79): 483–95. Another look at Faulkner from the perspective of film techniques which draws some examples from *Absalom, Absalom!*. Even when describing something static, Faulkner invests his language with motion, as in the opening description of Rosa.

Piacentino, Edward J. "Another Possible Source for *Absalom, Absalom!*" *Notes on Mississippi Writers*, 10 (Winter 1977): 87–94. Similarities between Sutpen and Miltaides Vaiden of T. S. Stribling's trilogy *The Forge*, *The Stone*, and *Unfinished Cathedral*.

Pilkington, John. "The Stubbornness of Historical Truth: *Absalom, Absalom!*" *The Heart of Yoknapatawpha*. Jackson: University Press of Mississippi, 1981, pp. 157–88. A largely superficial account of the novel's composition and reception, followed by a general consideration of the nature of the narrators and reflections on the book's ultimate meaning.

Pires, Mary Dolorine. "Plot Manipulation and Kaleidoscoping of Time as Sources of Tragic Perception in William Faulkner's *Absalom, Absalom!*" Diss. Saint Louis University, 1970. An intelligent *explication de texte* following a survey of theories of tragedy.

Pitavy, François. "The Gothicism of *Absalom, Absalom!*: Rosa Coldfield Revisited." *"A Cosmos of My Own": Faulkner and Yoknapatawpha, 1980*. Eds. Doreen Fowler and Ann J. Abadie. Jackson: University Press of Mississippi, 1981, pp. 199–226. Gothicism in *Absalom, Absalom!* reflects Rosa's methods of thinking, but on a deeper level it signals the dark side, the madness of the creative act. Some interesting comments about Rosa, though Pitavy is less persuasive in regarding Sutpen as a gothic hero.

———. "The Narrative Voice and Function of Shreve: Remarks on the Production of Meaning in *Absalom, Absalom!*" *William Faulkner's Absalom, Absalom!: A Critical Casebook*. Ed. Elisabeth Muhlenfeld. New York: Garland, 1984, pp. 189–205. Though Shreve both inflates and deflates the language of earlier narrators and his role is to provide distance from events, his view of the story is basically the same as Quentin's.

Poirier, Richard. "'Strange Gods' in Jefferson, Mississippi: Analysis of *Absalom, Absalom!*" *William Faulkner: Two Decades of Criticism*. Eds. Frederick J. Hoffman and Olga W. Vickery. East Lansing: Michigan State College Press, 1951, pp. 217–43; rpt. *Twentieth Century Interpretations of Absalom, Absalom!* Ed. Arnold Goldman. Englewood Cliffs, New Jersey: Prentice-Hall, 1971, pp. 12–31; *William Faulkner's Absalom, Absalom!: A Critical Casebook*. Ed. Elisabeth Muhlenfeld. New York: Garland, 1984. Includes a careful analysis of Rosa, showing how she is similar to Sutpen.

Polk, Noel E. Introduction. *William Faulkner Manuscripts 13: Absalom, Absalom!* New York: Garland, 1987. A description of materials in the facsimile edition of the typescript setting copy with a brief outline of the novel's composition.

———. "The Manuscript of *Absalom, Absalom!*" *Mississippi Quarterly*, 25 (Summer 1972), 359–67. Essay review of Langford which describes the manuscript and typescript of the novel in some detail. Langford's study is seriously flawed by his failure to take the typescript setting copy into account.

Porter, Carolyn. "Faulkner and His Reader." *Faulkner: The Unappeased Imagination, A Collection of Critical Essays*. Ed. Glenn O. Carey. Troy, New York: Whitstone Publishing Co., 1980, pp. 231–58. An analysis of Faulkner's method in *The Sound and the Fury*, *Light in August*, and *Absalom, Absalom!* as related to the concerns of modern painting. Faulkner's purpose in each work is to distance the reader from events, achieved through the flow of time in *Light in August* and through multiple perspectives in *The Sound and the Fury* and *Absalom, Absalom!*.

————. "Faulkner's America." *Seeing and Being: The Plight of the Participant Observer in Emerson, James, Adams, and Faulkner.* Middletown, Connecticut: Wesleyan University Press, 1981, pp. 207–76. An examination of the nature of the Southern planter class which draws upon *Absalom, Absalom!.* Porter sees the class as capitalistic with a paternal veneer. Sutpen, whom she relates to William C. Falkner, is both typically Southern and typically American.

Powers, Lyall H. *"Absalom, Absalom!" Faulkner's Yoknapatawpha Comedy.* Ann Arbor: University of Michigan Press, 1980, pp. 106–24. Adds parallels to the myth of Cadmus to an otherwise conventional look at the novel. The central theme is the "second chance" offered to several of the characters.

Price, Steve. "Shreve's Bon in *Absalom, Absalom!" Mississippi Quarterly,* 39 (Summer 1986): 325–35. Examines Shreve's role as storyteller, focusing on his creation of Bon's character.

Putzel, Max. "What is Gothic about *Absalom, Absalom!" Southern Literary Journal,* 4 (Fall 1971): 3–19. The gothic elements result from the emphasis on the decline of the Southern tradition of chivalry and on psychological terror, such as Quentin's at the novel's close.

Ragan, David Paul. " 'That Tragedy is Second-Hand': Quentin, Henry, and the Ending of *Absalom, Absalom!" Mississippi Quarterly,* 39 (Summer 1986): 337–50. Postulates that Quentin reacts so vehemently to his visit to Sutpen's Hundred because he recognizes in Henry a personification of Mr. Compson's defeatism.

Randel, Fred V. "Parentheses in Faulkner's *Absalom, Absalom!" Style,* 5 (Winter 1971): 70–87. A catalogue of the uses of parentheses which identifies four major functions: the opposition of the self and the external world; explanation of something otherwise ambiguous; allusions to another level of time; and "parentheses of confrontation and tension." Rosa's monologue employs the most parentheses.

Raper, J. R. "Meaning Called to Life: Alogical Structure in *Absalom, Absalom!" Southern Humanities Review,* 5 (Winter 1971): 9–23. A detailed examination of how Rosa's monologue uses techniques Faulkner could have learned from his work in film, such as the montage and slow motion.

Redekop, Magdalene. *"Absalom, Absalom!:* Through the Spectacles of Shreve McCannon." *William Faulkner: Materials, Studies, and Criticism,* 5 (August 1983): 17–45. Explores the personal and national characteristics which make Shreve an effective foil to Quentin in examining the Sutpen story.

Reed, Joseph W., Jr. *"Absalom, Absalom!" Faulkner's Narrative.* New Haven: Yale University Press, 1973, pp. 145–75. An examination of the novel as concerned with the fiction process as reflected in the characters' use of linked metaphors.

Rinaldi, Nicholas M. "Game Imagery in Faulkner's *Absalom, Absalom!" Connecticut Review,* 4 (October 1970): 73–79. Game images reveal Sutpen's approach to life and his competitive attitude toward other people, whom he merely exploits for his own ends. Rinaldi questions whether this attitude links Sutpen to the typical pursuit of the American Dream.

Robbins, Deborah. "The Desperate Eloquence of *Absalom, Absalom!" Mississippi Quarterly,* 34 (Summer 1981): 315–24. The characters use speech—talking—as an assertion of their significance and as a means of imposing order on their experience. Particularly good comments on Judith and Rosa.

Rodnon, Stewart. *"The House of the Seven Gables* and *Absalom, Absalom!:* Time, Tradition, and Guilt." *Studies in the Humanities,* 1 (1970): 42–46. Brief look at parallels between the two novels, including the influence of the past upon the present, the end of a tradition, and "a special view of the nature of good and evil." The article does not attempt to demonstrate influence; rather, it suggests "a common artistic intention."

Rollyson, Carl E., Jr. *"Absalom, Absalom!:* The Novel as Historiography." *Literature and History,* No. 5 (Spring 1977): 45–54; rpt. *William Faulkner's Absalom, Absalom!: A Critical Casebook.* Ed. Elisabeth Muhlenfeld. New York: Garland, 1984, pp. 157–72. A look at the historical method of the characters which concludes that "the form . . . remains true to the process of historical interpretation, even though the place it accords to the artistic imagination is out of keeping with traditional concepts of the historian's reconstruction of the past." A revision of the article, entitled "Historiography in *Absalom, Absalom!*," incorporates an extensive survey of critical opinion concerning the novel and detailed analysis of Sutpen and Rosa in particular; it is included in Rollyson's *Uses of the Past in the Novels of William Faulkner* (see below).

———— . "The Recreation and Reinterpretation of the Past in *Absalom, Absalom!*" *Uses of the Past in the Novels of William Faulkner*. Ann Arbor, Michigan: UMI Research Press, 1984, pp. 33–71. A rather long and wide-ranging consideration of various aspects of the novel with emphasis on how Quentin and Shreve rely on earlier narrators' theories in constructing their interpretation in chapter 8 and on what Quentin learned at Sutpen's Hundred. Also discusses Faulkner's use of Scott. The chapter incorporates revisions of three earlier articles: "Faulkner and Historical Fiction: *Redgauntlet* and *Absalom, Absalom!*" (*Dalhousie Review*, 56 [Winter 1976–77]: 671–81); "Quentin Durward and Quentin Compson: The Romantic Standard-Bearers of Scott and Faulkner" (*Massachusetts Studies in English*, 7 [1980]: 34–39); and "The Re-creation of the Past in *Absalom, Absalom!*" (*Mississippi Quarterly*, 29 [Summer 1976]: 361–74).

Rose, Maxine. "Echoes of the King James Bible in the Prose Style of *Absalom, Absalom!*" *Arizona Quarterly*, 37 (Summer 1981): 137–48. Demonstrates by comparing selected passages how stylistic techniques in *Absalom, Absalom!* reflect those of the Bible.

———— . "From Genesis to Revelation: The Grand Design of William Faulkner's *Absalom, Absalom!*" *Studies in American Fiction*, 8 (Autumn 1980): 219–28. The novel's title provides clues to how Faulkner shapes *Absalom, Absalom!* through allusions to the Bible. Several of the parallels here are strained to the point of gimmickry, though some are interesting.

Rosenman, John B. "Anderson's *Poor White* and Faulkner's *Absalom, Absalom!*" *Mississippi Quarterly*, 29 (Summer 1976): 437–38. Wash's murder of Sutpen bears striking resemblances to Joe Wainsworth's murder of Jim Gibson in Anderson's novel.

Ross, Stephen M. "Conrad's Influence on Faulkner's *Absalom, Absalom!*" *Studies in American Fiction*, 2 (1974): 199–209. A perceptive investigation into the influence of *Lord Jim* and *Heart of Darkness* on *Absalom*. *Lord Jim* mainly provided Faulkner technical devices and narrative viewpoint. *Heart of Darkness* may have suggested particular scenes. Quentin's journey to find Henry has much in common with Marlow's journey to discover Kurtz. Faulkner goes beyond Conrad by the use of Quentin, who expands "the rhetoric of Impressionism into psychological drama."

———— . "The Evocation of Voice in *Absalom, Absalom!*" *Essays in Literature*, 8 (Fall 1981): 135–49. The power of voice in the novel controls the narrative; "*Absalom* presumes an energetics of voice through which language can be transcended and reality rescued from erasure."

———— . "Faulkner's *Absalom, Absalom!* and the David Story: A Speculative Contemplation." *The David Myth in Western Literature*. Ed. Raymond-Jean Frontain and Jan Wojcik. West Lafayette, Indiana: Purdue University Press, 1980, pp. 136–53. The most extensive examination of the allusion in the title. Drawing upon Irwin, Ross demonstrates that easy parallels between Sutpen and David do not fit. Faulkner recreates the moral ambiguities inherent in the Old Testament and draws upon David's entire history, not just on his loss of Absalom.

———— . "Oratory and the Dialogical in *Absalom, Absalom!*" *Intertextuality in Faulkner*. Eds. Michel Gresset and Noel Polk. Jackson: University Press of Mississippi, 1985, pp. 73–86. Examines the rhetoric of *Absalom* in terms of Mikhail Bakhtin's theories concerning monological and dialogical speech. Ross suggests that dialogue becomes assault in some episodes.

Ruppersburg, Hugh M. "Chapter Four: *Absalom, Absalom!*" *Voice and Eye in Faulkner's Fiction*. Athens: University of Georgia Press, 1983, pp. 81–132. The most careful explication of the shifting narrative points of view in the novel. Ruppersburg also provides a useful vocabulary for discussing narrative problems in Faulkner generally.

Sabiston, Elizabeth. "Women, Blacks, and Thomas Sutpen's Mythopoeic Drive in *Absalom, Absalom!*" *Modernist Studies in Literature and Culture, 1920–1940*, 1 (1974–1975): 15–26. The novel's "twin themes of creativity and heredity" are embodied in its women and black characters.

Samway, Patrick, S. J. "Searching for Jason Richmond Compson: A Question of Echolalia and a Problem of Palimpsest." *Intertextuality in Faulkner*. Eds. Michel Gresset and Noel Polk. Jackson: University Press of Mississippi, 1985, pp. 178–209. An examination of what we can know about Mr. Compson from "That Evening Sun," *The Sound and the Fury*, and *Absalom*, in which he is less negative than in the earlier novel.

Scherer, Olga. "A Polygraphic Insert: Charles's Letter to Judith." *Intertextuality in Faulkner*. Eds. Michel Gresset and Noel Polk. Jackson: University Press of Mississippi, 1985, pp. 168–77. The letters included in the text must be read in context of the characters who wrote them and the characters they address.

Schmidtberger, Loren. "Names in *Absalom, Absalom!*" *American Literature*, 55 (March 1983): 83–88. A catalogue of names in the novel with a look at the importance attached to the act of naming by the narrators.

――――. "*Absalom, Absalom!*: What Clytie Knew." *Mississippi Quarterly*, 35 (Summer 1982): 255–63. A provocative inquiry into the extent of Clytie's knowledge concerning Bon, her treatment of Charles Etienne, and her (to Rosa at least) supernatural abilities. Her knowledge, which the narrators fail to give her credit for, may have been extensive.

Schoenberg, Estella. *Old Tales and Talking: Quentin Compson in William Faulkner's Absalom, Absalom! and Related Works*. Jackson: University Press of Mississippi, 1977. An interesting if somewhat superficial examination of the relationship between *Absalom, Absalom!* and *The Sound and the Fury*. Schoenberg conflates the chronology of the two books and hints at how the novel's narrative strategies developed from the Don-and-I stories, including "Evangeline," which she examines in some detail.

Schultz, William J. "Just Like Father: Mr. Compson as Cavalier Romancer in *Absalom, Absalom!*" *Kansas Quarterly*, 14 (Spring 1982): 115–23. A sound exploration of Mr. Compson's view of the Sutpen story. Compson is determined to find love between Judith and Bon, though the letter does not really reveal it. Quentin inherits his father's romanticizing tendencies.

Scott, Arthur L. "The Faulknerian Sentence." *Prairie Schooner*, 27 (Spring 1953): 91–98. Faulkner's style is a major component of the difficulty many readers find in his work. Scott analyzes the stylistic elements of *Absalom, Absalom!* by examining in detail the novel's second sentence. The style contributes to the meaning by suggesting the fluidity of time and serving as a metaphor of Faulkner's use of delayed revelation of information.

――――. "The Myriad Perspectives of *Absalom, Absalom!*" *American Quarterly*, 6 (Fall 1954): 210–20; rpt. *William Faulkner's Absalom, Absalom!: A Critical Casebook*. Ed. Elisabeth Muhlenfeld. New York: Garland, 1984, pp. 23–34. Largely outdated analysis of the novel's structure, redeemed by some interesting remarks on the similarity between *Absalom, Absalom!* and movements in the modern visual arts.

Seiden, Melvin. "Faulkner's Ambiguous Negro." *Massachusetts Review*, 4 (Summer 1963): 675–90. *Absalom, Absalom!* concerns "the ambivalent fascination and horror evoked by the obsession" with miscegenation. A typical look at the novel from the liberal vantage point of the civil rights controversies of the early sixties.

Sewall, Richard B. "*Absalom, Absalom!*" *The Vision of Tragedy*. New Haven: Yale University Press, 1959, pp. 133–47. An early examination of tragic elements in the novel, developed primarily though plot summary but exploring in some detail the differing conceptions of tragedy as related to Quentin and Sutpen.

Singleton, Marvin K. "Personae at Law and in Equity: The Unity of Faulkner's *Absalom, Absalom!*" *Papers on English Language and Literature*, 3 (Fall 1967): 354–70. Frequent references to terms from English common law and equity help delineate the characters and unify the novel. Rosa, for instance, pleads her case before Quentin, and Quentin and Shreve judge the actions of other characters.

Slabey, Robert M. "Faulkner's 'Waste Land': Vision in *Absalom, Absalom!*" *Mississippi Quarterly*, 14 (Summer 1961): 153–61. *Absalom, Absalom!* closes Faulkner's ten-year wasteland period. With Eliot, Faulkner shares the view of a world bereft of spiritual or moral value (though specific borrowings in the novel are few). The work of art itself becomes an affirmation of value.

Slatoff, Walter J. "*Absalom, Absalom!*" *Quest for Failure: A Study of William Faulkner*. Westport, Connecticut: Greenwood Press, 1960, pp. 198–203. The complexity and ambiguity of the novel are indicated by the "commentaries" on the Sutpen story provided by Quentin, Shreve, and Mr. Compson's letter at the end of the book.

Sowder, William J. "Colonel Thomas Sutpen as Existentialist Hero." *American Literature*, 33 (January 1962): 485–99. Uses existential terminology and parallels with characters in Sartre to examine Sutpen's design. Sutpen's failure results from his "vain attempt to define himself."

Stonum, Gary Lee. "The Fate of Design." *Faulkner's Career: An Internal Literary History*. Ithaca, New York: Cornell University Press, 1979, pp. 123–52. An essay which offers some interesting insights into the metaphor of design as an attempt to suspend motion employed by Sutpen and the narrators. The hypotheses concerning Faulkner's design over his material as a reflection of his personality are less convincing and less useful.

Strauss, Harold. "Mr. Faulkner Is Ambushed in Words." *New York Times Book Review* (November 1, 1936), p. 7. Review which attacks the obscurities of structure and style while praising certain "passages of great power and beauty."

Sullivan, Walter. "The Tragic Design of *Absalom, Absalom!*" *South Atlantic Quarterly*, 50 (October 1951): 552–66. *Absalom, Absalom!* embodies the tragic themes of the entire Yoknapatawpha series. Taking its cue from Cowley's theory of the myth of the South, the article refers to several theories of tragedy, including those of Hegel and Schopenhauer.

Swiggart, Peter. "A Puritan Tragedy: *Absalom, Absalom!*" *The Art of Faulkner's Novels*. Austin: University of Texas Press, 1962, pp. 149–70. Error-ridden essay suggesting that Sutpen's tragedy symbolizes "the failure of Southern society."

Tobin, Patricia Drechsel. "The Shadowy Attenuation of Time: William Faulkner's *Absalom, Absalom!*" *Time and the Novel: The Genealogical Imperative*. Princeton: Princeton University Press, 1978, pp. 107–32. Because of his views of the past, Quentin sees Sutpen as a father figure, and the characters are metaphorically linked. Draws upon Irwin.

———. "The Time of Myth and History in *Absalom, Absalom!*" *American Literature*, 45 (May 1973): 252–70. Objects that Sartre's view of Faulkner's use of time is too simplified. In *Absalom, Absalom!*, Sutpen is viewed within either a mythical or an historical context. He is mythologized by Rosa and Mr. Compson, viewed as a figure in historical time by Quentin and Shreve.

Torsney, Cheryl B. "The Vampire Motif in *Absalom, Absalom!*" *Southern Review*, 20 (July 1984): 562–69. Argues that references to vampires signal the theme of predatoriness.

Troy, William. "The Poetry of Doom." *Nation*, 143 (October 31, 1936): 524–25. Review which identifies the novel with the techniques of lyric poetry. *Absalom* is "not only the best that [Faulkner] has yet given us but one of the most formidable [novels] of our generation."

Tuso, Joseph F. "Faulkner's 'Wash.'" *Explicator*, 27 (November 1968), Item 17. The name of Sutpen's mare is changed from Griselda in "Wash" to Penelope in *Absalom, Absalom!*. Both represent fidelity and so are appropriate: the animal fulfills Sutpen's needs as Milly does not.

Vande Kieft, Ruth M. "Faulkner's Defeat of Time in *Absalom, Absalom!*" *Southern Review*, 6, New Series (October 1970): 1100–1109. The characters in the novel reflect Faulkner's own personality. Sutpen's attempt to gain immortality through his design parallels Faulkner's similar use of his art. The characters tend to sound alike because of their basis in the author's mind.

Vickery, Olga W. "The Idols of the South: *Absalom, Absalom!*" *The Novels of William Faulkner: A Critical Interpretation*. Rev. ed. Baton Rouge: Louisiana State University Press, 1964, pp. 84–102. General essay flawed by its insistence that Sutpen is representative of the South and that his children—including Judith—share in his peculiarly Southern design. The narrators reflect their own personalities and concerns.

Volpe, Edmund L. *"Absalom, Absalom!" A Reader's Guide to William Faulkner*. New York: Farrar, Straus and Giroux, 1964, pp. 184–212. General essay exploring the structure of the novel and providing character studies. Marred by numerous factual errors. A detailed chronology is appended.

Waggoner, Hyatt H. "The Historical Novel and the Southern Past: The Case of *Absalom, Absalom!*" *Southern Literary Journal*, 2 (Spring 1970): 69–85. A meditation on *Absalom, Absalom!* as an historical novel. Attacking the view of Sutpen in *Crowell's Handbook*, Waggoner contends that *Absalom* is not a conventional historical novel and that Sutpen is not exclusively representative of the Southern mentality; his faults are those of America in general or of Western man.

———. "Past as Present: *Absalom, Absalom!*" *William Faulkner: From Jefferson to the World*. Lexington: University of Kentucky Press, 1959, pp. 148–69; rpt. *Twentieth Century Views of William Faulkner*. Ed. Robert Penn Warren. Englewood Cliffs, New Jersey: Prentice-Hall, 1966. Though largely outdated, this general examination remains worth consulting, particularly for its comments on the form of the novel—related to lyric poetry—and on Shreve's role.

Wasson, Ben. *Count No 'Count: Flashbacks to Faulkner*. Jackson: University Press of Mississippi, 1983. Reminiscences of Wasson's long relationship with Faulkner, including a brief account of the author's preparation of the typescript setting copy of *Absalom, Absalom!*

Watkins, Evan. "The Fiction of Interpretation: Faulkner's *Absalom, Absalom!*" *The Critical Act: Criticism and Community*. New Haven: Yale University Press, 1978. A rather esoteric examination of how the language of the novel reveals the narrators' relationship to the story they tell and the author's relationship to the narrators. Special focus is upon Rosa and Shreve.

Watkins, Floyd C. "Thirteen Ways of Talking about a Blackbird." *The Flesh and the Word: Eliot, Hemingway, Faulkner*. Nashville: Vanderbilt University Press, 1971, pp. 216–33. Divides the characters in *Absalom, Absalom!* into two groups: those who talk (the narrators in 1909–10) and those who act (the participants in the Sutpen legend). Though the approach oversimplifies—Clytie and Rosa do act in 1909, for instance—Watkins makes some valid points about the terseness of conversations reported by the narrators.

———. "What Happens in *Absalom, Absalom!*" *Modern Fiction Studies*, 13 (Spring 1967): 79–87; rpt. *William Faulkner's Absalom, Absalom!: A Critical Casebook*. Ed. Elisabeth Muhlenfeld. New York: Garland, 1984, pp. 55–64. Cites various discrepancies in the novel and suggests that while many are oversights, others function to suggest the retold nature of the story, the impossibility of apprehending the past, the beginnings of myth.

Watson, James G. "'But Damn Letters Anyway': Letters and Fictions." *New Directions in Faulkner Studies: Faulkner and Yoknapatawpha, 1983*. Eds. Doreen Fowler and Ann J. Abadie. Jackson: University Press of Mississippi, 1984, pp. 228–53. Offers a brief consideration of the letters in *Absalom, Absalom!* within a more general study of letters in Faulkner's work and of Faulkner's own letter writing.

———. "Faulkner: Short Story Structures and Reflexive Forms." *MOSAIC*, 11 (Summer 1978): 127–37. Examines the impact of "Wash" on *Absalom* (and briefly mentions "Evangeline") in a general evaluation of the relationship between form and meaning in Faulkner's work.

———. "'If *Was* Existed': Faulkner's Prophets and the Patterns of History." *Modern Fiction Studies*, 21 (Winter 1975–76), pp. 499–507. Quentin, like most Faulkner characters, looks to the past for clues to the future, and he finds in the tale constructed by Rosa and Mr. Compson portents of his own demise.

Weatherby, H. L. "Sutpen's Garden." *Georgia Review*, 21 (Fall 1967): 354–69. Faulkner's characters have no possibility of redemption—of finding love in time—because Faulkner had inherited the vestiges of Christian tradition and possessed an incomplete understanding of it. Quentin is a primary example. He longs for the Garden (symbolized by the December garden outside Sutpen's library window) but does not know how to find it.

Weinstein, Arnold L. *Vision and Response in Modern Fiction*. Ithaca, New York: Cornell University Press, 1974, pp. 136–53. Interesting comments on *Absalom* within the book's larger concern with how literature bridges the gap between evidence and interpretation. The acquisition of understanding comes to Shreve and Quentin only as an act of love. Some perceptive comments about Rosa.

Weinstein, Philip M. "Precarious Sanctuaries: Protection and Exposure in Faulkner's Fiction." *Studies in American Fiction*, 6 (Autumn 1978): 173–91. Remarks on how Faulkner's characters retreat into sanctuaries when forced to confront the differences between the self and the not-self. The touch, like Rosa's touch of flesh with flesh, often breaks down those sanctuaries.

Weisgerber, Jean. "Faulkner's Monomaniacs: Their Indebtedness to Raskolnikov." *Comparative Literature Studies*, 5 (June 1968): 181–93. The monomaniacs of Faulkner's early novels may owe something to Raskolnikov in *Crime and Punishment*. Quentin of *The Sound and the Fury* is most directly influenced, but Sutpen also shares several traits, including a tendency to abstraction.

Whan, Edgar W. "*Absalom, Absalom!* as Gothic Myth." *Perspective*, 3 (Autumn 1950): 192–201. An early examination of the novel as an example of the gothic genre which flourished in the early nineteenth century. Faulkner both expands existing myths and creates new ones in his characters.

Wigley, Joseph A. "Imagery and Interpreter." *Studies in Interpretation*. Eds. Esther M. Doyle and Virginia Hastings Floyd. Amsterdam: Rodopi N. V., 1972, pp. 171–90. Surveys in detail animal imagery in *Absalom* as representative of Faulkner's careful use of image patterns for structural and thematic purposes.

Wilde, Meta Carpenter and Orin Borsten. *A Loving Gentleman: The Love Story of William Faulkner and Meta Carpenter*. New York: Simon and Schuster, 1976. Meta Carpenter's reminiscence of her affair with Faulkner, which began during the period of the composition of *Absalom, Absalom!*.

Williams, J. Gary. "Quentin Finally Sees Miss Rosa." *Criticism*, 21 (Fall 1979): 331–46. Argues that Quentin is moved most at the novel's end by his vision of Rosa returning to Sutpen's Hundred, not by meeting Henry. His interest in the Sutpen story links him with Rosa since he is most impassioned when thinking about her account, indifferent to his father and Shreve as narrators. A well-reasoned if not entirely convincing effort.

Williams, Philip. "Faulkner's Satan Sutpen and the Tragedy of *Absalom, Absalom!*" *English Language and Literature*, No. 45–46 (December 1964): 179–99. Because of his great sins, Sutpen can be viewed as a tragic hero only in the sense of Milton's Satan.

Wittenberg, Judith Bryant. "Faulkner and Eugene O'Neill." *Mississippi Quarterly*, 33 (Summer 1980): 327–41. Lists parallels between *Absalom, Absalom!* and *Mourning Becomes Electra* to demonstrate the possible influence of O'Neill on Faulkner.

_____ . "Portraits of the Artist at Work: *Pylon* and *Absalom, Absalom!*" *Faulkner: The Transfiguration of Biography*. Lincoln: University of Nebraska Press, 1979, pp. 130–55. Both *Pylon* and *Absalom, Absalom!* reflect Faulkner's own life, but *Absalom* more directly arises from the anguish and pain of the author's personality. The novel represents Faulkner's greater maturity both as man and artist since *The Sound and the Fury*. Most characters are artist figures, especially Quentin, who reflects aspects of Faulkner's own personality and relationship with his father—a rather unsuccessfully belabored thesis.

Young, Thomas Daniel. "Narration as Creative Act: The Role of Quentin Compson in *Absalom, Absalom!*" *Faulkner, Modernism, and Film: Faulkner and Yoknapatawpha, 1978*. Eds. Evans Harrington and Ann J. Abadie. Jackson: University Press of Mississippi, 1979, pp. 82–102; rpt. *Critical Essays on William Faulkner: The Compson Family*. Ed. Arthur F. Kinney. Boston: G. K. Hall, 1982, pp. 318–31. A look at how Quentin's view of Henry is related to his problems in *The Sound and the Fury*. The essay uses a conflated plot summary of the two novels as support and interprets Henry's fear of miscegenation as arising from Quentin's behavior in the creek scene when he and Caddy are children in *The Sound and the Fury*.

Zoellner, Robert H. "Faulkner's Prose Style in *Absalom, Absalom!*" *American Literature*, 30 (January 1959): 486–502. Excellent study which demonstrates how the novel's stylistic techniques are not designed to obfuscate; rather they reveal Faulkner's central thematic concerns.

Index

Names of characters in *Absalom, Absalom!* are given as they appear in the Genealogy appended to the novel. Character subentries are arranged chronologically insofar as possible, followed by other references arranged alphabetically.

DATE DUE

PRINTED IN U.S.A.